BR Swindon Type 1 0-6-0 Diesel-Hydraulic Locomotives Class 14

Cover: **D9520 (45) and D9548 (67), British Steel Corporation, Gretton Brook, Corby, 18 April 1979.** (Anthony Sayer)

D9523, British Steel Corporation, Glendon East, 18 April 1979. (Anthony Sayer)

BR Swindon Type 1 0-6-0 Diesel-Hydraulic Locomotives Class 14

Their Life in Industry

ANTHONY P. SAYER

PEN & SWORD TRANSPORT

AN IMPRINT OF PEN & SWORD BOOKS LTD.
YORKSHIRE – PHILADELPHIA

First published in Great Britain in 2022 by
Pen and Sword Transport
An imprint of
Pen & Sword Books Ltd.
Yorkshire - Philadelphia

ISBN 978 1 39901 917 0

A CIP catalogue record for this book is available from the British
Library.

Typeset in Palatino by SJmagic DESIGN SERVICES, India.

Printed and bound in India by Replika Press Pvt. Ltd.

Pen & Sword Books Ltd incorporates the imprints of Pen & Sword
Books Archaeology, Atlas, Aviation, Battleground, Discovery, Family
History, History, Maritime, Military, Naval, Politics, Railways, Select,
Transport, True Crime, Fiction, Frontline Books, Leo Cooper, Praetorian
Press, Seaforth Publishing, Wharncliffe and White Owl.

For a complete list of Pen & Sword titles please contact

PEN & SWORD BOOKS LIMITED
47 Church Street, Barnsley, South Yorkshire, S70 2AS, England
E-mail: enquiries@pen-and-sword.co.uk
Website: www.pen-and-sword.co.uk

or

PEN AND SWORD BOOKS
1950 Lawrence Rd, Havertown, PA 19083, USA
E-mail: Uspen-and-sword@casematepublishers.com
Website: www.penandswordbooks.com

CONTENTS

PREFACE

My book "BR Swindon Type 1 0-6-0 Diesel Hydraulic-Locomotives. Class 14: Their Life on British Railways" was my fifth in the Pen & Sword 'Locomotive Portfolios' series, and covered the early years of the locomotives over the period 1959 to 1969, the period when the requirement for a Type 1 diesel specifically to meet the needs of the Western Region was identified, developed, implemented and deployed. An initial identified requirement for up to 400 locomotives was gradually whittled-down such that only fifty-six machines were constructed at Swindon Works during 1964/65, and, ultimately, even these became redundant on British Railways by 1969.

It was fortuitous that a number of the heavy industrial concerns across the UK were starting the process of converting their steam fleets to diesel, and thus forty-eight of the Swindon Type 1s were sold into the coal, steel (iron-ore), oil and cement sectors, with most finding useful additional and active employment after their premature withdrawal from BR.

This 'companion' book, "Class 14: Their Life in Industry" covers this later period of activity, including the history of five locomotives which were transferred to continental Europe for further intended industrial duties after work in the UK diminished.

Extensive research has enabled significantly increased clarity and detail with respect to the industrial careers of these locomotives to be presented here. Many local Record Office and personal sources have been deployed, but by far the greatest resource accessed was the Industrial Railway Society (IRS) and their impressive array of books, periodicals and bulletins, together with their considerable 'vault' of archive material.

The IRS meticulously researches industrial locomotives and railways worldwide, with locomotive information largely centred around location chronology, so my IRS task was less one of finding the 'where' and 'when' information for the Swindon Type 1s, but more about extracting precise details of 'what' duties the locomotives undertook and 'why' the Class 14s, in particular, were purchased against the backdrop of numerous alternate industrial and redundant BR types available for purchase. The real task was extracting information regarding the relatively infinitesimal number of Swindon Type 1s from the unbelievable mass of other industrial information available!

Understanding the context was critical in terms of explaining 'Why the Swindon Type 1s were to be found at Ashington but not Horden?', for example. Suitably focused research has enabled the whole rationale of using the Swindon Type 1s at quite specific locations to be properly addressed; it was not by chance that twenty-three of these machines turned up in Lincolnshire and Northamptonshire.

In addition to the IRS information sources, enthusiast sightings and associated commentary have been absolutely crucial in determining locomotive status changes (e.g. working, out-of-use, etc). Unlike Rolling Stock Library details covering locomotive introduction, works visits, storage and withdrawal on BR, such official information in the industrial setting is not available. Any clarity on such information is virtually entirely reliant on enthusiast sightings. Unfortunately, despite the meticulous recording of events by many enthusiasts, the exact timing of the Class 14 status changes during their time in industry is significantly less precise than when owned by BR.

Despite the information shortcomings, sufficient sources have been found to enable the development of reasonably detailed histories for each of the forty-eight locomotives which moved into industry; space constraints have led to some abridgement but all information considered to be 'key' has been retained.

Enthusiast observations and photographs have been crucial particularly in identifying industry-specific detail differences and liveries.

The locomotives forming the subject of this book are variously described as Swindon Type 1s, Class 14s or 'Paxmans', the latter name being particularly popular amongst the industrial users and their staff.

Inside the cabs of the Class 14s, 'A Leading' or 'B Trailing' signage defined the locomotive ends and this apparently Western Region convention has again been used in this book. 'A Leading' equates to the No.1 end (where the radiator equipment is housed) and 'B Trailing' to No.2.

Finally, it should be noted that the post-industrial histories of the nineteen locomotives which survived into preservation are not included here on the basis that the locomotive owners themselves are much better placed to cover this part of the story. There are, however, a few photographs taken of Class 14s whilst in preservation which illustrate some of the new liveries and modifications now carried.

Anthony Sayer

D9502, NCB Ashington, 5 April 1986. (Anthony Sayer)

ACKNOWLEDGEMENTS

Most of the Class 14's productive time was spent in industry, notably the movement of coal and iron-ore, and as a consequence I looked to the Industrial Railway Society (IRS) for guidance and assistance which was both freely and enthusiastically given by all, officers and members alike. I must firstly thank Ian Bendall (Chairman of the IRS) for his very generous permission to research and reproduce information from the Society's extensive magazine and book sources, as well as giving me free access to all archive material, all thoroughly appreciated. I must also thank the following IRS officers for their considerable assistance: Adrian Booth (who compiles the excellent *Ex-BR Locos in Industry* books) for his ongoing help, not just with the locomotives themselves, but also geographical locations, detailed sightings, etc.; Andrew Smith (Treasurer) for his assistance with sourcing my specific photograph requirements; Martin Shill (*Bulletin* Editor) for his wonderful, if macabre, selection of photographs of locomotives dumped at Corby; Rob Pearman (Archivist) for his guidance around the hugely impressive Archive at Statfold Barn and for introducing new contacts; David Kitching (Administration)

for forwarding mail to potential new sources, together with Cliff Shepherd (*Industrial Railway Record* Editor), Roy Etherington (President), Roger West and Philip Cartwright. I also must not forget the late Colin Mountford for his help and guidance in the early days when this project was being hatched. I strongly recommend membership of this highly professional organisation, not only with respect to recording industrial locomotive history, but also the railways and industries in which they operated.

A number of other individuals have assisted greatly with each element of this book and my thanks is due to them all:

National Coal Board:
Trevor Scott has provided considerable assistance with the NCB North-East 'Paxmans. Trevor developed very close relationships with the local Traffic Managers and was able to regularly visit sites during the period 1975-90. He was fortunate in being able to obtain many fascinating documents, including a significant number of the Ashington Loco Shed Daily Reports. Trevor has very kindly allowed free use of this material.

British Steel Corporation:
Greg Evans has been similarly indispensable with respect to the BSC Corby and Glendon East operations, assisted greatly by his close contacts with former BSC employees, including Bill Warren, Neil Campbell, David Fursdon, David Kanes and Mick Browett.

Export: Mark Jones, Mike Kennard, Paul Spencer, Kevin Prince and Peter Hall (RCTS *Diesel Dilemmas*) have all provided insights into the Class 14s which found use abroad.

My continued use of the 'back to basics' approach has, by necessity, relied heavily on a massive amount of personal observation information in various forms. I have made every attempt to credit everyone concerned in the 'References and Sources' section. My thanks go to you all.

This book has used over 250 images to support the text. My thanks go to the following organisations, societies and individuals for the photographs used herein:

John Chalcraft (Rail-Photoprints), Paul Chancellor

(Colour-Rail), W. Gordon Davies and John Broughton (RCTS Archive), Robin Fell (Transport Treasury), Martin High (Transport Topics), Rail-Online and Old-Maps.co.uk.

Industrial Railway Society (John Gardner, M.J. Leah, Roger Monk, Cliff Shepherd, Martin Shill, G. Smith, Peter Stamper, Geoffrey Starmer, Eric Tonks, Jim Wade and Brian Webb).

Dan Adkins, Robin Barnes, Lewis Bevan, Adrian Booth, John Carter, Luis Rentero Corral, Chris Davis, Tom Dovey, P.J. Edwards, Billy Embleton, Derek Elston, Greg Evans

Collection, Adrian Freeman, David Ford Collection (inc. John Ford), Peter Foster, Bruce Galloway, Trevor Hall, Martyn Hearson (Renown), David Henderson, Robert von Hirschhorn, Douglas Johnson, Mark Jones, Steve Kemp, Kevin Lane, John Law, M. Liston, MasonPhenix19 Collection, Alistair Ness, Henry Pattison, Kevin Prince, Mike Richardson Collection (inc John Reay), my late father John Sayer, Trevor Scott Collection, Geoff Sharpe, Tony Skinner, Michael Urquhart, Pete Wilcox, George Woods, Phil Wormald, Ian (ijr65 (flickr)) and SlightlyReliable70 2010-2015 (flickr).

There are images from a very small number of photographers where it has proved impossible to obtain the appropriate permission to use their photographs despite every endeavour being made to track down the individuals concerned. In addition, there are a few images where the identity of the photographer is totally unknown; lack of accreditation on slides or prints has prevented any possibility of determining their provenance. In both cases, anyone who feels that they have inadequately credited should contact me via the publisher to ensure that the situation is corrected in future editions.

D9500(No.1), en route New Moor-Lynemouth, 2 November 1985. Ashington Colliery can be seen on the horizon to the left, with wagons stabled at New Moor Sidings visible in the far right distance. (Anthony Sayer)

ABBREVIATIONS

A	Amps.
APCM	Associated Portland Cement Manufacturers.
BLS	British Locomotive Society.
BR	British Railways / British Rail.
BRB	British Railways Board.
BSC	British Steel Corporation.
CTRL	Channel Tunnel Rail Link.
DP	Davey Paxman
FS	Ferrovie dello Stato (Italian National Railways).
hp	Horsepower.
IRS	Industrial Railway Society.
KESR	Kent & East Sussex Railway.
LCGB	Locomotive Club of Great Britain.
NCB	National Coal Board.
NVR	Nene Valley Railway.
OOU	Out of use.
RCTS	Railway Correspondence and Travel Society.
RENFE	Red Nacional de los Ferrocarriles Españoles (Spanish National Railways).
S&L or S&L(M)	Stewarts & Lloyd (Minerals) Ltd
SLS	Stephenson Locomotive Society.
SNCB	Société Nationale des Chemins de Fer Belges (Belgian National Railways).
V	Volts.

COLLIERY GLOSSARY

Shaft:	Vertical hole sunk from the surface to the coal seam or pit bottom.
Drift mine:	Tunnel leading from the surface to the coal in lieu of a shaft.
Screens:	Device with different size holes in plates for sorting coal into various sized pieces and grades.
Washery:	Facility where coal is cleaned of stone and other impurities by a mechanical process which uses water and take advantage of the difference in specific gravity of the coal and the impurities.
Coal preparation plant:	Facility that washes coal of impurities (washery), crushes it into graded sizes (screens), stockpiles various grades preparing it for transport to market, and, final loading into rail wagons, lorries, barges or ships. N.B. The more waste material that can be removed from coal, the lower its ash content, the greater its market value and the lower its transportation costs.
Spoil:	Waste material.

Chapter 1

INTRODUCTION: A NEW LIFE IN INDUSTRY

1.1 Industry Beckons.

The final chapter of my book "BR Swindon Type 1 0-6-0 Diesel-Hydraulic Locomotives. Class 14: Their Life on British Railways" entitled "Industry Beckons", provided a listing of the Class 14s which transferred into industry following completion of their work on British Railways. This list and the supporting text represented a final summary of their BR history, but also constituted an introduction for their forthcoming career in industry. As a consequence a short section of the "Industry Beckons" chapter is reproduced below.

1.2 A Second Career in Industry.

Forty-eight of the fifty-six Class 14s (85 per cent) found their way into industry after their short career with BR; only eight locomotives were immediately scrapped. Brian Haresnape, in his book *British Rail Fleet Survey: Western Region Diesel-Hydraulics*, was able to state: 'Fortunately BR was able to find ready purchasers for the majority of these engines'; very true, but it was seriously bad news for the manufacturers of industrial locomotives!

Put the other way around, only five of the twenty-three Class14s withdrawn from the Western Region were scrapped (i.e. D9501/6/9/19/22), and just three of the thirty-three Eastern Region contingent (D9543/6/50).

1.2.1 Disposal of the Hull Fleet (ER) into Industry.

D9503-5/7/10-2/5/6/20/3/5/9/32-4/7/9-42/4/5/7-9/51-4 (30, i.e. 91 per cent of the fleet)

Loco Nos.	Buyer	Movement
D9529	S&L Buckminster, Lincolnshire	08/68
D9552	S&L Buckminster, Lincolnshire	09/68
D9515	S&L Buckminster, Lincolnshire	11/68
D9510/2	S&L Buckminster, Lincolnshire	12/68
D9539	S&L Corby, Northamptonshire	10/68
D9507/16/32/7/44/9/53/4	S&L Corby, Northamptonshire	11/68
D9533/42/7/51	S&L Corby, Northamptonshire	12/68
D9503/41/8	S&L Harlaxton, Lincolnshire	11/68
D9520/3	S&L Glendon East, Northamptonshire	12/68

Loco Nos.	Buyer	Movement
D9504/25/40	NCB Philadelphia, Co. Durham	11/68
D9511	NCB Ashington, Northumberland	01/69
D9545	NCB Ashington, Northumberland	04/69
D9534	APCM Hope Cement Works, Derbyshire	09/68
D9505	APCM Hope Cement Works, Derbyshire	10/68

1.2.2 Disposal of the WR Fleet into Industry.
In total: D9500/2/8/13/4/7/8/21/4/6-8/30/1/5/6/8/55 (18, i.e. 78 per cent of the fleet)

a) Via W.H. Arnott Young & Co Ltd, Parkgate, Rotherham Scrapyard: D9513/31 (2)

Loco Nos.	Buyer	Movement
D9513/31	Hargreaves/NCBOE, Crigglestone, Yorkshire	11/68

b) Direct from WR Depots: D9500/2/8/14/7/8/21/4/6-8/30/5/6/8/55 (16)

Loco Nos.	Buyer	Movement (ex-86A)	Relevant BR/Buyer Meeting Dates
D9508/28	NCB Ashington, Northumberland (ex-86A)	06/03/69	BR/NCB Meeting 27/02/69
D9502/14/8/27	NCB Ashington, Northumberland (ex-86A)	30/06/69	BR/NCB Meeting ?
D9500/17	NCB Ashington, Northumberland (ex-86A)	17/11/69	BR/NCB Meeting 15/10/69
D9521/36	NCB Ashington, Northumberland (ex-86A)	04/03/70	BR/NCB Meeting 18/01/70
D9555	NCB Burradon, Northumberland (ex-86A)	04/03/70	BR/NCB Meeting 18/01/70
D9535	NCB Ashington, or, Burradon, Northumberland (ex-86A)	09/11/70	BR/NCB Meeting 18/09/70
D9524	BP Refinery Ltd, Grangemouth (ex-86A)	07/70	BR/BP Meeting?
D9530	Gulf Oil Co Ltd, Waterston (ex-86A)	11/69	BR/Gulf Meeting 05/11/69
D9538	Shell Haven Refineries, Thames Haven, Essex (ex-86A)	04/70	BR/Shell Meetings 26/11/69 and 19/12/69
D9526	APCM Westbury, Wiltshire (ex-86A)	01/70	BR/APCM Meeting 01/12/69

Note: 86A = Cardiff Canton.

Brian Penney (BR CM&EE Department, Cardiff) was heavily involved in the sale of the Western Region Class 14s to prospective industrial operators. He met representatives from a number of interested organisations over the period February 1969 to September 1970. Insights from Penney regarding these meetings is augmented by the specific dates which were quoted in David Clough's article 'Class 14s; the unlikely survivors' (*Rail* No.739) as a consequence of an interview he had with Penney.

First 'out of the blocks' was the NCB North East Area who

had major colliery systems in the Northumberland area. Representatives visited Cardiff on at least four occasions (see table above, fourth column), possibly even five, and as a result twelve Class 14s moved north in convoys of between one and four locomotives over the period March 1969 to November 1970.

Penney also had meetings with Gulf Oil, Shell, APCM (Westbury) and, presumably, BP all of which resulted in sales after the requisite locomotive inspections and demonstrations.

There were several instances where Class 14s were seen in traffic on BR after their official withdrawal date, either at Cardiff Canton (as depot pilots), on the main line between Canton and Radyr, and, indeed, undertaking weekend civil engineering duties (for example, D9524/35 on the route south of Craven Arms between Woofferton and Ludlow), based at Hereford). These duties ensured that locomotives were kept in operational condition for potential customer demonstrations, to ensure that locomotives were available for immediate use on delivery, and, possibly, for customer's driving staff familiarisation.

D9500, 16C Etches Park, Derby, November 1969. This photograph was purchased with no date and the suggestion that it was Derby. D2211, an early incarnation of the Class 04 design and adjacent to D9500, was allocated to 16C in May 1967 after Works repairs and a repaint into blue livery (w/e 27 May 1967 to be more precise) until July 1970 (stored w/e 11 July and withdrawn 19 July 1970, surplus to requirements). D9500 and D9517 were transferred from 86A Cardiff Canton to NCB Ashington between 17 and 25 November 1969, being sighted at 50A York on 22 November. Taken together, the photograph would appear to be D9500/17 at 16C Derby between 17 and 22 November 1969. (Author's Collection)

Chapter 2

LOCOMOTIVE HISTORIES (INDUSTRY – 1968–87)

2.1 Information Sources.

Information has come from a wide variety of sources:

2.1.1 Industrial Railway Society.

Information contained within various Industrial Railway Society publications form the central pillar of the locomotive histories, i.e.

- The *Industrial locomotives of.....* and *Industrial Railways and Locomotives of.....* books (latest editions),
- The *Ex-BR Diesels in Industry* books (particularly 7BRD and 8BRD),
- The quarterly *Industrial Railway Record* (IRRxxx) magazines, and,
- The IRS *Bulletins* (IRSxxx).
- CD-based repositories of member's observations.

I must once again thank the Chairman of the IRS, Ian Bendall, and the various Society Officers for their kind permission to use the full range of the society's resources in the production of this book; without their incredible generosity and kind help the level of detail presented in this Section would have not been possible.

Within the "Movements" section for each locomotive, where anomalies have been found the relevant source information is colour-coded as shown above. It must be stressed at this point that any anomalies and inconsistencies are in no way a reflectionof the quality of the IRS publications concerned; far from it, in fact! Considering the sheer numbers of locomotives that the IRS has dealt with over the years, the number of anomalies are incredibly small and mostly insignificant. The editors and authors of the various publications are absolutely first-rate professionals and complete experts in their field, and are to be fully applauded for their Herculean efforts.

In reality, many anomalies resulted from conflicting reports produced by the industries themselves (NCB and BSC to name but two), but by far the biggest number of anomalies in the context of the Class 14s relate to when locomotives worked on the Backworth, Burradon and Weetslade systems. Sightings of locomotives nominally allocated to any one of these systems were frequently seen on one or other of the other two systems over the years. This is not surprising because Burradon locomotives hauled spoil trains to Backworth, and Backworth locomotives hauled coal to Weetslade for washing! Equally locomotive shortages in one area could lead to short-term assistance from a neighbouring Shed. Both these factors led to an inevitable blurring of where locomotives were *believed* by enthusiasts to be effectively allocated on a given day and the effect of this can be seen in the information provided (particularly D9513 and D9535).

Information in IRS publications is highly reliant on enthusiast visits to industrial sites which were considerably less frequent than those visiting BR depots. The combined frequency of their visits to industrial establishments influenced the precision of information regarding the whereabouts of locomotives at any given time; in some cases there can unfortunately be significant time gaps between visits leading to some inevitable "fogginess" regarding locations, transfers and locomotive status.

Hopefully it can be understood that some anomalies are inevitable given the very 'nature of the beast'. The purpose of identifying such discrepancies here is purely as a trigger to encourage enthusiasts to dig out their records and to help with filling information gaps, resolving anomalies, and, adding to our general understanding of the industrial railway scene. Any help in this regard will be very much appreciated both by the IRS and myself.

2.1.2 Personal sightings.

The IRS information presented here is supported by a considerable quantity of additional personal sighting data. Most of the IRS locomotive information is based on the three critical items (i.e. Loco. No., Location, Date) but personal sightings can provide so much more (e.g. loco operational status, specific (micro) locations within a site, liveries, modifications, duties undertaken, etc). For the IRS to deal with all this additional information (for literally thousands of industrials in the UK) would be well nigh impossible; however, for me dealing with only a mere forty-eight industrial Class 14s, it is so much easier!

2.1.3 Photographic evidence.

Photographs are particularly useful for liveries and 'local' modifications.

2.1.4 Official Sources.

NCB Ashington Daily Reports, Signal Box registers (courtesy of Trevor Scott).

2.2 Information Presentation.

A few specific location comments are relevant here:

National Coal Board: Ashington. Ashington-based locomotives were also sub-shedded at Lynemouth for lengthy periods. Sightings at Lynemouth have been specifically marked as such, albeit still under the NCB Ashington heading. In most instances, locomotives listed at Lynemouth should be considered as being operational.

Other entries under the Ashington 'umbrella' are not specifically reported as such to avoid repetition, but, where available, anecdotal comments such as 'wkg', 'spare', 'OOU', 'reps', etc. are included to give an indication of a locomotive's operational status.

National Coal Board: Backworth, Burradon, Weetslade. The 'problem' here has already been described. Where locomotive have been noted on systems which are different from their nominally allocated Shed (as defined by the latest relevant IRS books), then they are specifically listed as such.

British Steel Corporation, Corby. Probably about 90% of

the observations of operational locomotives were made at Gretton Brook shed; however, where seen at quarries, locomotives are recorded accordingly.

2.3 Individual Industrial Histories.

Locomotive histories have been developed for each of the forty-eight Class 14 locomotives purchased by industrial concerns. Details are provided over the forthcoming pages.

Abbreviations used:

CPP	Coal Preparation Plant
CW	Central Workshops
DP	Disposal Point
GB	BSC Gretton Brook
LEW	NCB Lambton Engine Works, Philadelphia
Ly	NCB Lynemouth
OE	Opencast Executive (NCBOE)
dsm	Dismantled
Ldg	Ashington Leading loco
OOU	Out of use
rems	Remains
reps	Repairs
sdgs	Sidings
shed	Inside shed building
w/b	Weighbridge
wkg	Working
wtg	Waiting

Sightings:

Sighting dates are in the 'ddmmyy' format for clarity.

D9500

**D9500 (9312/92),
NCB Ashington,
Undated.** Based on the
livery and numbering,
sometime between about
November 1969 and June
1972. Very strange wagon
behind the Class 14;
its purpose.....for track
weed-killing, apparently.
(P.J. Edwards)

**D9500 (9312/92,
No.1), NCB Ashington,
2 November 1985.**
North East Area dark
blue livery with buffer-
beam (\\\\) stripes
replacing nose-end
chevrons. (Anthony Sayer)

NCB No.: No.1
Plant Registry No.: 9312/92

Movements:
Despatched from 86A Cardiff Canton: 17/11/69.
Sighted 50A York: 22/11/69, and, 52A Gateshead: 23/11/69 and 24/11/69 (with D9517).
Arrived NCB Ashington: 25/11/69.
To Ashington CW: early 06/72 (for repainting, completed by 07/06/72).
To NCB Ashington: by 07/06/72.
To BR South Gosforth: 07/12/72 (tyre-turning).
To Ashington CW: xx/12/72 (overhauled engine 620022/15 fitted).
To NCB Ashington: xx/10/73.
To BR South Gosforth: xx/04/77 (tyre-turning).
To NCB Ashington: 12/04/77.
To LEW Philadelphia: 12/07/78 (IRLNC/8BRD/IRR142).
To NCB Ashington: xx/09/78 (IRLNC).
To LEW Philadelphia: 10/11/78 (IRLNC) (for complete overhaul; fitted with new tyres, overhauled engine 620022/8, turbo-blower, transmission, heat exchangers, compressor and cleaned radiator 14/08/79) (NCB).
To NCB Ashington: 26/06/79 (IRLNC/8BRD), or, 14/08/79 (IRR142).
At NCB Ashington: Overhauled engine 630002/3 fitted 05/03/80 (NCB), or, 15/03/80 (IRR142).
To BR Thornaby: 14/05/82 (tyre-turning).
To NCB Ashington: 24/05/82.
To LEW Philadelphia: 12/05/83 (overhauled engine 630002/6 fitted).
To NCB Ashington Colliery: 21/07/83 (IRR142), or, 25/07/83 (IRLNC).
To Llangollen Railway (for preservation): 25/09/87.

Sightings:
NCB Ashington: 300370/180770 (Ly)/ 080970 (Ly)/ 140970 (Ly)/ 070572
Ashington CW: 250572
NCB Ashington: 270772/140872/ 221072
BR South Gosforth: Nil.
Ashington CW: 180873 (wtg engine)/190973 (wtg engine)
NCB Ashington: 120674/150774 (wkg)/ 240774/ 281074 (wkg)/ 040675 (wkg)/ 260975 (shed)/ 140676 (Ly)/ 280676 (Ly)
BR South Gosforth: Nil.
NCB Ashington: 190977 (wkg)/131177 (Ly)/ 250178 (shed, repairs)/ 210378/ 050478/ 150478 (shed)
LEW Philadelphia: Nil.
NCB Ashington: 291078
LEW Philadelphia: 250679/260679 (under reps / 050779
NCB Ashington: 281279 (shed)/180180 (wkg)/ 070580 (wkg, No.1 Ldg loco)/ 040780 (wkg)/ 080780 (Ly)/ 110780 (wkg)/ 061280/ 290381/ 100481 (outside shed)/ 130681 (shed)/ 190681 (shed)/ 140881 (shed)/ 05-060981

(full service)/ 120981 (wkg)/ 141081 (wkg)/ 271181 (wkg)/ 150182 (wkg)/ 260282 (wkg)/ 010382 (Ly)/ 130382 (Ly)/ 140482 (Ly)/ Departed for Thornaby 140582
BR Thornaby: 180582 (tyre-turning)
NCB Ashington: Arrived back from Thornaby 240582/ 010782 (shed, reps, wtg coupling-rod brasses)/ 240882 (side-rods fitted)/ 260882 (spare)/ 220982 (wkg)/ 011082 (Ly)/ 081182 (Ly)/ 291282 (shed)/ 200383/ 120583 (shed, later departed to LEW on low-loader)
LEW Philadelphia: 120583/140683/ 210783
NCB Ashington: 220783/280783 (shed)/ 150883 (ready to test post-overhaul)/ 180883 (wkg, test runs)/ 25-260883 and 300883 (overheating, LEW fitters in attendance)/ 100983 (serviceable, engine tests)/ 13-140983 (engine reps/tests)/ 150983 (wkg)/ 251083 (wkg)/ 151183 (wkg)/ 301183 (wkg, Ldg loco)/ 021283 (Ly)/ 231283 (wkg)/ 110184 (wkg, Ldg loco)/ 010284 (wkg)/ 130284 (wkg)/ 070784 (shed)/ 080285 (wkg)/ 060485/ 030585 (spare)/ 080585 (wkg)/ 110585 (wkg)/

150685 (shed)/ 270885 (wkg)/ 290885 (wkg, Ldg loco)/ 081085 (wkg)/ 201085 (shed)/ 021185 (wkg)/ 241185 (wkg, No.2 Ldg loco)/ 161285 (wkg, New Moor)/ 120186 (shed)/ 120286 (wkg)/ 180386 (wkg)/ 250386 (wkg)/ 050486 (wkg)/ 260486 (shed yard)/ 020586 (wkg)/ 150586 (shed)/ 160686 (outside shed)/ 270686 (wkg, Ldg loco)/ 170786 (wkg)/ 170986 (wkg, Ldg loco)/ 190986 (wkg, Ldg loco)/ 270986(wkg, New Moor)/ 081186 (wkg)/ 291186 (wkg, New Moor)/ 121286 (wkg)/ 181286 (wkg, New Moor)/ 301286 (shed)/ 050187 (wkg)/ 070187 (wkg)/ 230187 (spare, failing liners)/ 280187 (wkg)/ 300187 (wkg)/ 050287 (shed)/ 130287 (shed, spare)/ 150287 (wkg)/ 260287 (shed)/ 280287 (shed)/ 010387 (shed)/ 070387 (shed)/ 130387 (shed)/ 150387 (shed)/ 200387 (shed yard)/ 200487 (shed)/ 170587 (shed)/ 130687/ 030887 (shed)/ 100987/ 250987 (being loaded onto low-loader)

Liveries and numbers:

Renumbered 9312/92 on black panel over BR number by 27/01/70

Repainted in Ashington blue livery (with black/yellow chevrons on nose-end excluding headcode box glass (BR-dimensions)) and re-numbered No.1 at Ashington CW in 06/72 (completed by 07/06/72). Cabside details:

> **NCB**
> **Nº1**
> 9312/92

Repainted in North-East Area dark-blue livery including bonnet fronts (with white hand-rails, red coupling rods, black/yellow striped buffer beams [\ \ \ \ orientation]) and re-numbered 9312/92 at LEW, Philadelphia (completed by 26/06/79, or, 14/08/79).

Noted without 'No.1' on 07/05/80 through to 01/07/82. NCB Ashington shed staff restored the No.1 identity by 12/05/83. New cabside details:

> **NCB**
> **North East**
> **Area**
> 9312/92
> **Nº1**

Detail Differences:

Buffer-beam coupling-stick clips

Notes:

1. Fitted with Railway Executive registration plate (No.1433 of 1953).
2. Noted running with brake-tender 9300/2 on 04/06/75.
3. Ashington Periodic Reports:
   - Status, 24/11/81: Overhauled engine with high-capacity oil pump and CI heads fitted at Ashington on 05/03/80. Also overhauled turbo-blower, transmission, heat exchangers, compressor and cleaned radiators fitted 14/08/79; all done at Philadelphia Workshops. Tyre thickness 3/16" (BR exam 01/06/81).
   - Complaint, 23/08/83: "Came back (from Philadelphia) on July 21 [1983]. Took out for test runs on 18/8/83, 19/8/83, 22/8/83; engine cut out overheating each time. Philly Mechs to check engine on 25/8/83."
   - Status, 16/04/86: Working OK.
   - Status, 13/02/87: Engine tight. Tyres thick, but hollow. Generally OK but the engine will give trouble soon.

D9502

D9502 and D9540 (No.36), NCB Ashington, 28 April 1981. Recently delivered (with D9525) by BR from the closed Weetslade Washery. Note the roof mounted flashing light, which in NCB terms, was only a feature of Weetslade locomotives. Note also the absence of coupling rods for transit purposes. (Henry Pattison)

D9502, NCB Ashington, 7 March 1987. After 18 years in industry and still carrying its original BR livery. Note the redundant wiring above the cab side windows following the removal of the roof flashing lights. (Anthony Sayer)

NCB No.: -
Plant Registry No.: 9312/97

Movements:
Despatched from 86A Cardiff Canton: 30/06/69.
Sighted 85B Gloucester: 03/07/69 and 04/07/69 (with D9514/8/27) and Derby Midland: xx/07/69 (with D9514/8/27).
Arrived NCB Ashington: 19/07/69.
To NCB, Burradon Colliery: 06/09/69.
To Ashington CW: 24/07/73 (for overhaul).
To NCB Burradon: 14/03/74.
To NCB Weetslade CPP: xx/01/76 (IRR142 only) (Burradon loco shed closed 03/01/76).
To NCB Backworth (from Weetslade): 26/01/76 (for repairs) (IRR142 only).
To NCB Backworth (from Burradon): xx/01/76 (by 17/02/76) (IRLNC/8BRD).
To NCB Weetslade CPP: xx/06/76 (after 02/06/76).
To NCB Ashington: 24/04/81 (Weetslade operation closed 25/03/81).
To LEW Philadelphia: 28/04/83 (IRLNC/8BRD).
To BR Thornaby: 28/04/83 (tyre-turning) (IRR142).
To NCB Ashington (from Philadelphia): 12/05/83 (IRLNC/8BRD).
To NCB Ashington (from BR Thornaby): 12/05/83 (IRR142).
At NCB Ashington: OOU by 06/85, used as source of spares.
To Llangollen Railway (for preservation), 25/09/87.

Sightings:
NCB Ashington: 200769/010869/ 080869
NCB Burradon: 160969 (Weetslade)/051069 (shed)/ 171069 (wkg)/ 161169 (shed)/ 300370/ 230570/ 240570 (shed)/ 180770 (shed)/ 070870 (OOU)/ 150870 (shed)/ 210870 (OOU)/ 030970 (OOU, gearbox problems)/ 080970 (shed)/ 150970/ 180970/ 011070 (wkg)/ 181170 (Burradon-Weetslade)/ 101270 (wkg)/ 050371/ 240771/ 051071/ 251071 (shed)/ 190572/ 250572/ 140772 (shed)/ 120673 (shed)
NCB Ashington: 180873 (ex-Burradon, for ACW)
Ashington CW: 280973
NCB Burradon: 240174/260374 (shed)/ 120774 (Weetslade)/ 240774 (shed) / 281074 (Havannah Drift)
NCB Backworth (Eccles): 170276 (new arrival)/150576/ 150676 (shed)
NCB Weetslade: 200977 (Brenkley Drift)/131177/ 210378/ 050478 (wkg)/ 180778 (wkg)/ 291078/ 170479 (shed)/ 260679 (wkg)/ 090480 (spare)/ 300680 (wkg)/ 040780 (shed)/ 150381 (shed)
NCB Ashington: Arrived 240481 (from Killingworth Exchange Sdgs via BR, with D9525/40)/ 280481 (Landsale passbye, no rods)/ 130681 (shed)/ 180681 (shed yard)/ 190681 (shed)/ 140881 (shed)/ 2408-010981

(reps, inc cylinder heads/ governor)/ 120981 (Ly)/ 03-041081 (reps, full service)/ 271181 (Ly)/ 011281 (Ly)/ 081281 (wkg)/ 040182 (wkg)/ 150182 (wkg)/ 25-260182 (Ly)/ 28-290182 (wkg)/ 01-050282 (Ly)/ 10-130282 (wkg)/ 01-050382 (spare)/ 140482 (spare)/ 010782 (spare)/ 19-230782 (spare)/ 16-200882 (spare)/ 01-020982 (Ly)/ 06-100982 (Ly)/ 20-240982 (Ly)/ 27-300982 (Ly)/ 011082 (reps)/ 211082 (wkg)/ 011182 (wkg)/ 291282 (shed)/ 200383 (Ly)
LEW Philadelphia: Nil.
BR Thornaby: Nil.
NCB Ashington: Arrived 120583 (ex-LEW on low-loader)/ 14-170683 (wkg)/ 260683 (shed)/ 04-080783 (wkg)/ 220783/ 15-190883 (wkg)/ 100983 (Ly)/ 300983 (Ly)/ 251083 (wkg)/ 07-111183 (wkg)/ 291183 (wkg)/ 12-161283 (wkg)/ 110184 (New Moor)/ 23-270184 (wkg)/ 310184 (reps, cylinder head oil leak)/ 130284 (wkg)/ 020884 (Ly)/ 05-080285 (Ly)/ 11-120285 (Ly)/ 18-200285 (reps)/ 25-270285 (Ly)/ 060485/ 110485 (wtg scrap)/ 030585 ('scrap-line', dumped OOU)/ 110585 ('scrap-line')/ 150685 ('scrap-line', OOU)/ 290885 ('scrap-line')/ 051085 ('scrap-line', OOU)/ 201085 ('scrap-line')/ 021185 ('scrap-line')/ 241185 (OOU)/

011285 (being stripped of parts)/ 161285 ('scrap-line')/ 120186 ('scrap-line')/ 210286 ('scrap-line', OOU)/ 170386 (OOU, engine worn out, low oil pressure)/ 050486 ('scrap-line')/ 260486 ('scrap-line')/ 020586 ('scrap-line')/ 150586 ('scrap-line')/ 270686 ('scrap-line' / 200786 ('scrap-line')/ 260886 ('scrap-line')/ 170986 ('scrap-line')/ 270986 ('scrap-line')/ 081186 ('scrap-line')/ 291186 ('scrap-line')/ 121286 ('scrap-line')/ 301286 ('scrap-line')/ 050187 ('scrap-line')/ 230187 ('scrap-line', wtg scrap)/ 280187 ('scrap-line')/ 050287 ('scrap-line')/ 150287 ('scrap-line')/ 260287 ('scrap-line')/ 010387 ('scrap-line')/ 070387 ('scrap-line')/ 150387 ('scrap-line')/ 200487 ('scrap-line')/ 170587 ('scrap-line')/ 130687/ 030887 ('scrap-line')/ 310887/ 100987

Liveries and numbers:
Retained BR two-tone green livery (with black/yellow chevrons on the bonnet ends), with D9502 number and lion & wheel roundel, throughout period of NCB ownership.

Allocated Plant Registry No. 9312/97 never carried externally.

Detail Differences:
Buffer-beam coupling-stick clips

Roof-mounted flashing lights (x2) (Weetslade modification). Noted 30/06/80 at Weetslade, plus 28/04/81 immediately after arrival at Ashington from Weetslade. Subsequently removed.

Notes:
1. Ashington Periodic Report:
   - Status, 24/11/81: Engine overhaul unknown. Heat exchangers overhauled at Ashington Loco Shed on 28/05/81; overhauled compressor fitted 01/06/81. Tyre thickness $^3/_{16}''$ (BR exam 01/06/81).
2. Possible 1986 re-instatement? Ashington Daily Report information:
   - 19/03/86: "To be repaired. Parts to take off D9555."
   - 27/03/86: "OOU, engine worn out, low oil pressure."
   - 11/04/86: "To repair with parts off D9555."
   - 15/04/86: "D9502 and D9555 both 'standing for spares'".

D9503

**D9503, BSC Harlaxton,
23 December 1968.**
Lion and wheel roundel
painted out but BR
number retained.
(Pete Stamper [IRS])

**D9503 (65), BSC Corby
(Gretton Brook), 18
April 1979.** Modified
roof profile for working
at Harlaxton. Additional
footplate brackets
('A' end). (Anthony Sayer)

S&L/BSC Nos.: No.25 and 65.
S&L Plant No.: 8411/25

Movements:
Despatched from 50B Hull Dairycoates: xx/11/68. Booked transfer: 11/11/68.
Arrived S&L(M), Harlaxton Quarries, Lincolnshire: xx/11/68.
To BSC Tubes Division, Corby Quarries, Northamptonshire: 29/07/74.
At BSC Corby (Gretton Brook): Scrapped: xx/09/80 (by 24/09/80).

Sightings:

S&L/BSC Harlaxton: 221168/231268 (wkg)/ 180569/ 270969/ 080370/ 060770 (wkg)/ 150571 (outside shed, in pieces)/ 190671 (for spares)/ 270372 (wkg, Harlaxton-BSC/BR Casthorpe exchange sdgs)/ 060772 (wkg Casthorpe-Harlaxton incline)/ 210972 (shed yard)/ 160473 (shed, non-active due to strike at Stanton Ironworks)/ 260973 (shed, unavailable for work, unlikely to work at Harlaxton again)/ 160174 (outside shed, OOU)/ 190374 (shed yard)/ Departed for Corby 290774

BSC Corby: 080974 (GB)/ 221074 (being used for spares)/ 220275 (GB)/ 070575/ 010576 (GB, shed, OOU)/ 100776 (GB, shed)/ 300477
BSC Gretton Brook Dump (outside): 291277/ 050278/ 060478/ 150778/ 290878/ 180279/ 180479/ 120679/ 030879/ 230879/ 291279/ 160480/ 170580/ 270580/ 080680/ 180780/ 160880/ 220880/ Scrapped by 240980

Liveries and numbers:
D9503 to 06/70, No.25 from 06/70 to 10/74, 65 from 10/74.

BR two-tone green livery, black/yellow chevrons on nose-end, yellow buffer beams initially.

Panel below side cab window repainted dark green and 'No.25' applied 06/70.

Subsequently all Sherwood green replaced by dark green.

Detail Differences:
Cut-down roof profile (Harlaxton modification, retained at Corby).
Footplate brackets ('A' end) (Harlaxton modification).
Large spotlight mounted on bonnet ends (Harlaxton modification, retained at Corby).
No flashing lights on cab roof.
No buffer-beam lifting lugs, safety chains or coupling-stick clips fitted after arrival at Corby.

Notes:
1. Harlaxton, 13/09/71: "25(D9503) is being canniblased for spares for 26/7 (D9541/8)." (IRS137).
2. D9503/41/8: "They will go away by road [from Harlaxton to Corby] as the tyres are not in good enough condition to travel by BR." (IRS171).
3. Lack of Corby modifications suggest D9503 (65) was never used at Corby.

D9504

D9504, NCB Philadelphia, 1969.
(Colour-Rail)

D9504(506) with D9535 (37), NCB Ashington, 26 June 1983. Temporarily out of use awaiting spare parts for electrical repairs. Sealed-beam headlights, fitted at NCB Philadelphia and retained throughout industrial career. Note the absence of draw-gear and the redundant wiring above the cab side window which was associated with roof flashing lights used at its previous home at Weetslade Washery. Note also the side bonnet doors marked 'LF1', 'LF2', etc, to ensure correct positioning after removal.
(Anthony Sayer)

NCB No.: 506
Plant Registry No.: 2233/506

Movements:
Despatched from 50B Hull Dairycoates: 27/11/68.
Arrived NCB Philadelphia Loco Shed, Lambton Railway, Co. Durham: 29/11/68 (IRS Archive; official NCB records show 02/12/68).
To NCB Horden: 21/08/73 (IRLCD), or, to NCB Bolden: 21/08/73 (8BRD).
To NCB Philadelphia: 07/09/73 (IRLCD), or, LEW, Philadelphia: 07/09/73 (8BRD).
To NCB Boldon: xx/02/74 (IRLCD/8BRD).
To NCB Burradon (*via Backworth*): 17/12/74 (IRLCD/8BRD) (presumably departure date ex-Boldon).
To BR Cambois (for repairs): seen 03-06/01/75 (8BRD).
To NCB Burradon: 29/01/75 (IRLNC/8BRD) (delivered via Backworth exchange sidings per IRR142).
To NCB Weetslade CPP: 03/01/76 (after Burradon loco shed closure).
To LEW Philadelphia: 21/04/81 (after Weetslade system closure) (fitted with overhauled engine 620022/8).
To NCB Ashington: 11/09/81 (IRLNC/8BRD), or, 16/09/81 (IRR142).
At NCB Ashington: Overhauled engine fitted 20/03/86. One of last two locomotives in use; operated at Lynemouth during 03/87.
To Kent & East Sussex Railway, Tenterden (for preservation): 26/09/87.

N.B.: Reference to Horden (21/08/73-07/09/73) in IRLCD is believed to be an error for Boldon.
- Listed in IRLCD under Lambton Railway section as a sub-transfer (p233) but no listing under Horden Colliery.
- First move to Bolden (listed under Harton Railways, p157) in IRLCD is 02/74.

Sightings:
NCB Philadelphia: 010269 (shed)/080269 (shed yard)/ 100269 (wkg, Herrington)/ 110269 (shed yard)/ 140369 (shed)/ 080469 (wkg, Burnmoor)/ 150669/ 251069/ 010470/ 210870/ 080970 (wkg)/ 101270 (under reps)/ 160471 (repair shop)/ 260771 (wkg)/ 290771 (wkg)/ 240871/ 251071/ 020872 (shed)/ 300872/ 130673 (wkg)/ 170873 (wkg)
NCB Bolden: Nil.
LEW, Philadelphia: Nil.
NCB Bolden: 140674 (Westoe Loco Shed)
NCB Burradon: 171274 ("Moved here 17/12/74") (IRS188)
BR Cambois (Blyth): 030175/060175
NCB Burradon: 300575 (Fisher's Lane Crossing, light-engine)/ 260875
NCB Weetslade: 150676 (wkg)/280277 (wkg)/ 200977 (CPP)/ 131177/ 230278 (wkg)/ 210378/ 050478 (wkg, Brenkley)/ 080978 (wkg)/ 291078/ 260679/ 090480 (wkg)/ 300680 (wkg)/ 040780 (shed)/ 250281 (wkg)/ 150381 (shed)
LEW Philadelphia: 210481/180681 (inside)
NCB Ashington: 160981 (unloaded after LEW visit)/ 17-310981 (post-Works reps)/ 241181 (reps, electrical faults)/ xx1181 (wkg)/ 101281 (reps)/ 221281 (reps)/ 05-080182 (wkg)/ 25-290182 (wkg)/ 22-260282 (wkg)/ 02-050382 (wkg/spare)/ 140482 (shed, reps)/ 010782 (spare)/ 070782 (Ly)/ 13-160782 (Ly)/ 19-200782 (Ly)/ 21-230782 (reps)/ 16-200882 (reps)/ 23-270882 (reps)/ 310882 (reps)/ 0109-011082 (wtg reps)/ 19-221082 (standing for transmission/ coupling, wtg visit to LEW)/ 081182 (wtg visit to LEW)/ 291282 ('scrap-line')
LEW Philadelphia: ???
NCB Ashington: 200383/120583 (shed, reps)/ 14-170683 (reps)/ 260683 (near 'scrapline')/ 04-080783 (standing for spares)/ 18-190783 (standing for spares)/ 200783 (electrical reps started)/ 210783 (ready for test run)/ 220783/ 280783 (yard)/ 050883 (shed yard)/ 15-190883 (spare)/ 12-160983 (spare)/ 251083 (spare)/ 07-111183 (Ly) / 21-221183 (Ly)/ 281183 (reps, transmission coupling)/ 021283 (standing for transmission)/ 201283 (standing for new transmission to be fitted at LEW)/ 110184 (reps)/ 23-270184 (standing for new transmission/coupling)/ 010284 (standing for new transmission to be fitted at LEW)/ 130284 (receiving new transmission)
LEW Philadelphia: ???

NCB Ashington: 070784 (shed)/05-080285 (reps, new prop-shaft req'd)/ 25-270285 (reps, new prop-shaft req'd)/ 060485/ 030585 (reps)/ 150685 (shed)/ 290885 (shed)/ 16-200985 (reps, new prop-shaft req'd)/ 051085 (shed)/ 201085 (shed)/ 281085 (reps, prop-shaft sent to Barclays)/ 021185 ('scrap-line')/ 241185 (shed, reps)/ 011285 (shed, engine out)/ 161285 (shed)/ 080186 (reps, prop-shaft ready at Barclays)/ 120186 (shed)/ 210286 (shed, wtg re-conditioned engine to be fitted)/ 24-280286 (reps, prop-shaft and engine to fit)/ 070386 (reps, new engine fitted)/ 180386 (finishing off)/ 190386 (reps, ready to test)/ 200386 (on test)/ 210386 (wkg)/ 01-040486 (wkg)/ 050486 (shed)/ 21-250486 (wkg)/ 260486 (shed yard)/ 020586 (wkg)/ 150586 (shed yard)/ 190586 (wkg)/ 090686 (wkg)/ 270686 (shed, reps)/ 260886 (shed yard)/ 170986 (wkg)/ 190986 (wkg)/ 230986 (wkg, Ldg loco)/ 270986 (wkg, Ldg loco)/ 081186 (yard)/ 291186 (wkg, Ldg loco)/ 041286 (wkg)/ 181286 (wkg, Ldg loco)/ 301286 (shed)/ 050187 (wkg)/ 230187 (New Moor)/ 280187 (wkg)/ 300187 (wkg)/ 050287 (shed)/ 130287 (wkg, New Moor)/ 260287 (Ly)/ 070387 (spare)/ 130387 (spare)/ 150387 (shed)/ 200387 (shed yard)/ 200487 (shed)/ 170587 (shed)/ 130687/ 030887 (shed)/ 100987/ 130987/ 250987 (shed yard)

Liveries and numbers:
Re-numbered 506 xx/08/69.

Allocated Plant Registry No. never carried externally.

Repainted in Lambton emerald green with yellow buffer beams and black/yellow chevrons on the bonnet ends; date unknown (after 08/02/69). Carried through to preservation.

Detail Differences:
Buffer-beam coupling-stick clips

White headcode box panes, with two sealed-beam headlights fitted behind. Philadelphia modification; date unknown.

Roof-mounted flashing lights (x2) (Weetslade modification). Noted 25/02/81. Subsequently removed after transfer to Ashington.

Note:
1. Ashington Periodic Reports:
   - Status, 24/11/81: Standing with electrical faults.
   - Status, 16/04/86: OK pressure, good wheels, good transmission. Best locomotive of the lot.
   - Status, 13/02/87: Tyres OK and thick. New engine. Best loco on site.

D9505

D9534 and D9505, 31B March, May 1975.
En route from Hope, Derbyshire, to Belgium. The scars where nameplates have been removed can be seen on both locomotive cab sides. Rods removed. (Photographer unknown)

APCM No.: Nil; named 'MICHLOW'.

Movements:
Despatched from 50B Hull Dairycoates: 26/09/68.
Arrived APCM Hope Cement Works, Hope, Derbyshire: 26/09/68.
Departed Hope: 05/05/75.
Subsequently exported to Belgium (see Section 9).

Sightings:
APCM, Hope: 120471 (wkg)/170373/ 040973 (shed)/ 160674 (OOU, wtg spares)/131074 (stored at buffer stops behind wagons; OOU for some time)/ 120475 (OOU)/ Departed 050575 (en-route Harwich for export)

BR March MPD: 100575
Ipswich (passing): 100575 (9X35, hauled 37044, with D9534)
Harwich Docks: Nil.

Liveries and numbers:
No numbers; named 'MICHLOW' (initially as transfers, later cast plates on cabside).

APCM all-over dark green livery, black/yellow chevrons (reduced dimensions compared to BR), red shunter grab rails and couping rods and yellow buffer beams.

Detail Differences:
No external modifications.

Note:
1. "On 10/5 [1975].....D9505+D9534 were seen on a low loader in a siding south of March." (BLS0675)

D9507

D9507(55), BSC Corby, 18 April 1979. Bought for spares, but following heavy repairs was earning its living for BSC by at least 1975, and probably by late-1973. (Anthony Sayer)

S&L/BSC Nos.: 35 and 55.
S&L Plant No.: 8311/35

Movements:
Despatched from 50B Hull Dairycoates: xx/11/68.
Arrived S&L(M), Corby Quarries, Northamptonshire, xx/11/68.
To BSC Steelworks Disposal Site, Corby: xx/12/80.
At BSC Steelworks Disposal Site, Corby: Scrapped by Shanks & McEwan Ltd, Corby: xx/08/82 (IQM6) or xx/09/82 (ILoBBN/8BRD).

Sightings:
S&L/BSC Corby: 110169/241069/ 080370/ 060870 (GB, shed)/ 070871 (GB)/ 281071/ 200173 (GB, shed)/ 250973 (Pen Green workshops)/ 080974 (GB)/ 220275 (GB)/ 070575/ 161175 (wkg, Oakley Quarry)/ 020176 (GB, shed)/ 010576 (wkg)/ 100776 (GB, shed)/ 300477/ 220877 (GB, shed)/ 050278/ 150278 (wkg)/ 060478/ 150778 (GB, workable)/ 270778 (wkg)/ 180479 (GB, Repair Shed)/ 120679 (wkg)/ 030879 (GB, workable)/ 230879/ 291279 (GB, Repair Bay)/ 160480 (GB, shed)/ 080680 (GB, shed)/ 220880 (GB, shed)/ 090980 (GB, Repair Shop)/ 291080 (GB, shed)/ 261180 (GB, shed)
BSC Steelworks Disposal Site, Corby: 291280 (inside)/ 210181 (inside)/ 090581 (inside)/ 010881/ 270881/ 190981 (inside)/ 171181 (outside) / 230182 (outside, minus engine parts & some bodywork)/ 070282 (stripped)/ 120482/ 210582/ 080682/ 250882 (whole)

Liveries and numbers:
D9507 to xx/xx (noted numbered 35 on 11/01/69), 35 from xx/xx to 10/74, 55 from 10/74.

BR two-tone green livery, black/yellow chevrons on nose-end, yellow buffer beams initially.

Subsequently all Sherwood green replaced by dark green.

Detail Differences:
Twin spotlights mounted on bonnet ends (Corby modification).
Two flashing lights on cab roof (towards 'A' end) (Corby modification).
Fitted with buffer-beam lifting lugs, safety chains and coupling-stick clips (Corby modifications).

D9507 (55), BSC Corby Steelworks Disposal Point, 17 November 1981. (Martin Shill [IRS])

D9508

**D9508 (9312/99), NCB
Ashington Colliery,
17 July 1969.**
(Billy Embleton)

D9508 (No.9), NCB Ashington, 4 June 1975.
(Anthony Sayer)

NCB No.:	No.9
Plant Registry No.:	9312/99

Movements:
Despatched from 86A Cardiff Canton: 06/03/69.
Sighted 16A Toton: 09/03/69 (with D9528).
Arrived NCB Ashington: 14/03/69.
To Ashington CW: xx/06/72 (for repainting).
To NCB Ashington: xx/06/72.
To BR South Gosforth: 26/06/73 (tyre-turning).
To NCB Ashington: 29/06/73.
At NCB Ashington: Overhauled engine 640012/3 fitted xx/05/75.
To BR South Gosforth: xx/05/77 (tyre-turning).
To NCB Ashington: 02/06/77.
At Ashington: OOU from 07/05/80 (engine defects, heat exchangers needing overhaul and tyres requiring attention, source of spares).
At NCB Ashington: Withdrawn 11/83.
At NCB Ashington: Scrapped by D.Short Ltd, North Shields: 17/01/84.

Sightings:
NCB Ashington: 290369 (reps)/060469 (shed)/ 250569/ 140669 (shed)/ 290669/ 170769 (wkg)/ 200769/ 210769/ 010869/ 160969 (wkg)/ 300370/ 230570/ 240570/ 080970 (wkg, Ldg loco)/ 011070 (wkg)/ 290771 (shed)/ 010971/ 251071/ 250572/ 190672 (shed)/ 250772/ 140872
Ashington CW: Nil.
NCB Ashington: 221072
BR South Gosforth: Nil.
NCB Ashington: 180873 (wkg)/050973 (wkg)/ 230174/ 150774 (wkg)/ 240774/ 281074 (wkg)/ 100675 (wkg)/ 150676/ 280676 (wkg)
BR South Gosforth: 210577
NCB Ashington: 190977 (wkg)/131177/ 250178 (wkg)/ 210378/ 050478 (wkg)/ 291078 (Ly)/ 240279/ 281279 (wkg)/ 070580 (shed, spare)/ 040780 (shed)/ 110780 (spare)/ 060980 (shed)/ 061280/ 040181 (stabled near shed)/ 290381/ 130681 (adjacent to w/b)/ 180681 (under w/b)/ 190681 (under w/b)/ 140881 (under w/b)/ 240881 (standing for engines/tyres)/ 120981 ('scrap-line')/ 161281 (scrap for spares)/ 040182 (OOU)/ 010382 (OOU)/ 140482 ('scrap-line')/ 010782 ('scrap-line', being cannibalised for spares)/ 070782 ('scrap-line')/ 060982 (OOS)/ 081182 (OOU)/ 291282 (shed)/ 200383/ 120583 (OOU)/ 170683 (under w/b)/ 260683 (under w/b)/ 220783 (under w/b, wiring hanging out over loco)/ 280783 (OOU)/100983 (near entrance, OOU)/ 251083 (outside shed)/ 081183 (scrap, fitters taking parts off)/ 301183 (shed yard)/ 021283 (stored wtg disposal)/ 110184 ('scrap-line')/ 120184 (OOU)/ 150184 (part-cut)/ 170184 (cutting-up completed)

Liveries and numbers:
Renumbered 9312/99 on black panel over BR number by 17/07/69.

Repainted in Ashington blue livery (with black/yellow chevrons on nose-end excluding headcode box glass (BR dimensions)) and re-numbered No.9 at Ashington CW in 08-09/72. Carried through to withdrawal/disposal. Cabside details:

> **NCB**
> **Nº9**
> 9312/99

Detail Differences:
Buffer-beam coupling-stick clips

Notes:
1. Fitted with Railway Executive registration plate (No.1708 of 1953).
2. No NCB Workshop visits (apart from 06/72 repaint).
3. Noted running with brake-tender on 08/09/70.
4. Ashington Periodic Reports:
   - Status, 24/08/81: Standing for engine and wheels (tyres).
   - Status, 24/11/81: OOU. Engine. Tyres. Prop-shaft. Heat exchangers. Oil out of flywheel. Compressor taken off this loco and fitted to 9312/90 (D9521).
   - Status, 08/03/82: Engine badly worn; no oil pressure. Prop-shaft worn. Tyres very badly worn. Heat exchangers need repair. Compressor removed.
5. Photo of D9508 (No.9): part cut-up (*Rail* , May 1984).

D9510

D9510 (60), BSC Corby, 18 April 1979. Substantially cannibalised. When the indigenous supply of raw feedstock to the Tube Works ceased in 1980 and was replaced by hot-rolled coil from Teesside, D9510 became a potential candidate for conversion to a brake-tender for use alongside other Class 14s moving the heavy Teesside trains from the Corby BR/BSC Exchange sidings to the Slitting Plant. The BR trains were air-braked only, whereas the Class 14s were either vacuum-braked (at best) or incapable of continuously braking any trains at all (more likely after years of non-usage of the vacuum-brake equipment since purchase from BR).

The method of operation was defined as two locomotives on the front of the train (one under power, the other the brake-tender) with a third locomotive on the rear. D9551 (50) was selected as the powered partner for 60 and presumably both had operable or re-instated vacuum-braking equipment to facilitate use of the brakes 'in multiple' without recourse to double-manning. 60 apparently had an ingot 'installed' in the place of the Paxman engine to increase brake force.

Ultimately the brake-tender solution for train control was aborted. (Anthony Sayer)

S&L/BSC Nos.: 23 and **60**
S&L Plant No.: 8411/23

Movements:
Despatched from 50B Hull Dairycoates: xx/12/68.
Arrived S&L(M), Buckminster Quarries, Lincolnshire: xx/12/68 (N.B. AHBRDE5 specifically states 04/12/68).
BR Grantham station: 31/08/72 (8BRD, see Sightings and Note 1).
To BSC Tubes Division, Corby Quarries, Northamptonshire: 06/09/72.
To BSC Tube Works, Corby: xx/07/80 (by 10/07/80) (for conversion to brake-tender to work with D9551 (50), but project abandoned).
To BSC Steelworks Disposal Site, Corby: xx/xx/xx. (N.B. Movement not specifically reported but see Sightings below).
At BSC Steelworks Disposal Site, Corby: Scrapped by Shanks & McEwan Ltd, Corby: xx/08/82.

Sightings:
S&L/BSC Buckminster: 180469 (shed)/280969 (shed)/ 270170 (Stainby Quarry)/ 080370 (shed)/ 230971 (shed)/ 120172 (shed)/ 250272 (wkg, demolition train from Market Overton)/ 050472 (wkg, demolition train)/ Departed for Corby 130672
BR Grantham (in transit to Corby): 310872 (with D9512/5/29/52)
BSC Corby: 250973 (GB)/080974 (GB)/ 220275 (GB)/ 070575/ 010576 (GB, shed)/ 100776/ 071076 (GB, shed, dsm)/ 300477/ 050278/ 060478/ 150778 (GB, supplying parts for useable locos)/ 270778 (GB, shed, part dsm)/ 180479 (GB)/ 120679 (GB, shed)/ 030879 (GB, stored in shed, dsm)/ 230879/ 291279 (GB, OOU in shed)/ 160480 (GB, shed)/ 080680 (GB, shed)
BSC Corby (Tube Works): 180780 (for possible use as brake-tender)/ 220880 (Steelworks shed yard)/ 140980 (Steelworks shed yard)/ 021080/ 291080 (Steelworks shed yard)/ 091280/ 291280
BSC Steelworks Disposal Site, Corby: 210181 (outside)/ 090581 (outside)/ 010881/ 270881/ 190981 (outside)/ 230182 (outside, minus engine)/ 260182 (outside)/ 070282 (stripped)/ 120482/ 190582/ 080682

Liveries and numbers:
D9510 to 09/69, 23 from 09/69 to 10/74, 60 from 10/74.

BR two-tone green livery, black/yellow chevrons on nose-end, yellow buffer beams initially.

Panel below side cab window repainted dark green and '23' applied 09/69; also 'S&L' noted on cabside on 28/09/69 (later removed).

Subsequently all Sherwood green replaced by dark green.

Detail Differences:
Footplate brackets ('A' end) (Buckminster modification)
Large spotlight mounted on bonnet ends (Buckminster modification).
No flashing lights on cab roof.
No buffer-beam lifting lugs, safety chains or coupling-stick clips fitted after arrival at Corby.

Notes:
1. D9510/52 possibly moved to Corby in 06/72.
   - E.S. Tonks notes: 24/06/72: D9512 in yard, D9515/29 (20/22) in shed, D9510/52 (21/23) to Corby ("2-3 weeks ago").
   - IQM6/8: D9510/52 to Gretton Brook, Corby 6/1972, D9512/5/29 to Gretton Brook, Corby 9/1972
   - IRS148: Undated report (but 'surrounding' reports related to 06-07/72): "David Needham noted at Gretton Brook shed 21 and 23 from Buckminster."
2. BSC Corby, 18/07/80. "50 and 60 have been transferred to the steelworks; 60 is a shell but has good wheels and is to be converted to a brake-tender for use with 50 [D9551] on heavy trains." (IRS292)
3. BSC Corby (Tube Works), 02/10/80. "60 at Tube Works was loaded with ingots then used as a brake-tender." (IRS300)
4. Lack of Corby modifications suggest D9510 (60) was never used under power at Corby.

D9511

D9511 (9312/98), NCB Ashington, December 1972. An 0-6-0ST steam locomotive, (43, RSH7769), 'photo-bombed' by D9511! Note the fire-damage sustained at Havannah Drift by D9511 on the Burradon system in July 1972. (Billy Embleton)

D9511 (9312/98), NCB Ashington, 4 June 1975. Fire-damaged. Forward-facing lamp-iron reflecting its time at Hull. (Anthony Sayer)

NCB No.: -
Plant Registry No.: 9312/98

Movements:
Despatched from 50B Hull Dairycoates: xx/xx/69. Noted at Tyne Yard: 05/01/69.
Arrived NCB Ashington Colliery: 07/01/69 (first to arrive).
To NCB Bates, Blyth: 18/04/69 (on trial).
To NCB Burradon: 05/05/69.
At NCB Burradon: Caught fire at Havannah Drift during 07/72.
To Ashington CW: circa 10/72 (after 07/72) (for repairs, but found to be beyond economic repair).
To NCB Ashington: xx/xx/xx (used as source of spares).
At NCB Ashington: Remains scrapped 07/79. See sightings below.

Sightings:
NCB Ashington: 110169/050269 (shed yard)/ 040369/ 120369/ 290369 (driver-training)/ 060469 (shed)
NCB Bates (Blyth): Nil.
NCB Burradon: 090569 (wkg)/250569/ xx0669 (Havannah Drift)/ 280669 (wkg)/ 010769 (wkg)/ 200769/ 210769/ 080869/ 160969 (wkg)/ 051069/ 171069 (shed, reps)/ 161169 (shed)/ 300370 (Hazlerigg)/ 230570 (Havannah Drift)/ 240570 (Havannah Drift)/ 020770 (wkg)/ 180770 (shed)/ 150870 (shed)/ 030970 (wkg, Havannah Drift/ Weetslade/ 080970 (wkg)/ 150970/ 180970/ 101270 (wkg)/ 240771/ 051071/ 221071 (shed)/ 251071 (shed)/ 190572/ 250572/ 140772 (shed)

NCB Ashington: 221072 (burnt out)/xx1272 ('scrap-line', fire-damaged)/ 240773 (dumped OOU, part dsm for spares)/ 180873 (for scrap)/ 230174 ('scrap-line')/ 120674 ('scrap-line')/ 150774 (dumped/dsm)/ 240774 (dsm)/ 171174 ('scrap-line', gutted, no rods)/ 040675 ('scrap-line', fire-damaged, heavily cannibalised)/ 250875 (spares)/ 150576 ('scrap-line')/ 150676 ('scrap-line')/ 280676 ('scrap-line')/ 210577 ('scrap-line', dsm)/ 190977 (dsm)/ 131177/ 250178 (derelict/dsm)/ 210378 (OOU)/ 050478 (minus wheels)/ 180778 (OOU)/ 291078 (dsm)/ 240279 (stripped)/ 170479 ('scrap-line')/ 190579 ('scrap-line', derelict)/ 300779 (dsm)/ 230979 (fire-damaged). Not listed 281279.

Liveries and numbers:
Still numbered D9511 06/04/69. Re-numbered 9312/98 on black panel over BR number by 29/06/69, but, given the Plant Registry No., presumably re-numbered before departure to Bates/Burradon.

Retained BR two-tone green livery (including lion & wheel roundels) until withdrawal/disposal.

Detail Differences:
No external modifications.

Notes:
1. First Class 14 arrival at Ashington.
2. Fitted with Railway Executive registration plate (No.1750 of 1953).
3. April/May 1969 trials at Bates unsuccessful.
4. "At Ashington the dismantled ex-BR locos (D9511 and D9545).....have now been written off and are for disposal." (IRS277, 02/80)

D9512

D9512, BSC Corby, 1974. Proof that this loco never received the number 24. (Dan Adkins)

D9512 (63), BSC Corby Steelworks Disposal Point, 17 November 1981. (Martin Shill [IRS])

S&L/BSC Nos.: (24) and **60**
S&L Plant No.: 8411/24

Movements:
Despatched from 50B Hull Dairycoates: xx/12/68
Arrived S&L(M), Buckminster Quarries, Lincolnshire: xx/12/68.
At S&L(M), Buckminster Quarries, Lincolnshire: spares only, never used.
BR Grantham station: 31/08/72 (8BRD, see Sightings).
To BSC Tubes Division, Corby Quarries, Northamptonshire: 06/09/72.
At BSC Tubes Division, Corby Quarries, Northamptonshire: Used for spares.
To BSC Steelworks Disposal Site, Corby: 29/12/80.
At BSC Steelworks Disposal Site, Corby: Scrapped, circa 02/82.

Sightings:
S&L/BSC Buckminster: 180469 (shed yard)/280969 (shed yard, for spares)/ 270170 (for spares)/ 080370 (shed yard)/ 230971 (shed yard)/ 010172 (shed yard)/ 120172 (shed yard)/ 250272 (shed yard)/ 050472 (shed yard)/ 240672 (shed yard)/ 240772 (shed yard)/ Departed for Corby 050972
BR Grantham (in transit to Corby): 310872 (with D9510/5/29/52)
BSC Corby: 200173 (GB, shed yard, dsm, minus engine)/ 250973 (GB, back of shed)/ 080974 (GB)/ 221074 (GB, scrap lines, for spares)/ 220275 (GB)/ 070575/ 010576 (GB, shed, OOU)/ 100776 (GB, shed)/ 300477 (GB)
BSC Gretton Brook Dump (outside): 291277/ 050278/ 060478/ 160478/ 150778/ 180279/ 180479/ 120679/ 030879/ 230879/ 291279/ 160480/ 170580/ 080680/ 180780/ 160880/ 220880/ 190980/ 121080/ 291080/ 261180
BSC Steelworks Disposal Site, Corby: 291280 (inside)/ 210181 (inside)/ 090581 (inside)/ 010881/ 270881/ 190981 (inside)/ 171181 (outside)/ 230182 (outside, minus parts of engine)/ 260182 (outside)/ 070282 (derelict)

Liveries and numbers:
D9512 to 10/74 (assumed), 63 from 10/74 (assumed). N.B. The first allocated number (24) was never carried.

BR two-tone livery retained throughout BSC ownership; lion & wheel roundels retained until renumbered direct to 63 in 1974.

Detail Differences:
No footplate brackets ('A' end) fitted whilst at Buckminster.
No spotlights mounted on bonnet ends.
No flashing lights on cab roof.
No buffer-beam lifting lugs, safety chains or coupling-stick clips fitted after arrival at Corby.

Notes:
1. Buckminster, 24/07/72. D9512/5/29. ".....due to go to Corby when system closes 2/9/72, though gent in charge felt deadline will not be met." (IRS150)
   See also Note 1 for D9510.
2. Never used at Buckminster or Corby.
3. BSC Corby, 190582. "63 (*D9512*).....has been cut up as it was in the way of the demolition of a nearby building." (E.S. Tonks)

D9513

**D9513 (D1/9513),
NCBOE British Oak,
Crigglestone, Undated.**
'Jinty' 47445 shunting
D9513 or vice versa?
(Geoff Sharpe)

Hargreaves No.: D1/9513

NCB No.: 38
Plant Registry No.: 2100/524

Movements:
Despatched from 85A Worcester: 18/07/68.
Arrived W.H.Arnott Young & Co Ltd, Parkgate, Rotherham: xx/xx/68.
Re-Sold to Hargreaves (West Riding) Ltd, NCBOE British Oak DP, Crigglestone.
To Hargreaves (West Riding) Ltd, NCBOE British Oak DP, Crigglestone: xx/11/68.
To Hargreaves (West Riding) Ltd, NCBOE Bowers Row DP, Astley/Swillington: 05/09/69.
Sold to NCB North East Area: xx/xx/xx.
To Allerton Bywater CW, West Yorkshire: xx/10/73 (for overhaul).
York: 12/01/74 (in transit)
Arrived Ashington CW: 21/01/74 (outshopped retaining Hargreaves orange/black livery and running number D1/9513).
To NCB Ashington: xx/05/74.
To NCB Backworth: 10/06/74 (for repainting).
To NCB Burradon: xx/07/74 (after 04/07/74, by 12/07/74).

D9513 (38), NCB Lynemouth, 2 November 1985. (Anthony Sayer)

To NCB Backworth: 03/01/76 (IRLNC) (after closure of Burradon shed), or, 05/01/76 (8BRD).
To NCB Weetslade CPP: 12/01/76 (ex-Burradon) (IRR142 only).
To NCB Weetslade CPP: xx/xx/76 (after 17/02/76) (ex-Backworth) (IRLNC only).
To NCB Backworth: by 15/05/76 (IRLNC only).
To NCB Weetslade CPP: by 13/11/76 (IRLNC (only).
To LEW Philadelphia: 22/11/76 (ex-Backworth (IRLCD/8BRD) / ex Weetslade (IRLNC/IRR142).
To NCB Ashington: 14/02/77 (IRLCD/8BRD), or, 22/02/77 (IRR142) (N.B. LEW records show 04/02/77).
To LEW Philadelphia: 19/04/77 (IRR142) (tyres turned during visit), or, 08/09/77 (IRLNC/IRLCD/8BRD).
To NCB Ashington: 14/11/77 (IRLNC/IRLCD/8BRD), or, 15/11/77 (IRR142).
At NCB Ashington: Overhauled engine number 630002/6 fitted 06/78.
At NCB Ashington: Overhauled engine fitted 29/06/82, then to Lambton Engine Works next day (IRR142).
To LEW Philadelphia: 29/06/82 (IRLCD), or, 30/06/82 (8BRD/IRR142), or, 26/09/82 (IRLNC) (for bottom-end engine overhaul). (N.B. Despatched ex-Lambton Engine Works: 17/12/82 (per LEW records) (IRR142).
To BR Thornaby: ?? (IRLNC/IRR142 only)(tyre-turning) (explanation for gap between departure ex-LEW and arrival Ashington?).
To NCB Ashington: 17/02/83 (IRLNC/IRR142 only).
At NCB Ashington: In use until late 01/87 when engine problems caused it to be stopped.
Sold to C.F.Booth, Rotherham: 09/87; re-sold for preservation.
To Embsay & Bolton Abbey Railway (for preservation): 12/10/87.

Sightings:
NCBOE British Oak DP, Crigglestone: 241268/ 190169/ 130269 (OOU)/ 010369/ 090369 (fitter working on engine)/ 100369 (shed)/ 230369 (wtg reps)/ 260369 (wtg reps)/ 060469/ 160469/ 270469 (shed, OOU)/ 110569 (reps)/ 240769 (dsm, contract reps)/ 100869 (outside shed)/ 180869 (wkg)/ 300869/ 310869 (parked in yard)/ 010969
NCBOE Bowers Row DP, Astley/Swillington: 080969 (wkg)/ 150969/ 021069 (failed, aux. generator)/ 051069 (OOU)/ 301069 (OOU)/ 201169 (wkg)/ 290570 (wkg)/ 211070/090273/ 070473/ 111073
Allerton Bywater CW: Nil.

York: 120174 (in northbound freight hauled by D178)

NCB Ashington: 230174 (wtg access to Ashington CW?)
Ashington CW: Nil.
NCB Backworth (Eccles): 040774 (being repainted)/ 120774 (workshops, freshly repainted)
NCB Burradon: 240774 (shed)/281074 (Seaton Burn)
NCB Ashington: 040675
NCB Burradon: xx1075 (Seaton Burn)
NCB Backworth (Eccles): 170276 (new arrival)/150576/ 150676 (shed)
NCB Weetslade: Nil.
LEW Philadelphia: Nil.
NCB Ashington: 210577 (shed)

LEW Philadelphia: 200977 (Workshops)/131177/ 141177
NCB Ashington: 210378 (Ly)/050478 (Ly)/ 080978 (near shed)/ 291078/ 240279/ 170479 (shed)/ 300779 (shed)/ 281279 (shed)/ 070580 (wkg, No.2 Colliery loco)/ 040780 (wkg)/ 110780 (wkg)/ 061280/ 230181 (wkg/shed yard)/ 290381/ 080481 (wkg)/ 100481 (wkg)/ 130681 (shed)/ 180681 (wkg)/ 190681 (wkg)
BR Thornaby: 250781/260781 (tyre-turning)
NCB Ashington: 140881 (wkg)/240881 (low oil pressure, engine on way out)/ 01-230981 (succession of reps, inc. full service)/ 271181 (wkg)/ 011281 (wkg)/ 081281 (Ly)/ 190182 (Ly)/ 290182 (Ly)/ 01-160282 (reps)/ 170282 (wkg)/ 22-260282 (Ly)/ 02-050382 (wkg)/ 080382 (spare)/ 140482 (Ly)/ Departed for LEW 300682
LEW Philadelphia: 010782/130782/ 040882 (outside wtg attention)/ 010982/ 081182/ 291282/ 100183 (outside)
BR Thornaby: Nil.
NCB Ashington: 140383 (wkg)/200383/ 120583 (wkg, No.1 Colliery loco)/ 140683 (wkg)/ 260683 (shed)/ 210783 (wkg)/ 170883 (wkg)/ 100983 (spare)/ 230983 (wkg)/ 251083 (wkg)/ 071183 (wkg)/ 021283 (wkg)/ 231283 (wkg)/ 110184 (wkg, Duke St. battery)/ 230184 (wkg)/ 240184 (derailed all wheels, inspection)/ 250184 (wkg)/ 010284 (wkg)/ 130284 (wkg)/ 070784 (shed)/ 05-080285 (wkg)/ 180285 (Ly)/ 270285 (Ly)/ 030585 (Ly)/ 290885 (Ly)/ 160985 (wkg)/ 170985 (Ly)/ 051085 (Ly)/ 021185 (Ly)/ 241185 (Ly)/ 011285 (Ly)/ 161285 (Ly)/ 120186 (shed)/ 210286 (Ly)/ 24-260286

(reps)/ 270286 (Ly)/ 250386 (behind shed)/ 020486 (reps, standing for brake blocks)/ 050486 (shed)/ 150486 (reps, standing for brake blocks)/ 160486 (wkg, low oil pressure)/ 020586 (wkg)/ 08-090586 (Ly)/ 150586 (shed)/ 090686 (Ly)/ 270686 (Ly, wtg reps)/ 170986 (Ly)/ 190986 (Ly, wtg reps)/ 270986 (Ly)/ 291186 (Ly, failed; dragged to Ashington)/ 181286 (shed, reps)/ 301286 (shed)/ 050187 (shed)/ 230187 (wkg, Ldg loco)/ 280187 (shed)/ 300187 (shed)/ 050287 (shed)/ 130287 (shed, spare)/ 260287 (shed)/ 280287 (shed)/ 010387 (shed)/ 070387/ 130387 (shed, reps)/ 140387 (shed)/ 150387 (shed)/ 200387 (shed yard)/ 200487 (shed)/ 170587 (shed)/ 130687/ 030887 (shed)/ 100987/ 250987 (shed)/ 270987 (shed)/ 081087/ 101087 (outside shed)

Liveries and numbers:
Repainted in Hargreaves black/orange livery, with Hargreaves logos positioned over BR roundel and behind the headcode box glasses, and re-numbered D1/9513 (BR 'D' prefix removed and replaced by 'D1/') by 13/02/69. Carried out at Crigglestone.

Repainted in Backworth/Burradon dark blue livery (with white handrails, red coupling rods, black/yellow chevrons on the bonnet ends including headcode box glass (BR dimensions) and dark red buffer beams) and renumbered 38 at NCB Backworth between 10/06/74 and xx/07/74. Cabside details:

> **N.C.B.**
>   **38**
> D1/9513

Maybe Backworth misinterpreted the D1/9513 number as a Plant Registry No.?

Detail Differences:
Buffer-beam coupling-stick clips

Notes:
1. BR registration plate, NC No.77 fitted but date unknown.
2. Ashington Periodic Reports:
   - Status, 24/11/81:Overhauled engine fitted June 1978 with CI heads, also turbo-blower. Overhauled heat exchangers fitted 14/05/79; overhauled prop-shaft fitted 25/05/79.
   - Status, 08/03/82: Engine and prop-shaft need repair. Side-rods. Tyres.
   - Status, 16/04/86: Working but oil pressure poor.
   - Status, 23/01/87: Poor condition: Bent coupling-rods (1-2 side), tyres thin and hollow, erratic loco brake air pressure, tendency to boil over and shut down.
   - Status, 13/02/87: Tyre thickness ½"; very hollow. Bent side-rod (done at Lynemouth about 3 years ago but does not affect performance). Some minor faults: brake air pressure, overheating, side-rod knuckle joints loose, excessive play in rods.

D9514

D9514 (No.4), NCB Ashington Colliery, 16 August 1976. (Trevor Hall)

D9514 (No.4/ 9312/96)), NCB Ashington, 2 November 1985. In late-1983 this locomotive was set aside pending a complete overhaul at Philadelphia Workshops; repairs were not forthcoming and D9514 was scrapped two years later in December 1985, just over three weeks after this photograph was taken.
(Anthony Sayer)

NCB No.: No.4
Plant Registry No.: 9312/96

Movements:
Despatched from 86A Cardiff Canton: 30/06/69.
Sighted 85B Gloucester: 03/07/69 and 04/07/69 (with D9502/18/27), and, Derby Midland: xx/07/69 (with D9502/18/27).
Arrived NCB Ashington: 19/07/69.
At NCB Ashington: Overhauled engine 630002/5 fitted 04/72.
To Ashington CW: xx/06/72 (for repainting).
To NCB Ashington: xx/06/72.
To BR Gosforth Depot: 12/10/72 (tyre-turning).
To NCB Ashington: 26/10/72.
To BR South Gosforth: 11/10/75 (IRLNC/8BRD), or, 13/10/75 (IRR142) (tyre-turning).
To NCB Ashington: xx/11/75 (IRLNC/IRR142), or, by 21/11/75 (8BRD).
To LEW Philadelphia: circa 08/77 (for engine repairs [six new alloy cylinder heads fitted] and new tyres).
To NCB Ashington: 23/12/77 (IRR142), or, xx/01/78 (IRLNC), or, xx/xx/78 (8BRD).
To LEW Philadelphia: xx/09/80.
To NCB Ashington: 03/12/80.
At NCB Ashington: Overhauled engine 620010/3 fitted 23/01/81.
To BR Thornaby: xx/10/82 (tyre-turning).
To NCB Ashington: xx/10/82.
At NCB Ashington: OOU from 24/11/83.
At NCB Ashington: Scrapped by Robinson and Hannon Ltd, Blaydon: 05-16/12/85.

Sightings:
NCB Ashington: 200769/010869/ 080869/ 171069/ 230570/ 240570/ 090870 (Ly)/ 140970 (Ly)/ 251071/ 070572/ 250572
Ashington CW: Nil.
NCB Ashington: Nil.
BR South Gosforth: Nil.
NCB Ashington: 221072/310373 (wkg)/ 190573/ 180873 (wkg)/ 120674/ 150774 (shed)/ 240774/ 040675
BR South Gosforth: 011175
NCB Ashington: 150576 (wkg)/160876 (wkg)/ 210577 (shed)/ 190977 (shed)
LEW Philadelphia: 131177/141177
NCB Ashington: 250178 (shed)/210378 (Ly)/ 050478/ 150478 (shed)/ 291078/ 240279/ 310579 (wkg)/ 281279 (shed)/ 070580 (shed, spare)/ 040780 (shed)/ 110780 (spare)/ 060980 (wkg)
LEW Philadelphia: Nil.
NCB Ashington: 061280/040181 (outside shed)/ 230181 (wkg)/ 290381 (Ly)/ 100481 (Ly)/ 180681 (wkg)/ 190681 (wkg)/ 140881 (Ly)/ 120981 (Ly)/ 271181 (Ly)/ 040182 (Ly)/ 110182 (Ly, to Ashington for reps)/ 12-150182 (reps)/ 180182 (wkg)/ 200182 (Ly)/ 190282 (Ly)/

22-260282 (full service)/ 010382 (wkg)/ 080382 (wkg)/ 140482 (spare)/ 010782 (Ly)/ 070782 (Ly)/ 130782 (Ly)/ 190782 (Ly)/ 160882 (Ly)/ 280982 (Ly)/ 300982 (standing for tyres)/ 011082 (tyres)
BR Thornaby: 101082
NCB Ashington: 191082 (side-rods to fit)/211082 (side-rods to fit)/ 011182 (wkg)/ 041182 (spare)/ 291282 (shed)/ 200383/ 120583 (shed, reps)/ 140683 (spare)/ 170683/ 260683 (shed)/ 150783 (Ly)/ 220783 (Ly)/ 150883 (Ly)/ 230983 (Ly)/ 251083 (Ly)/ 07-151183 (reps)/ 161183 (spare)/ 221183 (spare)/ 231183 (Ly)/ 241183 (exhaust reps)/ 281183 (standing for complete overhaul at LEW)/ 021283/ 030184 (complete overhaul required)/ 110184/ 130284 (reps)/ 050484 (shed yard, derailed all wheels)/ 070784 ('scrap-line')/ 250285 (complete overhaul required)/ 060485/ 030585 ('scrap-line', OOU)/ 110585 ('scrap-line')/ 150685 ('scrap-line', OOU)/ 290885 ('scrap-line', dumped wtg scrapping)/ 250985 ('scrap-line')/ 051085 ('scrap-line', OOU)/ 141085 ('scrap-line')/ 201085 ('scrap-line')/ 021185 ('scrap-line')/ 221185 (shed, draining oil/fuel)/ 241185 (OOU)/ 011285 (being stripped of parts)/ 161285 (final stages of scrapping)

Liveries and numbers:
Still numbered D9514 on 08/08/69. Renumbered 9312/96 on black panel over BR number by 30/08/69.

Repainted in Ashington blue livery (with black/yellow chevrons on nose-end excluding headcode box glass (BR dimensions)) and renumbered No.4 at Ashington CW during 06/72 (completed by 19/06/72). Carried until withdrawal/disposal. Cabside details:

NCB
Nº4
9312/96

Detail Differences:
Buffer-beam coupling-stick clips

Notes:
1. Fitted with Railway Executive registration plate (No.1474 of 1953) and BR registration plate NC No.80.
2. Ashington Periodic Report:
   • Status, 24/11/81: New engine with CI heads and big capacity oil pump, and, turbo-blower fitted 23/01/81. Tyre thickness ¼" (BR exam 01/06/81). Holset coupling and prop shaft fitted 15/01/81 at Ashington Loco Shed.
3. Written-off 26/09/85.

D9515

D9515 (S&L 22), S&L Buckminster (Sewstern shed), 28 September 1969. (Robin Barnes)

D9515 (62), BSC Corby, 18 April 1979. Note how the spotlight at 'A' end is much lower than 'B' end. Maybe the mounting bracket has been damaged causing the 'sagging' effect, or, perhaps the light was of a different design. Note also the engine compartment door steps. (Anthony Sayer)

S&L/BSC Nos.: 22 and **62**
S&L Plant No.: 8411/22

Movements:
Despatched from 50B Hull Dairycoates: xx/11/68. Noted Newark 02/11/68.
Arrived S&L(M), Buckminster Quarries, Lincolnshire: 02/11/68
BR Grantham station: 31/08/72 (8BRD, see Sightings)
To BSC Tubes Division, Corby Quarries, Northamptonshire: 06/09/72
To BSC Steelworks Disposal Site, Corby: 29/12/80
To Hunslet Engine Co. Ltd, Leeds: xx/12/81

Subsequently exported to Spain (see Section 9).

Sightings:
S&L/BSC Buckminster: 180469 (outside Workshop)/ 250469 (shed yard)/ 270969 (shed yard)/ 280969 (shed yard)/ 270170 (workshop)/ 080370 (Works, under reps)/ 140971 (wkg)/ 230971 (wkg)/ 010172 (WRC enthusiast's special)/ 060172 (wkg)/ 120172 (wkg)/ 250172 (Stainby Sdgs)/ 250272 (shed)/ 050472 (shed)/ 240672 (shed)/ 240772 (shed)/ Departed for Corby 050972
BR Grantham (in transit to Corby): 310872 (with D9510/2/29/52)
BSC Corby: 250973 (GB, then derailment recovery work)/ 080974 (GB)/ 220275 (GB)/ 070575/ 010576 (shed)/ 100776 (wkg)/ 250876 (wkg, Park Lodge Quarry)/ 071076 (wkg)/ 300477 (wkg)/ 250677 (wkg)/ 050278/ 060478/ 120678 (outside Pen Green Workshops)/ 150778 (workable)/ 270778 (wkg)/ 260279 (wkg)/ 180479 (wkg)/ 060579 (wkg, Shotley Quarry)/ 120679 (wkg)/ 140779 (wkg)/ 030879 (wkg)/ 230879 (GB)/ 291279 (GB, workable)/ 160480 (GB, shed)
BSC Corby (Works): 080580 (wkg, shunting steel bars)/ 270580 (wkg)
BSC Corby: 080680 (GB, shed)/180780 (GB, shed)/ 220880 (GB, shed)/ 090980 (GB, shed)/ 291080 (GB, shed)/ 261180 (GB, shed)
BSC Steelworks Disposal Site, Corby: 291280 (inside)/ 210181 (inside)/ 090581 (inside)/ 010881/ 270881/ 190981 (inside)/ 171181 (shunting D9548 [67] onto low-loader for movement to Hunslet, Leeds)/ Departed xx1281 to Hunslet, Leeds

Liveries and numbers:
D9515 to 09/69, 22 from 09/69 to 10/74, 62 from 10/74.

BR two-tone green livery, black/yellow chevrons on nose-end, yellow buffer beams initially.

Panel below side cab window repainted dark green and '22' applied 09/69; also 'S&L' noted on cabside on 28/09/69 (later removed).

Subsequently all Sherwood green replaced by dark green.

Detail Differences:
Footplate brackets ('A' end) (Buckminster modification)
Large spotlight mounted on bonnet ends (Buckminster modification, retained at Corby).
Two flashing lights on cab roof (towards 'A' end) (Corby modification).
Fitted with buffer-beam lifting lugs, safety chains and coupling-stick clips after arrival at Corby.

Note:
1. Buckminster, 24/07/72. D9512/5/29. "…..due to go to Corby when system closes 2/9/72, though gent in charge felt deadline will not be met." (IRS150)
   See also Note 1 for D9510.

D9516

D9516 (56), BSC Corby, 18 April 1979. D9516 was one of three originally bought for the Corby operation as a spares locomotive, the others being D9507 and D9512, with the possibility of at least one good locomotive being brought into traffic from the three. Available sightings of D9516 give no indication of working activity until mid-1979 but following heavy repairs it sprang into action for a few months prior to cessation of all ironstone activities at Corby in January 1980. D9507 also saw service, so two out of three wasn't bad! Very thick tyres. (Anthony Sayer)

S&L/BSC Nos.: 36 and 56
S&L Plant No.: 8311/36

Movements:
Despatched from 50B Hull Dairycoates: xx/11/68.
Arrived S&L(M), Corby Quarries, Northamptonshire: xx/11/68.
To BSC Steelworks Disposal Site, Corby: 29/12/80.
To Great Central Railway, Loughborough (for preservation): 17/10/81 (8BRD) or 19/10/81 (ILoBBN).

Sightings:
S&L /BSC Corby: 110169/241069/ 080370/ 060870/ 070871 (GB)/ 281071/ 200173 (GB)/ 080974 (GB)/ 220275 (GB)/ 070575/ 010576 (GB, shed)/ 100776 (GB, shed)/ 071076 (GB, shed, dsm)/ 300477/ 200977 (GB, shed)/ 050278/ 060478/ 150778 (GB, supplying parts for useable locos)/ 270778 (GB, shed, part dsm)/ 180479 (GB, running shed)/ 120679 (Pen Green Shops)/ 030879 (wkg)/ 230879/ 291279 (GB, workable)/ 160480 (GB, shed) / 080680 (GB, shed)/ 180780 (GB, shed)/ 220880 (GB, shed)/ 090980 (GB, shed, believed to be in working order)/ 291080 (GB, shed)/ 261180 (GB, shed)
BSC Steelworks Disposal Site, Corby: 291280 (inside)/ 210181 (inside)/ 090581 (outside)/ 010881/ 270881/ 190981 (outside)

Liveries and numbers:
D9516 to xx/xx (noted numbered 36 on 11/01/69), 36 from xx/xx to 10/74, 56 from 10/74.

BR two-tone green livery, black/yellow chevrons on nose-end, yellow buffer beams initially.

Subsequently all Sherwood green replaced by dark green.

Detail Differences:
Twin spotlights mounted on bonnet ends (Corby modification).
No flashing lights on cab roof.
Fitted with buffer-beam lifting lugs, safety chains (assumed) and coupling-stick clips (Corby modifications).

D9517

D9517 (No.8), NCB Ashington, 4 June 1975. (Anthony Sayer)

D9517 (No.8), NCB Ashington, 24 February 1979. (Anthony Sayer)

NCB No.: No.8
Plant Registry No.: 9312/93

Movements:
Despatched from 86A Cardiff Canton: 17/11/69.
Sighted 50A York: 22/11/69 (with D9500), and, 52A Gateshead: 23/11/69 and 24/11/69 (with D9500).
Arrived NCB Ashington: 25/11/69.
At NCB Ashington: Overhauled engine 620010/19 fitted 04/71.
To Ashington CW: xx/06/72 (for repainting).
To NCB Ashington: xx/06/72.
To BR South Gosforth: 30/01/74 (tyre-turning).
To NCB Ashington: 04/02/74.
At NCB Ashington: Overhauled engine 620022/21 fitted 06/76.
To LEW Philadelphia: 14/06/77.
To NCB Ashington: 20/07/77 (IRR142), or, 05/09/77 (IRLNC/8BRD).
To NCB (OE) Butterwell opencast site (on loan) whilst NBL27588 was receiving repairs: xx/09/77.
To NCB Ashington: xx/09/77.
To BR South Gosforth: xx/09/79 (tyre-turning).
To NCB Ashington: 12/09/79.
At NCB Ashington: OOU by 24/04/81 (with engine defects and requiring new tyres), Withdrawn 11/83.
At NCB Ashington: Scrapped by D. Short Ltd, North Shields: 23-24/01/84.

Sightings:
NCB Ashington: 300370 (Ly)/230570/ 240570/ 180770 (shed)/ 080970/ 011070 (shed)/ 251071 (Ly)/ 200572 (wkg)/ 250572/ 190672 (wkg)/ 270772/ 140872
Ashington CW: Nil.
NCB Ashington: 180873 (wkg)
BR South Gosforth: Nil.
NCB Ashington: 240774/281074 (wkg)/ 040675 (shed yard)/ 260975 (shed)/ 150576 (shed)/ 280676 (wkg)/ 210577 (shed yard)
LEW Philadelphia: Nil.
NCB Ashington: 131177/250178 (wkg)/ 210378/ 050478 (wkg)/ 150478 (shed)/ 080978 (Ly)/ 291078/ 240279
BR Tyne Yard: 010979
BR South Gosforth: 080979
NCB Ashington: 281279 (wkg)/070580 (shed, spare)/ 040780 (Ly)/ 110780 (Ly)/ 060980 (wkg, taking D9531 to Ashington Shed)/ 061280/ 290381/ 130681 (shed)/ 140881 (shed)/ 240881 (stopped for engine/wheels)/ 120981 (shed)/ 241181 (OOU)/ 161281 (to scrap for spares)/ 160282 (scrap for spares)/ 140482 ('scrap-line') / 010782 ('scrap-line')/ 070782 ('scrapline')/ 160882 (OOU)/ 011082 (OOU) / 081182 (OOU)/ 291282 ('scrap-line')/ 200383/ 120583 (OOU)/ 170683 ('scrap-line')/ 260683 ('scrap-line')/ 220783 ('scrap-line')/ 280783 (OOU)/ 050883 ('scrap-line')/ 100983 ('scrap-line')/ 251083 (being transferred from shed to scrap-line by D9521 after cannibalisation)/ 081183 (scrap, fitters taking parts off)/ 301183 (shed yard, being stripped)/ 021283 (stored wtg disposal)/ 110184 ('scrap-line')/ 200184 (scrap)

Liveries and numbers:
Renumbered 9312/93 on black panel over BR number by 28/01/70.

See photo of D9517 (as 9312/93) at NCB Ashington on 20/05/72 in *Looking Back at Western Region Hydraulics*, p73.

Repainted in Ashington blue livery (with black/yellow chevrons on nose-end excluding headcode box glass (BR dimensions)) and renumbered No.8 at Ashington CW during 08/72. Carried until withdrawal/disposal. Cabside details:

NCB
Nº8
9312/93

Detail Differences:
Buffer-beam coupling-stick clips

Notes:
1. Fitted with a Railway Executive registration plate (No.1597 of 1953) and BR registration plate NC 79.
2. Ashington Periodic Reports:
   - Status, 24/08/81: Standing for engine and wheels (tyres).
   - Status, 24/11/81: OOU, Engine seized. Tyres. Prop Shaft. Heat exchangers.
   - Status, 08/03/83: Engine seized. Tyres badly worn. Prop-shaft and heat exchangers need repair. Reported transmission overheating.

D9518

D9518 (No.7) and D9528 (No.2), NCB Ashington, 24 February 1979. 'Scrap-line'; No.7 awaiting new tyres. Remains of D9545 just visible to the left of the picture. (Anthony Sayer)

NCB No.: No.7
Plant Registry No.: 9312/95

Movements:
Despatched from 86A Cardiff Canton: 30/06/69.
Sighted 85B Gloucester: 03/07/69 and 04/07/69 (with D9502/14/27) and Derby Midland: xx/07/69 (with D9502/14/27).
Arrived NCB Ashington: 19/07/69.
To Ashington CW: 15/09/69.
To NCB Ashington: by 10/69.
At NCB Ashington: Overhauled engine fitted 10/70.
To Ashington Central Workshops: xx/06/72 (for repainting).
To NCB Ashington: xx/06/72.
To BR South Gosforth: 22/05/73 (for tyre-turning).
To NCB Ashington: xx/05/73.
To LEW Philadelphia: 01/05/75 (IRLNC), or, xx/05/75 (IRR142), or, 06/75 (8BRD) (fitted with overhauled engine 630002/6 and tyres turned).
To NCB Ashington: 02/06/75 (IRLNC), or, xx/09/75 (8BRD/IRR142).
At NCB Ashington: Overhauled engine number 620010/19 with CI cylinder heads fitted 16/05/77.
To LEW Philadelphia: 29/08/80 (IRR142), or, 05/09/80 (IRLNC/8BRD) (new tyres fitted).
To NCB Ashington, 03/12/80 (IRLNC/8BRD), or, 05/12/80 (IRR142).
At NCB Ashington: Withdrawn 17/04/86 requiring engine change.
To Rutland Railway Museum, Cottesmore (for preservation): 26/09/87.

D9518 (No.7), NCB Ashington, 27 February 1987. Dumped out of use; engine repairs were commenced in mid-1986 but were never completed. Compare the tyre thickness with the previous picture. (Bruce Galloway)

Sightings:
NCB Ashington: 200769/010869/ 080869
Ashington Central Workshops: Nil.
NCB Ashington: 171069/300370/ 230570/ 240570/ 220970 (shed)/ 011070 (wkg)/ 290771 (outside shed)/ 010971/ 250572/ 270772
Ashington CW: Nil.
NCB Ashington: 140872/221072
BR South Gosforth: Nil.
NCB Ashington: 180873 (wkg)/050973 (wkg)/ 230174 (wkg)/ 120674/ 240774/ 281074 (wkg)/ 040675

LEW Philadelphia: 290875 (Works yard)
NCB Ashington: 150576 (shed yard)/150676/ 280676 (wkg)/ 210577 (shed)/ 190977 (shed)/ 250178 (wkg)/ 050478 (wkg)/ 150478 (outside shed)/ 080978 (Ly)/ 291078/ 240279 ('scrap-line')/ 170479 ('scrap-line')/ 190579 ('scrap-line')/ 310579 (OOU)/ 300779 (OOU)/ 230979 ('Scrap-line')/ 281279 ('scrap-line')/ 070580 ('scrap-line', wtg overhaul and new tyres)/ 040780 (OOU)/ 110780 (dsm)/ 240780 (dsm)

LEW Philadelphia: 120980 (outside)/041280 (departed for Ashington)

NCB Ashington: 061280/290381/ 100481 (wkg)/ 180681 (wkg)/ 190681 (wkg)/ 140881 (shed)/ 240881 (standing for transmission)/ 120981/ 040182 (standing for reps)/ 010282 (standing for reps)/ 010382 (standing for reps)/ 080382 (reps)/ 010782 (shed, reps)/ 130782 (reps)/ 190782 (standing for spare parts)/ 011082 (standing for spare parts)/ 191082 (wkg)/ 221082 (wkg)/ 011182 (overheating, reps)/ 021182 (wkg)/ 081182 (reps)/ 291282 (shed)/ 220283 (wkg)/ 200383/ 120583 (wkg, No.1 Ldg loco)/ 140683 (wkg)/ 220783/ 150883 (wkg)/ 100983 (spare)/ 251083 (wkg)/ 021283 (wkg)/ 110184 (spare)/ 010284 (wkg)/ 130284 (wkg)/ 070784 (shed)/ 070285 (wkg)/ 060485/ 030585 (spare)/ 110585 (wkg)/ 150685 (shed)/ 290885 (wkg, Colliery 'battery' loco)/ 300885 (wkg)/ 160985 (wkg)/ 250985 (wkg)/ 051085 (wkg/shed)/ 141085 (shed)/ 201085 (shed)/ 021185 (wkg)/ 241185 (wkg, No.2 Colliery loco)/ 011285 (shed)/ 161285 (wkg)/ 120186 (shed)/ 210286 (wkg, Colliery loco)/ 240386 (wkg)/ 250386 (shed)/ 050486 (wkg)/ 160486 (oil leak from flywheel, low oil pressure)/ 290486 (fitters working on engine 620022/8 to be fitted into No.7)/ 020586 (shed)/ 070586 (pulled into position to take top off)/ 150586 (shed)/ 200786 (shed yard)/ 170986 (shed)/ 190986 (reps, new engine to be fitted)/ 270986 (shed)/ 081186 (shed, reps)/ 291186 (shed, engine out)/ 181286 (shed, engine change)/ 301286 (shed)/ 050187 (shed)/ 230187 (shed, minus engine, repaired engine available but not fitted)/ 280187 (shed, engine out)/ 300187 (shed, minus engine)/ 050287 (dumped between w/b and shed)/ 130287 (near w/b, engine out, repair work ceased, OOU)/ 260287 (shed yard, OOU)/ 280287 (outside shed)/ 010387 (shed)/ 070387 (shed yard (east))/ 130387 (siding near w/b, OOU)/ 150387 (shed yard)/ 110487 (shed yard)/ 200487 (dumped, shed yard)/ 170587 (shed)/ 130687/ 030887 (shed)/ 100987/ 250987 (shed)

Liveries and numbers:

Still numbered D9518 08/08/69. Renumbered 9312/95 on black panel over BR number by 15/09/69.

Repainted in Ashington blue livery (with black/yellow chevrons on nose-end excluding headcode box glass (BR dimensions)) and renumbered No.7 at Ashington CW during 07-08/72. Carried until withdrawal/disposal. Cabside details:

NCB
Nº7
9312/95

Detail Differences:
Buffer-beam coupling-stick clips

Notes:
1. Fitted with Railway Executive registration plate (No.1430 of 1953).
2. Ashington Periodic Reports.
   - Status, 24/08/81: Standing for transmission.
   - Status, 24/11/81: OOU, Transmission, standing at Ashington. Transmission over-heating and cutting out the engine. Old transmission oil run off and new put in but still the same.
   - Status, 16/04/86: Oil leak from fly wheel. Very low oil pressure. About 30ltr oil required per shift. Will not run much longer.
   - Status, 13/02/87: OOU. Engine out; new engine available but repair work ceased. Condition unknown.

D9520

D9520 (45), BSC Corby, 18 April 1979.
Gretton Brook fuelling point. Note the small
'Plant Registry No.' plaque under the 'B'-end
forward-facing cab window; this was the
standard position for such plaques, although
from photographic evidence it would appear
that not all locomotives were so fitted.
After entering preservation, D9520 returned
to industry on at least two occasions for
enthusiast events; Scunthorpe Steelworks was
visited in May 2008 (courtesy of the Appleby-
Frodingham RPS) and Hope Cement Works
hosted the locomotive in September 2008.
(Anthony Sayer)

S&L/BSC Nos.: 24 and 45
S&L Plant No.: 8311/24

Movements:
Despatched from 50B Hull Dairycoates: xx/12/68.
Arrived S&L(M), Glendon Quarries, Northamptonshire: 16/12/68.
To Stewarts & Lloyds Minerals Ltd, Corby Quarries, Northamptonshire: 12/01/70.
To BSC Tube Works, Corby: xx/09/80.
To North Yorkshire Moors Railway (for preservation): arrived 16/03/81 (via BR, with D9529).

Sightings:
S&L/BSC Glendon: 110169/270469/ 241069
S&L/BSC Corby: 080370/060870/ 070871 (GB)/ 281071/
200173 (GB)/ 250973 (Pen Green Workshops)/ 080974
(GB)/ 220275 (GB)/ 020176 (wkg)/ 010576 (wkg)/
100776/ 071076 (wkg)/ 161076 (wkg)/ 300477/ 250677
(Pen Green Workshop yard)/ 220877 (wkg)/ 200977
(wkg)/ 050278/ 060478/ 150778 (GB, Repair Shop)/
270778 (GB, Repair Shop)/ 180479 (wkg)/ 120679

(wkg)/ 030879 (GB, workable)/ 150879 (wkg)/ 230879/
031179 (GB, shed)/ 040180 (wkg, ore-crusher)/ 160480
(wkg, ore-crusher)/ 080680 (GB, shed)/ 220880 GB,
shed)/ 090980 (GB, Repair Shop). Not seen 291279
(at Pen Green Workshops?).
BSC Corby (Tube Works): 240980 (wkg)/291080/
311080/ 091280/ 291280 / 210181 (outside Tube Works
shed)/ Departed 150381 (for NYMR)

Liveries and numbers:
D9520 to xx/xx (retained until arrival at Corby?), 24 from xx/xx to 10/74, 45 from 10/74.

BR two-tone green livery, black/yellow chevrons on nose-end, yellow buffer beams initially.
Subsequently all Sherwood green replaced by dark green.

Detail Differences:
Twin spotlights mounted on bonnet ends (Corby modification).
Two flashing lights on cab roof (towards 'A' end) (Corby modification).
Fitted with buffer-beam lifting lugs, safety chains and coupling-stick clips (Corby modifications).

D9521

D9521(No.3) and D9545, NCB Ashington, 12 June 1974. (John Sayer)

NCB No.: No.3
Plant Registry No.: 9312/90

Movements:
Despatched from 86A Cardiff Canton: 04/03/70.
Noted at Tyne Yard 05/03/70 (with D9536).
Arrived NCB Ashington: 06/03/70.

At Ashington: Overhauled engine fitted 12/71.
To Ashington CW: xx/06/72 (for repainting, completed by 07/06/72).
To NCB Ashington: xx/06/72.
To BR South Gosforth: 10/06/74 (tyre-turning).
To NCB Ashington: xx/06/74.
To BR South Gosforth: 11/03/76 (tyre-turning).
To NCB Ashington: 17/04/76.
To LEW Philadelphia: 15/11/77 (IRR142), or, 30/11/77 (8BRD), or, xx/11/77 (IRLNC) (overhauled engine 620010/2 and new tyres fitted).
To NCB Ashington: 06/04/78 (IRLNC/IRR142), or, by xx/10/78 (8BRD).
To LEW Philadelphia: xx/11/78 (IRLNC only).
To NCB Ashington: xx/xx/78 (IRLNC only).
At NCB Ashington: Engine 620010/2 removed 03-04/79 whilst transmission repairs were carried out; eventually put back 12/04/79.
At NCB Ashington: CI cylinder heads fitted to engine 620010/2 on 29/03/80.
At NCB Ashington: Overhauled engine 620022/15 fitted 17/09/80.

To LEW Philadelphia: 06/01/82 (IRR142), or, 07/01/82 (IRLNC/8BRD) (for overhaul including tyre-turning; overhauled engine 620010/18 fitted, repainted).
To NCB Ashington Colliery: 26/06/82 (IRLNC), or, 30/06/82 (IRR142/8BRD).
To LEW Philadelphia: xx/03/83 (transmission faults).
To NCB Ashington: 24/03/83.
At NCB Ashington: Numerous difficulties experienced with this locomotive at this time; only worked one day (16/09/83) until 30/11/83.
At NCB Ashington: 20/01/84 (returned from Lynemouth with transmission faults).
At NCB Ashington: Still serviceable in 03/87 seeing use at Lynemouth.
Sold to C.F.Booth, Rotherham: 09/87; resold for preservation.
To Rutland Railway Museum, Cottesmore (for preservation), 14/10/87.

Sightings:
NCB Ashington: 060370 (see Note 2)/300370 (Ly)/ 160570 (wkg)/ 230570/ 240570/ 180770 (wkg)/ 270770 (shed yard)/ 290771 (shed)/ 251071/ 250572
Ashington CW: Nil.
NCB Ashington: 221072/180873 (wkg)/ 120674 ('scrap-line', rods removed)
BR South Gosforth: Nil.
NCB Ashington: 150774 (shed)/281074 (wkg)/ 200575 (Ly)/ 100675 (Ly)
BR South Gosforth: 100476
NCB Ashington: 150576 (shed yard)/150676 (shed)/ 280676/ 131177
LEW Philadelphia: 250178/190378 (Works yard)/ 050478 (due back at Ashington 060478)
NCB Ashington: 291078
LEW Philadelphia: Nil.
NCB Ashington: 240279/170479 (wkg)/ 070580 (wkg, No.2 Ldg loco)/ 040780 (wkg)/ 110780 (wkg)/ 060980 (shed, minus engine)/ 061280/ 290381/ 100481 (wkg)/ 130681 (shed)/ 180681 (wkg)/ 190681 (wkg)/ 140881 (Ly)/ 12-130981 (shed, full service)/ 141081 (wkg)/ 271181 (wkg)/ 040182 (wkg)/ 050182 (sanders off ready to go to LEW)/ 060182 (loaded up, sent to LEW)
LEW Philadelphia: 070182/140182 (wheels)/ 260282/ 140482/ 090682 (being repainted, rods off D9536)
NCB Ashington: Arrived from LEW 300682/ 010782 (wkg, No.2 Ldg loco)/ 070782 (stabled, ex-Works)/ 13-160782 (reps)/ 190782 (wkg)/ 310882 (wkg)/ 250982 (wkg)/ 011082 (wkg)/ 191082 (standing for new transmission)/ 081182 (wtg to go to LEW for new transmission)/ 291282 (shed)
LEW Philadelphia: 100383 (Works yard)/200383 (Works yard)

NCB Ashington: 120583 (wkg, No.2 Ldg loco)/ 170683/ 210683 (wkg)/ 220683 (prop-shaft failed)/ 260683 (shed)/ 010783/ 220783/ 220883 (prop-shaft failed)/ 01-120983 (LEW fitters replacing prop-shaft and refitting engine)/ 130983 (ready to test)/ 14-160983 (tests)/ 190983 (wkg)/ 251083 (wkg, shunting withdrawn Class 14s)/ 071183 (spare)/ 291183 (spare)/ 021283 (Ly)/ 191283 (wkg)/ 040184 (Ly)/ 110184 (Ly)/ 190184 (Ly)/ 200184 (transmission drive coupling turning on shaft)/ 010284 (transmission fault)/ 130284 (repairs)/ 050484 (shed yard)/ 070784 (outside back of shed)/ 050285 (OOU, transmission prop-shaft fault)/ 270285 (transmission fault)/ 060485/ 030585 (reps)/ 150685 (shed)/ 290885 (shed)/ 160985 (wkg)/ 051085 (shed)/ 141085 (wkg)/ 021185 (wkg)/ 241185 (wkg, No.1 Ldg loco)/ 011285 (shed)/ 161285 (wkg)/ 120186 (shed)/ 070286 (wkg)/ 210286 (shed, badly worn generator to replace)/ 240286 (new generator fitted)/ 260286 (wkg)/ 250386 (wkg)/ 020486 (wkg)/ 050486 (Ly)/ 020586 (Ly)/ 080586 (compressor repaired)/ 150586 (Ly)/ 090686 (wkg)/ 270686 (Ly)/ 260886 (shed yard)/ 170986 (shed)/ 190986 (spare)/ 270986(wkg, Duke St./Battery loco)/ 081186 (shed))/ 291186 (wkg, Ldg loco)/ 121286 (wkg)/ 181286 (wkg, Duke St./Battery loco)/ 301286 (shed)/ 050187 (wkg)/ 070187 (wkg, accident with van on crossing E of Ashington, continued in service)/ 230187 (Ly)/ 280187 (Ly)/ 300187 (Ly)/ 050287 (Ly)/ 130287 (Ly)/ 260287 (shed)/ 280287 (shed)/ 010387 (shed)/ 130387 (shed)/ 150387 (shed)/ 200487 (shed)/ 170587 (shed)/ 130687/ 030887 (shed)/ 310887/ 250987 (shed)/ 270987 (shed)/ 081087/ 101087 (outside shed)

Liveries and numbers:
Still D9521 30/03/70.
Renumbered 9312/90 on black panel over BR number by 16/05/70.
Repainted in Ashington blue livery (with black/yellow chevrons on nose-end excluding headcode box glass
(BR dimensions)) and re-numbered No.3 at Ashington CW in 06/72 (completed by 07/06/72). Cabside details:

> NCB
> Nº3
> 9312/90

Repainted in North-East Area dark blue livery including bonnet fronts (with red hand-rails, red coupling rods,
black/yellow striped buffer beams [/// orientation]) and renumbered 9312/90 at LEW, Philadelphia (completed by
30/06/82). Noted without "No.3" on 01/07/82; NCB Ashington staff restored the No.3 identity to the locomotive
sometime after its return. New cabside details:

> NCB
> North East Area
> 9312/90
>   Nº3

Detail Differences:
Buffer-beam coupling-stick clips

Notes:
1. Fitted with Railway Executive registration plate (No. 1705 of 1953).
2. Photograph in *D for Diesels: 7* (p15): NCB Ashington Colliery: 06/03/69 (*sic 06/03/70?*) (numbered D9521)
   Loco positioned between BR Diesel Brake-Tender and HTO wagon; just arrived from Western Region?
3. Ashington Periodic Reports:
   - Status, 24/11/81: New engine fitted at Ashington shed on 17/09/80 with CI heads and big capacity pump.
     Overhauled turbo-blower fitted 17/09/80. Tyre thickness ¼" (BR exam 01/06/81).
   - Complaint, 22/06/83: "New engine fitted 29/06/82, wheels done; new transmission fitted 31/03/83. Prop-
     shaft gone on 20/06/83; new shaft required."
   - Complaint, 22/08/83: "This engine came back and only ran for 3 shifts, then prop-shaft went. Standing from
     16 June 1983 for Philly Mechs to do repairs."
   - Status, 16/04/86: Working OK.
   - Status, 13/02/87: Engine condition unknown, but it has a coolant fault and will not run any distance without
     overheating.
4. Lynemouth, 23/01/87. "No.3 was shunting at Lynemouth, and is confined there since it will boil over if it goes on
   the main line." (IRS Archive)

D9523

D9523, BSC Glendon East, 18 April 1979. Note the small '25' number near to top of the footsteps at the 'A' end. This locomotive was always kept in immaculate external condition by the local personnel; internally, as well, there never appear to have been any significant issues, no trip to Gretton Brook for major repairs, and no substitute locomotives from Corby to cover for major failures. IQM6 does, however, make the comment: "The pattern of railway operations was altered according to production requirements and the locomotive power available". This flexibility may, therefore, have disguised some availability issues with D9523! (Anthony Sayer)

S&L/BSC Nos.: 25 and (46)
S&L Plant No.: 8311/25

Movements:
Despatched from 50B Hull Dairycoates: xx/12/68.
Arrived S&L(M), Glendon East Quarries, Northamptonshire: 16/12/68.
To BSC Tubes Division, Corby Quarries, Northamptonshire: 28/05/80.
To BSC Steelworks Disposal Site, Corby: 29/12/80.
To Great Central Railway, Loughborough (for preservation): 17/10/81.

Sightings:
S&L/BSC Glendon: 110169/270469/ 241069/ 080370/ 270974 (wkg)/ 160476/ 250476/ 100776/ 300378 (wkg)/ 150478/ 270778 (wkg)/ 180479 (wkg)/ 030879 (wkg)/ 230879/ 131179 (wkg, Barford East)/ 191279 (wkg)/ 311279 (wkg, last train)/ 280580 (moved 'Steelman' 20 to BR/BSC Exchange Sdgs)
Transfer BSC Glendon East-BSC Corby (Lloyds sidings): 280580 (hauled by BR loco, with 'Steelman' 20)

BSC Corby: 080680 (GB, shed)/180780/ 220880 (wkg, p.way)/ 090980 (wkg, Steelworks)/ 240980 (tracklifting)/ 291080 (GB, shed)/ 261180 (GB, shed)
BSC Steelworks Disposal Site, Corby: 291280 (inside)/ 210181 (inside)/ 090581 (inside)/ 010881/ 270881/ 190981 (inside)

Liveries and numbers:
BR two-tone livery with black/yellow chevrons on nose-end and lion & wheel roundels and number D9523 retained throughout BSC career.

Number '25' carried on footplate fuel tank at 'A' end (very small digits) as late as 18/04/79.

The allocated 10/74 number (logically 46) was never carried.

Detail Differences:
Twin spotlights mounted on bonnet ends (Corby/Glendon modification).
No flashing lights on cab roof.
Fitted with buffer-beam lifting lugs, safety chains and coupling-stick clips (Corby/Glendon modifications).

Note:
1. Glendon East to Corby (via BR), 28/05/80 (with 'Steelman' 20); under own power (IQM6), or, haulage by BR (IRS291)?

D9524

BP No.: No.8
BP Plant No.: 144-8

Movements:
Despatched from 86A Cardiff Canton: xx/xx/70.
Arrived BP Refinery Ltd, Grangemouth: xx/07/70.

D9524 (No.8, 144-8),
Scottish Railway
Preservation Society,
Falkirk, 25 June 1983.
Preserved but still in
BP livery at this time.
(Anthony Sayer)

Fitted with Dorman 8QT 500h.p. engine and electrical system modified to 24V, by Andrew Barclay, Sons & Co Ltd, Kilmarnock (unknown whether work was undertaken at Grangemouth or Kilmarnock).
To BR Grangemouth: circa 11/71 (for repairs).
To BP Refinery Ltd, Grangemouth: xx/xx/xx.
To BR Eastfield: xx/03/78 (for repairs).
To BP Refinery Ltd, Grangemouth: xx/xx/78
To Scottish Railway Preservation Society (SRPS), Falkirk (for preservation): 09/09/81.
Fitted with Rolls Royce type DV8 450hp engine.

Sightings:
BP Refinery Ltd, Grangemouth: Nil.
Andrew Barclay, Kilmarnock: ???
BR Grangemouth: Nil.
BP Refinery, Grangemouth: 280274 (wkg)/270676 (OOU, broken windows, no coupling rods, no engine covers)/ 070777 (stabled in middle of complex, OOU)

BR Eastfield: 240378/250378/ 270378 (rods removed)

BP Refinery, Grangemouth: 100980 (outside shed, OOU, for disposal)
SRPS, Falkirk: Arrived 090981 (via BR)

Liveries and numbers:
No.8 on door pillar at No.1 end of cab.

144-8 on box on footplate just forward of the cab towards No.1 end.

"B.P. REFINERY (GRANGEMOUTH) CO. LTD" above side access doors on No.1 end bonnet.

Large BP logo below cab side windows.

All-over light blue livery with black/yellow chevrons (BR dimensions) and striped black/yellow buffer beams (\ \ orientation) and red roof hatch.

Detail Differences:
No external modifications.

Notes:
1. "D9524 was sold to BP Chemicals, Grangemouth, from Cardiff during July (*1970*)" (RO0171)
2. BP Refinery, Grangemouth: "Locos are all flame-proofed except ex-BR D9524." (IRS150)
3. BP Refinery, Grangemouth, 07/07/77: "No.8.....is stabled OOU, as difficulty has been experienced in getting it flame-proofed." (IRS226)
4. Serious Dorman engine failure precipitated sale into preservation.

D9525

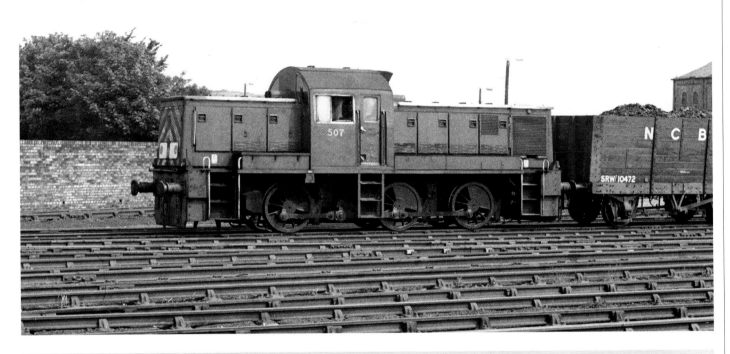

D9525 (507), NCB Ashington, 4 June 1975.
(Anthony Sayer)

D9525(507) and D9540(No.36), NCB Ashington, 14 August 1981. Both Class 14s are standing on the 'Landsale passbye' line and had relatively recently arrived at Ashington following the closure of Weetslade; both locomotives are without coupling rods for transit purposes. Four flashing lights carried by D9525 and two by D9540, fitted for use whilst at Weetslade.
(Trevor Scott Collection)

NCB No.: 507
Plant Registry No.: 2233/507

Movements:

Despatched from 50B Hull Dairycoates: 28/11/68.
Arrived NCB Philadelphia Loco Shed, Lambton Railway, Co. Durham: xx/xx/68 (official NCB records show 02/12/68).
To NCB Burradon: 07/03/75 (IRLCD/IRLNC/8BRD only) (see comment below).
To NCB Ashington: 14/03/75 (IRLNC/8BRD only).
To NCB Backworth: 13/12/75 (ILRNC/IRR142), or, 15/12/75 (8BRD).
To NCB Ashington: 15/05/80 (ILRNC(Ashington list) only), or, 15/08/80 (IRLNC(Backworth list)/8BRD only).
To NCB Weetslade CPP: xx/08/80 (direct from Backworth) (IRR142), or, xx/01/81(from Ashington) (ILRNC/8BRD).
To NCB Ashington: 24/04/81 (IRLNC/8BRD/IRR142).
To LEW Philadelphia: 21/07/83 (IRR142), or, 25/07/83 (ILRCD/ILRNC/8BRD) (overhauled engine fitted).
To NCB Ashington: 19/12/83 (per LEW records [IRR142]), or, 07/02/84 (IRLCD/IRLNC/8BRD) (02/84 per Ashington records).
At NCB Ashington: Overhauled engine fitted 16/01/86.
To Kent & East Sussex Railway, Tenterden (for preservation): 29/09/87.

Comment:

Trevor Scott believes that the Philadelphia to Burradon move prior to Ashington (03/75) did not actually happen and comments that "Ashington records show it as being received from Philadelphia under its own power".

Sightings:

NCB Philadelphia: 010269 (shed)/080269 (shed yard)/ 100269 (shed, being repainted)/ 150269 (shed yard, fully repainted, no numbers)/ 140369 (wkg)/ 150669/ 251069/ 010470 (wkg)/ 210870/ 101270 (reps)/ 160471 (shed yard)/ 290771 (shed, minor reps)/ 300872 ((stabled)/ 130673 (shed, reps)/ 170873 (wkg)/ 230873 (wkg, BR/NCB Penshaw Exchange)/ 240774 (shed)
BR South Gosforth: 170874 (side-rods removed)
NCB Philadelphia: 290175 (shed)
NCB Burradon: Nil.
NCB Ashington: 040675 (wkg)/280875
NCB Backworth (Eccles): Arrived 131275/150576/ 150676 (shed)/ 131177/ 230278 (wkg)/ 050478 (wkg)/ 291078 (shed)/ 130379 (wkg)/ 030779 (reps)/ 090480 (wkg)
NCB Ashington: Nil.
NCB Weetslade: 051180 (wkg)/010181/ 150381 (shed)
NCB Ashington: Arrived 240481 (from Killingworth Exchange Sdgs via BR, with D9502/40)/ 130681 (shed yard)/ 180681 (outside shed)/ 190681 (outside shed)/ 140881 ('scrap-line', rods off)/ 24-260881 (reps, side-rods refitted)/ 300881 (reps, brake blocks removed for wheels to be cut)/ 120981 (shed)

BR Thornaby: 071181
NCB Ashington: 271181 (reps)/011281 (reps)/ 221281 (reps)/ 04-080182 (standing)/ 11-150182 (reps)/ 18-220182 (reps)/ 250182 (electrical faults)/ 01-050282 (reps)/ 22-260282 (reps)/ 01-050382 (reps)/ 080382 (completed full service)/ 140482 (shed, reps)/ 010782 (Ly)/ 13-160782 (spare)/ 210782 (reps, no oil pressure)/ 06-100982 (new engine required, waiting to go to LEW)/ 221082 (new engine and overhaul)/ 081182 (wtg to go to LEW)/ 291282 ('scrap-line')/ 200383/ 120583 (OOU)/ 170683 ('scrap-line', OOU)/ 260683 ('scrap-line')/ 070783 (wtg to go to LEW, engine prop-shaft, tyres to cut)/ 210783 (loaded up for LEW)
LEW Philadelphia: 220783/241083 (Erecting Shop)/ 021283/ 110184/ 010284
NCB Ashington: 130284/070784 (shed)/ 05-080285 (wkg)/ 25-270285 (wkg)/ 030585 (wkg, arrived on shed with "terminal complaint")/ 110585 ('scrap-line')/ 150685 ('scrap-line')/ 290885 ('scrap-line')/ 16-200985 (new engine required)/ 051085 ('scrap-line')/ 141085 ('scrap-line')/ 201085 ('scrap-line')/ 021185 ('scrap-line')/ 24-261185 (new engine required)/ 011285 (shed)/ 161285 (shed)/ 030186 (LEW fitters installing

new engine)/ 06-090186 (LEW fitters installing new engine)/ 100186 (turbo-blower fitted)/ 120186 (shed)/ 160186 (test run, found OK)/ 170186 (wkg)/ 20-240186 (wkg)/ 070286 (wkg)/ 17-210286 (wkg)/ 210286 (wkg, Ldg loco)/ 03-050386 (wkg)/ 06-070386 (Ly)/ 10-110386 (Ly)/ 19-200386 (wkg, on test with British Engines' (BE) engineer, low oil pressure)/ 240386 (repairs, low oil pressure)/ 250386 (wkg)/ 01-040486 (wtg BE engineer)/ 050486 (shed)/ 07-110486 (wtg BE engineer)/ 14-150486 (wtg BE engineer)/ 160486 (oil pressure poor, engine noisy, max 1200rpm)/ 21-240486 (wtg BE engineer)/ 25+280486 (BE wkg on loco)/ 2904-010586 (wtg BE engineer)/ 020586 (outside shed)/

060586 (engine running)/ 07-090586 (wkg)/ 150586 (wkg)/ 140686 (wkg)/ 270686 (wkg, Colliery loco)/ 170986 (wkg)/ 190986 (reps)/ 270986 (shed)/ 081186 (shed)/ 291186 ('scrap-line', wtg reps)/ 121286 ('scrap-line', OOU)/ 181286 ('scrap-line', OOU)/ 301286 ('scrap-line')/ 050187 ('scrap-line', OOU))/ 230187 ('scrap-line', OOU)/ 280187 (towed into shed)/ 300187 (shed)/ 050287 (shed)/ 130287 (shed, under reps, new turbo bracket being fitted)/ 260287 (shed, under reps)/ 280287 (shed)/ 010387 (shed)/ 070387 (shed, repairs)/ 130387 (shed)/ 140387 (shed)/ 150387 (shed)/ 200487 (shed)/ 170587 (shed)/ 130687/ 030887 (shed)/ 100987/ 250987 (shed)

Liveries and Numbers:

Re-numbered 507 xx/08/69.

Allocated Plant Registry No. never carried externally.

Repainted in Lambton emerald green with yellow buffer beams and black/yellow chevrons on the bonnet ends (BR dimensions); date unknown (circa 02/69). Carried through to preservation.

Detail Differences:

Buffer-beam coupling-stick clips

White headcode box panes, with two sealed-beam headlights fitted behind. Philadelphia modification; date unknown (after 16/04/71, headcode box glass painted over with black/yellow chevrons on this date).

Roof-mounted flashing lights (x4) (Weetslade modification). Noted 05/11/80, plus 14/08/81 after transfer to Ashington. Subsequently removed.

Re-profiled buffer beam bottom corners (No.2 end only).

Notes:

1. Class 11 12084 brought in to Philadelphia Loco Shed from Hylton Colliery 03/03/75, to replace D9525 (507) which departed 07/03/75 to Northumberland.
2. Backworth. "NCB Backworth finished steam working on approx 13/12/75 with the arrival of two ex-BR D95xx. D9555 had arrived by 9/12, but not in use immediately, whilst a second one (*subsequently identified as D9525*) arrived on 13/12." (IRS Archive)
3. Ashington Periodic Reports:
   - Status, 24/11/81: OOU. Engine overhaul details unknown.
   - Status, 08/03/82: Engine oil pressure low. Prop-shaft. Tyres.
   - Status, 05/07/83: Standing for repair at Philadelphia. Engine prop-shaft. Tyres to cut.
   - Status, 08/04/86: Engine overhauled at British Engines. Oil pressure poor, engine noisy. Engine will not exceed 1200rpm.
   - Status, 13/02/87: Tyres very thin but profile OK. Rods have slight side play.
4. Probably the last loco to undergo repairs at Ashington (new turbo-blower bracket).

D9526

**D9526, APCM
Westbury, 26 February
1977.** (Adrian Booth)

**D9526, APCM,
Westbury, 16 October
1977.** (Rail-Photoprints)

APCM No.: -

Movements:
Despatched from 86A Cardiff Canton: xx/xx/69.
Arrived APCM, Westbury, Wiltshire: xx/01/70.
To APCM, Dunstable: 28/05/71.
To APCM, Westbury: 24/11/71.
To West Somerset Railway (for preservation): 03/04/80.

Sightings:
Westbury: xx1269 ("D9526 spent at least a week at Westbury depot during December.")

APCM Westbury: 080370
Booked transfer: APCM Westbury to Brent: 280571
APCM Houghton Regis, Dunstable: 030771/ 311071 (Factory [not quarry shed], being overhauled and repainted)

APCM Westbury: 130272/120573/ 010174/ 230874/ 030575 (possibly OOU)/ 090775/ 271075/ 260376/ 150476/ 310876/ 120277/ 180277/ 260277/ 161077/ 221177 (moved from previous position)/ 230379 (covered over, wtg preservation)
Huntworth, Somerset: 020480 (on low-loader, en-route to West Somerset Railway)
West Somerset Railway: Arrived 030480

Liveries and numbers:
D9526 carried on cabside within the Blue Circle logo.

All-over dark green (except area beneath cab side windows painted yellow), black/yellow chevrons on nose-ends and yellow buffer-beams. Cabside logo, containing 'D9526':

APCM L^td
O
Westbury Works

Grey primer when returned from Dunstable to Westbury in November 1971; repainted as above at Westbury.

Detail Differences:
Large spotlight on nose-ends .

Notes:
1. "D9526 is still at APCM Westbury works, but is doing little or no work." (RO0570)
2. "Class 14 D9526 was scheduled to be transferred from APCM Westbury to Dunstable under its own power on 28.5 [1971]." (LCGB0771)
3. "On 31st October [1971] D9526 was present at APCM Houghton Regis works, Dunstable, being repainted and overhauled." (RO0372)
4. "D9526 was returned from APCM Dunstable to APCM Westbury on 26/11 [1971] under its own power." (LCGB0272)
5. Photo in CD&E18 of unidentified Class 14 at Newbury (actually Thatcham) allegedly in 1964; loco appears to be in primer (certainly no chevrons on No.1 bonnet end. Large headlight on bonnet roof.
   Given track curvature, the loco was travelling westwards towards Westbury, so the photograph was probably of D9526 returning from Dunstable to Westbury in November 1971.
6. Same photo in *Class 14: The Cinderellas of the Diesel-Hydraulic Era* (2nd Edition) (D&EG, 1982).
   Caption: "Possibly the last Class 14 to run on BR under power, D9526 returns from Dunstable to Westbury past Thatcham on 27th January 1973. Note the grey livery". Another date but, given sightings, certainly not 1973.
7. Believed stored after December 1976 (difficult to start, low power). (D9526 Brochure)

D9527

D9527 (No.6, 9312/94), NCB Ashington, 15 June 1976. Operating with brake-tender. Still carrying the cab accident damage sustained in BR days (see page 161). (Anthony Sayer)

NCB No.: No.6
Plant Registry No.: 9312/94

Movements:
Despatched from 86A Cardiff Canton: 30/06/69.
Sighted 85B Gloucester: 03/07/69 and 04/07/69 (with D9502/14/8) and Derby Midland: xx/07/69 (with D9502/14/8).
Arrived NCB Ashington: 19/07/69.
At NCB Ashington: Overhauled engine fitted 08/71.
To Ashington CW: xx/06/72 (for repainting).
To NCB Ashington: xx/06/72.
To BR South Gosforth: 03/05/73 (tyre-turning).
To NCB Ashington: 05/05/73.
To BR South Gosforth: 19/03/75 (tyre-turning).
To NCB Ashington: xx/03/75.
At NCB Ashington: Overhauled engine 620010/3 fitted xx/11/75.
To LEW Philadelphia: 29/05/77 (for overhaul).

To NCB Ashington: 20/09/77.
At NCB Ashington: Wheel sets changed with those from D9545 on 27/09/77.
To LEW Philadelphia: 05/09/78.
To NCB Ashington: 21/09/78 (IRR142), or, xx/10/78 (IRLNC/8BRD).
At NCB Ashington: Overhauled engine 620010/13 with CI cylinder heads fitted 19/12/79.
At NCB Ashington: OOU from 12/09/83, Withdrawn 11/83.
At NCB Ashington: Scrapped by D. Short Ltd, North Shields: 20-23/01/84.

Sightings:
NCB Ashington: 200769/010869/ 080869/ 160969 (wkg)/ 171069/ 161169 (shed, reps)/ 300370/ 240570/ 220970 (wkg)/ 011070 (wkg)/ 251071/ 200572/ 250572/ 270772
Ashington CW: Nil.
NCB Ashington: 140872/221072
BR South Gosforth: Nil.
NCB Ashington: 190573/180873 (wkg)/ 230174/ 240774
BR South Gosforth: Nil.
NCB Ashington: 040675/260975 (shed, engine out)/ 150576 (shed yard)/ 150676 (wkg)/ 280676 (wkg)
LEW Philadelphia: 200977 (Workshops)
NCB Ashington: 131177/250178 (Ly)/ 210378/ 050478 (Ly)
LEW Philadelphia: 050978 (A1(M) southbound near Durham, on low-loader, en route to LEW)
NCB Ashington: 251078 (wkg)/291078/ 240279/ 170479 (shed)/ 281279 (shed)/ 070580 (Ly)/ 040780 (shed)/ 110780 (spare)/ 060980 (shed)/ 011080 (wkg)/ 061280/

230181 (shed yard)/ 290381/ 080481 (wkg)/ 100481 (wkg)/ 130681 (shed)/ 140881 (shed)/ 120981 (shed)/ 250981 (engine low pressure)/ 241181 (reps)/ 011281 (reps)/ 081281 (spare)/ 221281 (wkg)/ 110182 (wkg)/ 120182 (Ly)/ 220182 (Ly)/ 250182 (wkg)/ 080282 (spare)/ 090282 (Ly)/ 080382 (Ly)/ 140482 (wkg, No.1 Ldg loco)/ 010782 (wkg, No.1 Ldg loco)/ 13-160782 (wkg)/ 200782 (Ly)/ 310882 (Ly)/ 010982 (reps)/ 06-140982 (new generator fitted)/ 200982 (spare)/ 191082 (wkg)/ 291282 (shed)/ 200383 (Ly)/ 120583 (spare)/ 140683 (Ly)/ 140783 (Ly)/ 15-210783 (spare)/ 280783 (shed yard)/ 050883 (shed yard)/ 15-220883 (spare)/ 23-310883 (Ly)/ 01-090983 (Ly)/ 120983 (standing for complete overhaul)/ 220983 (standing for complete overhaul)/ 251083 (half under w/b)/ 081183 (standing to go to LEW)/ 091183 (scrap for spare parts only)/ 301183 (under w/b, being stripped)/ 021283 (stored wtg disposal)/ 231283 (scrap)/ 110184 ('scrap-line')/ 200184 (scrap)

Liveries and numbers:
Still numbered D9527 on 16/09/69.

Renumbered 9312/94 on black panel over BR number by 03/11/69.

Repainted in Ashington blue livery (with black/yellow chevrons on nose-end excluding headcode box glass (BR dimensions)) and re-numbered No.6 at Ashington CW in 07-08/72. Carried until withdrawal/disposal. Cabside details:

NCB
Nº6
9312/94

Detail Differences;
Buffer-beam coupling-stick clips

Notes:
1. Fitted with Railway Executive registration plate (No.1772 of 1953) and BR registration plate NC 78.
2. Noted running with brake tender 9300/2 on 15/06/76 and 28/06/76.
3. Ashington Periodic Report:
   • Loco Status, 24/11/81: Loco under repair. CI heads and big capacity pump fitted. Work left to do: Oil pipes to fit, filters to fit, etc. This loco had a new engine fitted on 19/12/79 (620010/13).

D9528

D9528 (No.2), NCB Ashington, 12 June 1974. Coupling rods removed; batteries also removed from the running plate mounted boxes at the near 'B' end. The running plate box at the far ('A') end is one of three fuel tanks; another fuel tank was positioned on the opposite running plate, and the third beneath the radiator, giving 338-gallons in total. Thin tyres. (John Sayer)

NCB No.: No.2
Plant Registry No.: 9312/100

Movements:
Despatched from 86A Cardiff Canton: 06/03/69.
Sighted 16A Toton: 09/03/69 (with D9508).
Arrived NCB Ashington: 14/03/69.
To Ashington CW: xx/06/72 (for repainting).
To NCB Ashington: xx/06/72 (by 25/06/72).
To BR South Gosforth: 31/10/72 (tyre-turning).

D9528 (No.2, 9312/100), NCB Ashington, 19 June 1981. Scrapped six months later.
(Peter Wilcox)

To NCB Ashington: 23/11/72.
At NCB Ashington: Part overhauled engine fitted 12/72.
At NCB Ashington: Overhauled engine 620010/13 fitted 09/74.
To BR South Gosforth: 11/03/76 (tyre-turning).
To NCB Ashington: 10/04/76.
To LEW Philadelphia: 14/06/77 (for repairs).
To NCB Ashington: 12/10/77.
At NCB Ashington: OOU by 02/78 and used as source of spares.
At NCB Ashington: Scrapped 12/81.

Sightings:
NCB Ashington: 250369/290369 (wkg, No.1 Ldg loco)/ 060469 (shed)/ 250569/ 140669 (shed)/ 290669/ 200769/ 080869/ 300370/ 230570/ 240570/ 220970 (shed)/ 011070 (shed)/ 290771 (shed)/ 251071/ 070572/ 250572
Ashington CW: Nil.
NCB Ashington: 190672 (wkg)/270772/ 140872/ 221072
BR South Gosforth: Nil.
NCB Ashington: 310373 (wkg)/190573/ 180873 (wkg)/ 230174/ 120674 (batteries/rods removed)/ 150774 (shed)/ 240774/ 200575 (Ly)/ 100675 (Ly)
BR South Gosforth: Nil.
NCB Ashington: 150576 (Ly)/150676 (shed)/ 280676/ 210577 (shed)
LEW Philadelphia: Nil.

NCB Ashington: 190977 (shed)/131177/ 250178 (shed, reps)/ 210378/ 050478/ 150478 (shed, engine out)/ 291078/ 240279 (partially stripped)/ 170479 ('scrap-line')/ 190579 ('scrap-line', derelict)/ 300779 (dsm)/ 230979 ('scrap-line')/ 281279 ('scrap-line')/ 070580 ('scrap-line', engine removed)/ 040780 ('scrap-line', being stripped for spares)/ 110780 (dsm)/ 240780 (dsm)/ 060980 ('scrap-line')/ 261080 ('scrap-line')/ 061280 (dsm)/ 040181 ('scrap-line')/ 230181 ('scrap-line')/ 290381 ('scrap-line', dsm)/ 100481 ('scrap-line')/ 130681 ('scrap-line')/ 190681 ('scrap-line', dsm)/ 140881 ('scrap-line', engine out)/ 120981 ('scrap-line', dsm)

Liveries and numbers:
Renumbered 9312/100 on black panel over BR number by 25/03/69.

Repainted in Ashington blue livery (with black/yellow chevrons on nose-end excluding headcode box glass (BR dimensions)) and re-numbered No.2 at Ashington CW in 06/72 (by 07/06/72). Carried until withdrawal/ disposal. Cabside details:

NCB
Nº2
9312/100

Detail Differences;
Buffer-beam coupling-stick clips

Notes:
1. Fitted with Railway Executive registration plate (No. 1404 of 1953).
2. Authorised for disposal on receipt of redundant locomotives from Backworth.

D9529

D9529 (61), BSC Corby, 18 April 1979. Devoid of cab roof lights, somewhat surprising for an operational loco at this late stage. WR-style sideways-facing lamp-irons retained despite its time at Hull. Steps on third engine compartment door.
(Anthony Sayer)

S&L/BSC Nos.: 20 and **61**
S&L Plant No.: 8411/20

Movements:

Despatched from 50B Hull Dairycoates: xx/08/68.
To S&L(M), Buckminster Quarries, Lincolnshire: 26/08/68.
BR Grantham station: 31/08/72 (8BRD, see Sightings).
To BSC Tubes Division, Corby Quarries, Northamptonshire: 06/09/72.
To BSC Steelworks Disposal Site, Corby: 29/12/80.
To North Yorkshire Moors Railway, Grosmont (for preservation): arrived 16/03/81 (via BR, with D9520).

Sightings:
S&L/BSC Buckminster: 260868 (on trial from BR)/ 180469 (wkg)/ 280969 (shed)/ 270170 (wkg, Stainby Quarry)/ 080370 (shed)/ 230971 (wkg)/ 120172 (shed)/ 250272 (shed)/ 050472 (shed)/ 240672 (shed)/ 240772 (shed)/ Departed for Corby 050972
BR Grantham (in transit to Corby): 310872 (with D9510/2/5/52)
BSC Corby: 200173 (GB, not used)/250973 (GB)/ 080974 (GB)/ 220275 (GB)/ 070575/ 081175 (shed)/ 010576 (wkg)/ 100776 (wkg)/ 071076 (wkg)/ 161076 (wkg)/ 300477/ 250677 (track-panels)/ 050278/ 300378 (wkg)/ 150778 (workable)/ 270778 (wkg)/ 180479 (wkg)/ 090679/ 120679 (wkg)/ 030879 (workable)/ 230879/ 101279/ 121279 (wkg)/ 291279 (GB, workable)/ 020180 (wkg)/ 160480 (wkg, Park Lodge)/ 170580 ("Farewell to Corby" railtour, with D9537 [52])/ 080680 (GB, shed)/ 180780 (GB, shed, see Note 3)/ 160880 (GB, shed)/ 220880 (GB, shed)/ 090980 (GB, shed)/ 240980 (GB, Repair Shop)/ 291080 (GB, shed)/ 261180 (GB, shed)
BSC Steelworks Disposal Site, Corby: 291280 (inside)/ 210181 (inside)/ Departed 150381 (for NYMR)

Liveries and numbers:
D9529 to 09/69, 20 from 09/69 to 10/74, 61 from 10/74.

BR two-tone green livery, black/yellow chevrons on nose-end, yellow buffer beams initially.

Panel below side cab window repainted dark green and '20' applied 09/69; also 'S&L' noted on cabside on 28/09/69 (later emoved).

Subsequently all Sherwood green replaced by dark green.

Detail Differences:
Footplate brackets ('A' end) (Buckminster modification)
Large spotlight mounted on bonnet ends (Buckminster modification)).
No flashing lights on cab roof whilst at Corby.
Fitted with buffer-beam lifting lugs, safety chains and coupling-stick clips after arrival at Corby.

Notes:
1. Buckminster, 24/07/72. D9512/5/29. ".....due to go to Corby when system closes 2/9/72, though gent in charge felt deadline will not be met." (IRS150)
   See also Note 1 for D9510.
2. 17/05/80, "Farewell to Corby" railtour, Gretton Brook to Wakerley and return, with D9537 (52). (IRS291)
3. BSC Corby, 18/07/80. "61 and 64 [D9529 and D9549] are.....working in the steelworks, solo, but return to Gretton Brook shed after duty." (IRS292)

D9530

D9530, Swndon Works ('A' Shop), 13 August 1971. (Anthony Sayer)

Gulf Oil No: -

NCB No.: -
Plant No.: -

Movements:
Despatched from 86A Cardiff Canton: xx/xx/69. N.B. Noted: 86A Cardiff Canton: 19/10/69 and 26/10/69, and, 87E Landore 29/11/69.
To Gulf Oil Co Ltd, Cardiff Roath Docks: circa 09/69 for short [trial?] period (see Section 7.2.1).
Arrived Gulf Oil Co Ltd, Waterston, Pembrokeshire: 26/09/69 (see Section 7.2.2).
To BR Swindon Works: 05/08/71.
To Gulf Oil Co Ltd, Waterston, Pembrokeshire: 07/10/71.
To BR Cardiff Canton: xx/xx/75.
Arrived NCB Mardy Colliery, Glamorgan: 28/10/75 (ILoMSG)/ after 16/11/75 (8BRD).
To BR Canton Depot and BR Ebbw Junction: xx/07/76 to 16/08/76.
To NCB Mardy Colliery: 16/08/76.
To BR Cardiff Canton: 01/10/77 (for Open Day, and, presumably, repairs).
To NCB Mardy Colliery: circa 12/77.
At NCB Mardy: Scrapped: xx/03/82 (8BRD), or, xx/04/82 (ILMSW).

2030B. D9530, 86A Cardiff Canton, 22 October 1977. (Transport Treasury [G.H. Taylor])

Sightings:
Gulf Oil Co. Ltd., Waterston: 240570
BR Swindon Works ('A' Shop): 050871 (for overhaul)/ 110871/ 130871 ('A' Shop)/ 180871/ 270871 ('A' Shop)
Gulf Oil Co. Ltd., Waterston: 200173

BR Cardiff Canton: 221075/261075/ 081175/ 161175/ 061275
NCB Mardy: 040576 (shed)
BR Ebbw Junction: 250776/160876
En route Ebbw Junction to NCB Mardy: 160876 (allegedly under own power)

NCB Mardy: 160277 (OOU, electrical faults)/ 170377 (outside workshops)
BR Cardiff Canton: 011077/221077/ 071177/ 131177 (wtg reps)
NCB Mardy Colliery: 170478/100279/ 151179 (OOU)/ 190280 (OOU, BR/NCB exchange sdgs)/ 010680 (OOU, exchange sdgs)/ 190680/ 060780 (dumped, OOU)/ 220980 (dumped, OOU)/ 270181/ 230781 (dumped, exchange sdgs)/ 090981 (exchange sdgs)

Liveries and numbers:
Gulf Oil.
Retained BR two-tone green livery with black/yellow chevrons on nose-ends and yellow buffer beams, together with D9530 numbers and lion & wheel roundels until at least 13/08/71.

Painted all-over light blue with black/yellow chevrons on nose-ends (BR Dimensions) and yellow buffer beams whilst at Swindon August 1971.

NCB
Retained light blue livery. No number carried but the following was carried on the cabside:

NCB MARDY
SOUTH WALES
    AREA

Also 'NCB' on cab end near roof (at least on No.2 end).

Detail Differences:
No external modifications.

Notes:
1. Mardy.
   - Undated. "The new arrival, ex-BR D9530, has not been reported at work yet.....D9530 was reported in the shed 5/76." (IRS203)
   - "Ex-BR D9530 has not been reported in traffic yet. It returned from visits to BR Canton and Ebbw Jcn for maintenance 16/8/76 under its own power." (IRS206)
   - "Ex-BR D9530 carries a board "On hire from A.R. Adams" so is not a NCB loco." (IRS253)
   - 10/02/79. "D9530 out of use (now for over a year); too expensive to repair." (IRS Archive)
   - 15/11/79. "It is rumoured that D9530 may be sent to Ashington for use as a source of spare parts." (IRS277)
   - Undated. "D9530 was cut up about 2 months ago." (IRS Archive, letter dated 14/06/82)

D9531

D9531(D2/9531), NCB Lynemouth, February 1980. 'B' end denting of front access doors. (John Ford (David Ford Collection))

D9531(2100/523, No.31), NCB Ashington, 2 November 1985. Despite a major overhaul in 1981, D9531 still has that dent in the front end. 'No.31' applied locally underneath the Plant Registry No. (Anthony Sayer)

Hargreaves No.: D2/9531

NCB No.: No.31
Plant Registry No.: 2100/523

Movements:
Despatched from 85A Worcester: 18/07/68.
Arrived W.H.Arnott Young & Co Ltd, Parkgate, Rotherham: xx/xx/68.
Re-Sold to Hargreaves (West Riding) Ltd, NCBOE British Oak DP, Crigglestone.
To Hargreaves (West Riding) Ltd, NCBOE British Oak DP, Crigglestone: xx/11/68.
Sold to NCB North East Area: xx/xx/xx.
Arrived NCB Burradon Colliery: 10/10/73 (8BRD), or, 19/10/73 (IRLNC), or, arrived Ashington CW: 19/10/73 (IRR142).
To NCB Ashington: by xx/03/74 (IRLNC/8BRD/IRR142).
At NCB Ashington: Overhauled engine 620022/19 fitted 20/01/77.
To BR South Gosforth: xx/07/77 (tyre-turning) (IRR142 only).
To NCB Ashington: 09/07/77 (IRR142 only).
To BR South Gosforth: xx/06/79 (IRR142 only).
To NCB Ashington: 29/06/79 (IRR142 only).
To LEW Philadelphia: 26/08/81 (IRLNC), or, 15/09/81 (IRR142), or, 26/09/81 (8BRD) (for repairs, repainted).
To NCB Ashington: 27/10/81.
To BR Thornaby: xx/10/81 (tyre-turning) (IRLNC/IRR142 only).
To NCB Ashington: 06/11/81 (IRLNC/IRR142 only).
At NCB Ashington: Overhauled engine 620022/15 fitted 02/84.
Sold to C.F.Booth, Rotherham: 09/87; re-sold for preservation.
To East Lancashire Railway, Bury (for preservation): 02/10/87 (IRLNC), or, 031087 (8BRD).

Comment:
Some doubt surrounding whether D9531 moved from Crigglestone to Burradon or Ashington Central Workshops in 10/73.

Sightings:
NCBOE British Oak DP, Crigglestone: 241268/ 190169/ 130269 (OOU)/ 010369/ 090369 (shed)/ 230369 (wtg reps)/ 260369 (wtg reps)/ 060469/ 120469 (wtg reps)/ 160469/ 270469 (wkg)/ 110569 (wkg)/ 240769 (wkg)/ 100869 (wtg overhaul)/ 300869/ 310869 (engine out, reps in shed)/ 010969/ 080969 (wtg reps)/ 270969 (wtg spares to begin overhaul)/ 161069 (reps)/ 231169 (wkg)/ 300170/ 080270 (wkg)/ 060370 (wkg)/ 090470 (wkg)/ 180470/ 160570 (wkg)/ 040770 (wkg)/ 211070/ 011170/ 040871/ 020971/ 160973 (rods removed)/ 111073 (departure date)

NCB Ashington: 230174/150774 (wkg)/ 240774/ 281074 (wkg)/ 100675 (wkg)/ 150576 (shed)/ 150676 (wkg)/ 280676 (shed yard)
BR South Gosforth: Nil.

NCB Ashington: 131177/250178 (Ly)/ 210378/ 050478 (wkg)/ 150478 (outside shed)/ 180778 (stabled)/ 080978 (wkg)/ 291078 (Ly)/ 240279 (Ly)/ 170479 (wkg)
BR South Gosforth: Nil.
NCB Ashington: 281279 (shed)/180180 (Ly)/ 070580 (Ly)/ 040780 (Ly)/ 080780 (Ly)/ 110780 (Ly)/ 060980 (being dragged to Ashington Loco Shed by D9517 [No.8])/ 061280/ 200181 (Ly)/ 230181 (wkg)/ 290381 (Ly)/ 130681 (shed)/ 140881 (shed)/ 240881 (standing for tyres)/ 100981 (side-rods taken off and sanders made ready to load up for LEW)/ 120981 (shed)/ 150981 (loaded onto trailer, sent to LEW)
LEW Philadelphia: Nil.
BR Thornaby: Nil.
NCB Ashington: 271181 (ex-Works, wkg)/181281 (wkg)/ 221281 (reps, to have snow ploughs fitted)/

080182 (reps, water in transmission)/ 11-140182 (standing for reps)/ 200182 (reps)/ 250182 (electrical faults)/ 260182 (wkg)/ 260282 (wkg)/ 080382 (wkg)/ 140482 (wkg, No.1 Ldg loco)/ 010782 (wkg, No.1 Ldg loco)/ 160882 (wkg)/ 020982 (wkg)/ 150982 (fan unit from D9535 [37] fitted)/ 210982 (wkg)/ 300982 (wkg)/ 011082 (Ly)/ 081182 (Ly)/ 291282 (shed)/ 140383 (wkg)/ 200383/ 120583 (Ly)/ 220783 (Ly)/ 15-180883 (reps)/ 230883 (wkg, then reps)/ 070983 (standing for new engine)/ 080983 (shed, engine being dis-connected)/ 140983 (engine 620022/19 lifted out ready to send to Workshops for overhaul)/ 190983 (engine despatched off-site)/ 230983 (fitters working on prop-shaft)/ 251083 (shed, reps)/ 021283 (reps)/ 061283 (prop-shaft fitted, ready for new engine)/ 071283 (new engine 610022/15 fitted)/ 110184 (reps)/ 180184 (mech. work complete)/ 190184 (elec. work complete)/ 300184 (lid to put on and test)/ 130284 (reps)/ 290284 (wkg)/ 070784 (shed)/ 050285 (wkg)/ 270285 (wkg)/ 060485/ 030585 (spare)/ 150685 (shed)/ 120885 (wkg)/ 290885 (shed)/ 16-200985 (Ly)/ 23-260985 (electrical fault)/ 300985 (wkg)/ 051085 (shed)/ 141085 (wkg)/ 201085 (shed)/ 021185 (wkg, Ldg loco)/ 241185 (wkg, No.3 Ldg loco)/ 011285 (shed)/ 161285 (Ly)/ 02-030186 (Ly)/ 080186 (Ly)/ 120186 (shed)/ 270286 (Ly)/ 280286 (turbo-blower to fit)/ 030386 (turbo-blower fitted)/ 120386 (Ly)/ 050486 (Ly)/ 110486 (Ly)/ 1404-060586 (reps, inc cylinder heads)/ 070586 (wkg)/ 150586 (wkg)/ 090686 (wkg)/ 170686/ 270686 (Ashington for reps, ex-Lynemouth)/ 170786 (wkg)/ 260886 (shed)/ 170986 (shed)/ 190986 (spare)/ 270986 (shed)/ 081186 (spare)/ 291186 (shed)/ 181286 (Ly)/ 301286 (shed)/ 050187 (shed)/ 230187 (spare)/ 280187 (shed)/ 300187 (shed))/ 050287 (dumped OOS, under w/b)/ 130287 (under w/b, OOS)/ 260287 (under w/b)/ 280287 (under w/b)/ 010387 (under w/b)/ 070387 (under w/b)/ 130387 (under w/b)/ 110487 (under w/b)/ 200487 (under w/b)/ 170587 (shed)/ 130687/ 030887 (shed)/ 100987/ 250987 (shed yard)/ 270987 (shed yard)/ 011087

Liveries and numbers:
Repainted in Hargreaves black/orange livery with Hargreaves logos positioned over BR roundel and behind the headcode box glasses. Renumbered D2/9531 (BR 'D' prefix removed and replaced by 'D2/') by 13/02/69. Carried out at Crigglestone.

Repainted in North East Area dark blue (with red handrails, red coupling rods, black/yellow striped buffer beams (/// orientation) (all-over dark blue nose-ends including headcode box glass) and renumbered 2100/523 at LEW, Philadelphia by 27/10/81. Ashington shed staff added their own identity No.31 sometime after this. Cabside details:

> **NCB**
> **North East Area**
> **2100/523**
> **No.31**

Detail Differences;
Buffer-beam coupling-stick clips

Notes:
1. "NCBOE, Crigglestone. "D2/9514 (*sic*) has been purchased by the NCB and was moved somewhere in Cumberland (*sic*) on 11th October (*1973*), according to the driver (at Crigglestone)." (IRS73/5095)
2. Fitted with Railway Executive registration plate (No.1440 of 1953).
3. Ashington Periodic Reports:
   - Status, 24/08/81: Standing for wheels (tyres).
   - Status, 24/11/81: New engine fitted 20/01/77 with CI heads.
   - Status, 16/04/86: Working OK but standing for brake blocks.
   - Status, 13/02/87: Tyres thickness about ¾", but very poor profile.

D9532

D9532(57), BSC Corby, 18 April 1979. Heavily cannibalised with Paxman engine parts and batteries neatly placed on the floor. Spotlights removed from 'A' end (securing bolts still visible), although just visible at 'B' end. (Anthony Sayer)

S&L/BSC Nos.: 37 and 57
S&L Plant No.: 8311/37

Movements:
Despatched from 50B Hull Dairycoates: xx/11/68.
Arrived S&L(M), Corby Quarries, Northamptonshire: xx/11/68.
To BSC Steelworks Disposal Site, Corby: 29/12/80.
At BSC Steelworks Disposal Site, Corby: Scrapped by Shanks & McEwan Ltd, Corby: xx/02/82.

Sightings:
S&L/BSC Corby: 110169/241069/ 080370/ 060870/ 070871 (GB)/ 200173 (GB)/ 250973 (wkg)/ 080974 (GB)/ 220275 (GB)/ 070575/ 010576 (wkg)/ 100776/ 071076 (wkg)/ 300477 (wkg)/ 220877 (GB, shed)/ 050278/ 060478/ 150778/ 270778 (GB, shed, part dsm)/ 180479 (GB, running shed)/ 120679 (GB, shed)/ 030879 (GB, stored in shed, dsm)/ 230879/ 291279 (GB, shed, OOU)/ 160480 (GB, shed)/ 080680 (GB, shed)/ 180780 (GB, shed)/ 220880 (GB, shed)/ 291080 (GB, shed)/ 261180 (GB, shed)

BSC Steelworks Disposal Site, Corby: 291280 (inside)/ 210181 (inside)/ 090581 (inside)/ 010881/ 270881/ 190981 (inside)/ 171181 (outside)/ 230182 (outside, minus engine)/ 070282 (missing engine)/ 190582

Liveries and numbers:
D9532 to xx/xx (noted numbered 37 on 11/01/69), 37 from xx/xx to 10/74, 57 from 10/74.

BR two-tone green livery, black/yellow chevrons on nose-end, yellow buffer beams initially. Subsequently all Sherwood green replaced by dark green.

Detail Differences:
Twin spotlights mounted on bonnet ends (Corby modification).
No flashing lights on cab roof .
Fitted with buffer-beam lifting lugs, safety chains and coupling-stick clips (Corby modifications).

Note:
1. BSC Corby, 19/05/82. "63 (*D9512*).....has been cut up as it was in the way of the demolition of a nearby building." (IRS Archive)

N.B. Presumably the same explanation also applied to D9532 [57]).

D9533

D9533 (26), S&L Corby, 2 June 1969. (Author's Collection)

D9533 (26), BSC Corby (Gretton Brook Road Stockyard), 16 November 1970. Greg Evans commentary: 'Perhaps the most serious incident at Corby was when the driver of 26, ex-BR D9533, let the loco roll away whilst he was running round a train of stone on 16th November 1970. He had just come out of Earltrees Pit, and was off the loco pulling the points when she rolled away and hit the stop-blocks. I understand there was some transmission damage to this loco.' (Greg Evans Collection)

S&L/BSC Nos.: 26 and 47
S&L Plant No.: 8311/26

Movements:
Despatched from 50B Hull Dairycoates: xx/12/68.
Arrived S&L(M), Corby Quarries, Northamptonshire: xx/12/68.
To BSC Steelworks Disposal Site, Corby: 29/12/80.
At BSC Steelworks Disposal Site, Corby: Scrapped by Shanks & McEwan Ltd, Corby: xx/09/82.

Sightings:
S&L/BSC Corby: 110169 (GB, shed)/020669 (GB, shed yard, under reps)/ 241069 (wkg)/ 080370/ 060870/ 161170 (derailed at Gretton Brook Road Stockyard)/ 070871 (GB)/ 281071/ 130172 (GB, shed)/ 200173 (GB)/ 250973 (wkg)/ 080974 (GB)/ 220275 (GB)/ 070575/ 010576 (GB, in shed)/ 100776/ 300477/ 050278/ 060478/ 150778 (GB, supplying parts for useable locos)/ 270778 (GB, shed, waiting reps and/or supplying parts)/ 180479 (GB, running shed)/ 120679 (GB, shed)/ 030879 (GB, stored in shed, dsm)/ 230879/ 291279 (GB, shed, OOU)/ 160480 (GB, shed)/ 080680 (GB, shed)/ 180780 (GB, shed)/ 160880 (GB, shed)/ 220880 (GB, shed)/ 121080 (GB)/ 291080 (GB, shed)/ 261180 (GB, shed)
BSC Steelworks Disposal Site, Corby: 291280 (inside)/ 210181 (inside)/ 090581 (inside)/ 010881/ 270881/ 190981 (inside)/ 171181 (outside)/ 230182 (outside, minus parts of engine)/ 260182 (outside)/ 070282 (part-stripped)/ 230282 (outside)/ 120482/ 190582/ 080682/ 250882 (whole)

Liveries and numbers:
D9533 to xx/xx (noted still numbered D9533 on 11/01/69), 26 from xx/xx to 10/74, 47 from 10/74.

BR two-tone green livery, black/yellow chevrons on nose-end, yellow buffer beams initially.
Subsequently all Sherwood green replaced by dark green.

Detail Differences:
Twin spotlights mounted on bonnet ends (Corby modification).
No flashing lights on cab roof.
Fitted with buffer-beam lifting lugs, safety chains and coupling-stick clips (Corby modifications).

D9534

APCM No.: Nil, named **'ECCLES'**.

Movements:
Despatched from 50B Hull Dairycoates: xx/10/68.
Arrived APCM Hope Cement Works, Hope, Derbyshire: xx/10/68.
Departed Hope: 05/05/75.
Subsequently exported to Belgium (see Section 9).

Sightings:
APCM, Hope: 120169 (wkg)/291269 (Earles Sdgs)/
071170/ 120471 (wkg)/ 021071/ 170373/ 250373 (OOU,
yielding parts to keep *Michlow* [D9505] working)/
040973/ 160674 (OOU, wtg spares)/ 131074 (stored at
buffer stops behind wagons; OOU for some time)/ 120475
(OOU)/ Departed 050575 (en-route Harwich for export)

BR March MPD: 100575
Ipswich (passing): 100575 (9X35, hauled 37044, with
D9505)
Harwich Docks: Nil.

Liveries and numbers:
No numbers; named 'ECCLES' (initially as transfers, later cast plates on cabside).

APCM all-over dark green livery, black/yellow chevrons (reduced dimensions compared to BR), red shunter grab rails and couping rods and yellow buffer beams.

Detail Differences:
No external modifications.

Note:
1. "On 10/5 [1975].....D9505+D9534 were seen on a low-loader in a siding south of March." (BLS0675)

Above left: **D9534, APCM Hope, 12 January 1969.** Named *Eccles* whilst still carrying the full BR livery. (Pete Stamper [IRS])

Above right: **D9534, APCM Hope, 17 March 1973.** Nameplate fitted. Reduced size chevron warning panel. Stored out of use. Note the accident damage to the 'B' end shunter recess grab rails. (G. Smith [IRS])

D9535

D9535(37), NCB Weetslade, circa November 1973. Test run from Backworth following repairs and full repaint (including red buffer beam). A189 road under construction in the background. (Trevor Scott)

NCB No.:37
Plant Registry No.: 9312/59

Movements:
Despatched from 86A Cardiff Canton: 09/11/70.
Arrived NCB Ashington: xx/11/70 (8BRD), or, Arrived NCB Burradon: 12/11/70 (IRLNC/IRR142).
To NCB Burradon: xx/01/71 (8BRD only).
To Ashington CW: 25/05/73 (IRLNC/IRR142), or, circa 03/74 (8BRD only).
To BR South Gosforth: 11/10/73 (tyre-turning) (IRLNC/IRR142 only).
To NCB Burradon: xx/10/73 (IRLNC/IRR142 only).
To NCB Backworth: by 24/10/73 (IRLNC only), or, circa 06/74 (for repainting) (IRR142 only).
To NCB Burradon: by 26/03/74 (IRLNC), or, circa 06/74 (8BRD/IRR142).

D9535 (37) with D9504 (506), NCB Ashington, 26 June 1983. Red buffer beam repainted yellow and now very faded. Thin tyres. (John Sayer)

To NCB Weetslade CPP: 03/01/76 (IRLNC), or, 05/01/76 (8BRD), or, xx/01/76 (IRR142).
To NCB Backworth: 08/01/76 (IRR142), or, circa 05/76 (by 15/05/76) (IRLNC/8BRD).
To NCB Ashington: 15/08/80 (IRR142), or, by 06/09/80 (IRLNC), or, 13/09/80 (8BRD).
To BR Thornaby: 05/12/80 (tyre-turning) (IRR142 only).
To NCB Ashington: 17/12/80 (IRR142 only).
To LEW Philadelphia: xx/12/80 (IRR142), or, 05/12/80 (IRLNC/IRLCD/8BRD).
To NCB Ashington: by 08/04/81 (IRLNC), or, 23/04/81 (8BRD), or, 23/05/81 (IRR142).
At NCB Ashington: Withdrawn 11/83.
At NCB Ashington: Scrapped by D. Short Ltd, North Shields: 18-20/01/84.

Comments:
Conflicting data re. D9535's first industrial port of call in November 1970; the 9312 Plant Registry No. supports Ashington.
Conflicting data re. D9535's return to work after repainting in 1973.

Sightings:
NCB Burradon: 101270* (wkg)/040171/ 240771/ 051071/ 221071 (wkg, Weetslade-Burradon)/ 251071 (shed)/ 050472/ 190572/ 250572/ 140772 (shed)/ 020872 (wkg, Havannah Drift)/ 020173. Not listed 120673 (at Ashington for repairs).
Ashington CW: 180873/280973.

BR South Gosforth: 131073
NCB Backworth (Eccles): 241073 (workshop, grey undercoat). N.B. Here for repainting only.
NCB Burradon: 231173* (wkg, Weetslade, repainted blue)/ 240174 (blue)/ 260374 (shed)/ 120774 (wkg, Weetslade)/ 281074

NCB Burradon: 160575 (wkg, Burradon-Eccles)/ 300575 (wkg, Fisher's Lane Crossing, light-engine)
NCB Weetslade: Nil.
NCB Backworth (Eccles): 150576/280277 (wkg, Weetslade)/ 131177/ 050478 (shed)/ 180778/ 291078 (wkg)/ 030779 (wkg)/ 090480 (reps, brake block renewal and leaky radiator)
NCB Ashington: 060980 ('scrap-line', looking OOU)/ 261080 ('scrap-line'). Not listed 061280.
BR Thornaby: Nil. Did it go?
NCB Ashington: 040181 ('scrap-line', OOU). Not listed 230181.
LEW Philadelphia: Nil. Did it go?
NCB Ashington: 290381 ('scrap-line')/080481 ('scrap-line', "ex-Lambton")/ 100481 ('scrap-line')/ 130681 ('scrap-line')/ 190681 ('scrap-line')/ 140881 ('scrap-line')/ 240881 (standing for engine)/ 120981 ('scrap-line')/ 161281 (scrap, for spares)/ 040182 (scrap, for spares)/ 160282 (scrap, for spares)/ 080382 (scrap, for spares)/ 140482 ('scrap-line')/ 010782 ('scrap-line')/ 070782 ('scrap-line')/ 160882 (OOU)/ 011082 (OOU)/ 081182 (OOU)/ 291282 ('scrap-line')/ 140383/ 120583 (OOU)/ 170683/ 260683 (near 'scrap-line', thin tyres)/ 220783 ('scrap-line')/ 280783 (OOU)/ 050883 ('scrap-line')/ 100983 ('scrap-line')/ 251083 (being transferred from shed to 'scrap-line' [after cannibalisation] by D9521 [No.3])/ 081183 (scrap, fitters taking parts off)/ 301183 ('scrap-line')/ 021283 (stored wtg disposal)/ 231283 (scrap)/ 110184 ('scrap-line')/ 120184 (scrap)

Liveries and Numbers:
BR two-tone green livery (including lion & wheel roundels) and numbered D9535 until mid-1974.

Repainted North East Area dark blue (with white hand rails, red buffer beams, red coupling rods and black/yellow chevrons on bonnet ends (BR dimensions) and renumbered 37 at NCB Backworth by 23/11/73 (see below).

Plant registry number not carried externally. Buffer beams repainted yellow between 1976 and 1978.

Cabside details:

N.C.B.
37

Detail Differences:
Buffer-beam coupling-stick clips

Notes:
1. * Sighting date 10/12/70. Listed in correspondence as "All four Paxman's on the road the day we arrived thanks to sterling work by fitters here." Assumed to be D9502/11/35/55.
2. * Report for Burradon 23/11/73 listed D9555, No.36 (D9540) and another Class 14 ("repainted blue"); assumed to be D9535 (37).
3. D9535 on 'scrap-line' on 06/09/80 and 26/10/80, then 04/01/81. An intervening trip to BR Thornaby *seems* to have revealed the impossibility of turning the tyres given D9535's immediate return to the 'scrap-line' on its return to Ashington. A trip to LEW *appears* to have resulted in a decision to store the loco as, once again, on return to Ashington it was instantaneously dumped on the 'scrap-line'. If these two statements are correct, then D9535 was one of only three NCB North East locomotives never to have worked at Ashington, the others being D9540/5.
4. Ashington Periodic Reports:
   • Status, 24/08/81: Standing for engine.
   • Status, 24/11/81: Engine; liners worn, water in sump. Prop-shaft. Heat exchangers.
   • Status, 08/03/82: Water in engine. No oil pressure. Prop-shaft worn. Heat exchangers worn. Tyres.

D9536

D9536 (No.5) and D9528 (No.2), NCB Ashington, 23 January 1974. Rods removed from D9536. (Anthony Sayer)

NCB No.: No.5
Plant Registry No.: 9312/91

Movements:
Despatched from 86A Cardiff Canton: 04/03/70.
Noted Tyne Yard: 05/03/70 (with D9521).
Arrived NCB Ashington: 06/03/70.
To Ashington CW: xx/06/72 (for repainting).
To NCB Ashington: xx/06/72.
To BR South Gosforth: 16/08/73 (tyre-turning).
To NCB Ashington: 18/08/73.
At NCB Ashington: Overhauled engine 610035/1 fitted 06/74.
To LEW Philadelphia: 28/01/77.
To NCB Ashington Colliery: 15/05/77.
To LEW Philadelphia: xx/01/78 (IRLNC/8BRD/IRR142) (for attention to damaged cab. Cab fitted from D9545; cab only repainted).
To NCB Ashington: 31/01/78 (IRR142), or, xx/06/78 (IRLNC/8BRD).

D9536 (No.5), NCB Ashington, November 1985. Note the revised cabside identification, following the fitting of the cab from D9545 in early-1978. The cab was also painted into a darker shade of blue although this is not evident here following the accumulation of over seven years of grime. Final disposal (very) imminent, but were the wheelsets retained given their decent thickness? (Steve Kemp)

To LEW Philadelphia: 16/09/81 (new tyres fitted).
To NCB Ashington: 05/01/82 (IRLNC), or, 06/01/82 (IRR142).
At NCB Ashington: Overhauled engine installed during 1983.
At Ashington: OOU by 03/84.
At NCB Ashington: Scrapped by Robinson and Hannon Ltd, Blaydon: between 05-16/12/85.

Sightings:
NCB Ashington: 060370 (see Note 2)/300370/ 180770 (Ly)/ 080970/ 220970 (shed)/ 011070/ 010971/ 251071/ 250572
Ashington CW: Nil.
NCB Ashington: 270772/221072/ 190573
BR South Gosforth: 180873
NCB Ashington: 190973 (new engine required, side-rods removed)/ 230174 (rods removed)/ 120674/ 190674 (wkg)/ 150774 (shed)/ 240774/ 040675/ 150576 (shed)/ 150676 (shed)/ 280676
LEW Philadelphia: Nil.
NCB Ashington: 190977 (wkg)/131177
LEW Philadelphia: Nil.
NCB Ashington: 250178 (shed)/210378/ 050478/ 150478 (OOU)/ 291078/ 240279/ 310579 (wkg)/ 281279

(shed)/ 070580 (shed yard, spare)/ 040780 (shed)/ 110780 (spare)/ 060980 (shed)/ 061280/ 230181 ('scrap-line')/ 290381 ('scrap-line')/ 100481 ('scrap-line')/ 130681 ('scrap-line')/ 190681 ('scrap-line', OOU)/ 140881 ('scrap-line')/ 240881 (standing for transmission/ wheels)/ 120981 ('scrap-line')/ 150981 (being made ready for transfer to LEW)/ 160981 (loaded and sent to LEW)
LEW Philadelphia: Nil.
NCB Ashington: 060182 (unloaded after visit to LEW, to check over)/ 07-140182 (reps)/ 150182 (wkg)/ 090282 (wkg)/ 080382 (wkg)/ 140482 (wkg, No.2 Ldg loco)/ 200582 (wkg)/ 010782 (shed, reps)/ 130782 (wkg)/ 310882 (wkg)/ 011082 (wkg)/ 221082 (wkg)/ 021182 (wkg)/ 291282 (shed)/ 200383/ 120583 (Ly)/

170683 (wkg)/ 260683 (shed)/ 060783 (wkg)/ 220783/ 180883 (wkg)/ 220883 (reps)/ 070983 (reps)/ 080983 (wkg)/ 130983 (wkg)/ 140983 (spare)/ 230983 (spare, run on engine only)/ 251083 (spare)/ 071183 (spare)/ 15-171183 (Ly)/ 251183 (spare)/ 021283 (reps)/ 051283 (Ly)/ 231283 (Ly)/ 110184 (Ly)/ 010284 (Ly)/ 130284 (Ly)/ 050484 (shed yard)/ 070784 ('scrap-line')/ 050285 (transmission prop-shaft)/ 250285 (transmission prop-shaft)/ 060485/ 030585 ('scrap-line', dumped OOU)/ 110585 ('scrap-line')/ 150685 ('scrap-line'/ 290885 ('scrap-line')/ 051085 ('scrap-line'/ 141085 ('scrap-line')/ 201085 ('scrap-line')/ 021185 ('scrap-line')/ 221185 (shed, being drained of oil/fuel)/ 241185 (OOU)/ 011285 (being stripped of parts)/ 161285 (final stages of scrapping)

Liveries and Numbers:
Still numbered D9536 30/03/70.

Renumbered 9312/91 on black panel over BR number by 15/05/70

Repainted in Ashington blue livery (with black/yellow chevrons on nose-end excluding headcode box glass (BR dimensions)) and re-numbered No.5 at Ashington CW during 06/72. Carried until withdrawal/disposal. Cabside details:

> **NCB**
> **Nº5**
> 9312/91

Cab fitted from D9545 after sustaining collision damage. Cab only repainted in North East Area dark blue with revised identification. Released to traffic from Lambton Engine Works, Philadelphia during 01/78 (see Note 3). Retained until withdrawal/ disposal. New cabside details:

> **NCB**
> **North East Area**
> **Nº5**
> **9312/91**

Detail Differences:
Buffer-beam coupling-stick clips

Notes:
1. Fitted with Railway Executive registration plate (No.1544 of 1953).
2. Photograph in *D for Diesels: 7* (p16): NCB Ashington Colliery: 06/03/69 (*sic 06/03/70?*) (numbered D9536) Just arrived from Western Region with D9521?
3. Clarity required regarding fitment of cab from D9545.
   - ILNRC/8BRD/IRR142 all show D9536 to Lambton Engine Works, Philadelphia: xx/01/78. IRR142 shows return to Ashington: 31/01/78, with IRLNC/8BRD showing xx/06/78.
   - Trevor Scott visit to Ashington, 05/04/78: "During 1977 No.5 [D9536] received the cab from D9545 after being involved in an accident. This engine now has a darker cab and a different lettering style to the other members of the same class."
4. Ashington Periodic Reports:
   - Status, 24/08/81: Standing for transmission and wheels (tyres).
   - Status, 24/11/81: OOU, Transmission and Tyres. Loco at Philadelphia Workshops, sent Wed 16/09/81.
5. Written-off 26/09/85.

D9537

D9537(52), BSC Corby Gretton Brook, 17 May 1980. Industrial Railway Society ironstone special. (Transport Treasury [John Tolson])

S&L/BSC Nos.: 32 and 52
S&L Plant No.: 8311/32

Movements:
Despatched from 50B Hull Dairycoates: xx/11/68.
D9539 sighted passing Toton on 18/11/68 (with D9553) (RO0169); this is a recording error, believed to have been D9537.
Arrived S&L(M), Corby Quarries, Northamptonshire: xx/11/68.
To BSC Pen Green Crane Depot, Corby: by 15/08/81 (used for shunting wagons for scrapping) (ILoBBN) , or, 05/82 (used for demolition work) (IQM6), or, circa 11/81 (8BRD).
To Gloucestershire & Warwickshire Railway (for preservation): 23/11/82.

Sightings:

S&L/BSC Corby: (110169)/241069/ 080370/ 060870/ 070871 (GB)/ 200173 (GB)/ 250973 (wkg)/ 080974 (GB)/ 220275 (GB)/ 070575/ 081175 (wkg, Priors Hall Quarry)/ 010576 (wkg)/ 100776 (wkg)/ 140477 (GB, outside shed)/ 300477/ 290977 (wkg)/ 050278/ 060478/ 150778 (GB, workable)/ 270778 (wkg)/ 180479 (GB, Repair Shed)/ 120679 (wkg)/ 030879 (wkg)/ 230879/ 291279 (GB, workable)/ 020180 (wkg)/ 040180 (wkg, Park Lodge (last day))/ 160480 (GB, in shed)/ 170580 ("Farewell to Corby" railtour, with D9529 [61])/ 270580 (GB, shed)/ 080680 (GB, shed)/ 180780 (GB, shed)/ 090980 (GB, shed, working order)

BSC Corby (Works): 240980 (wkg)/021080 (wkg)/ 291080 (p.w. work)/ 311080 (p.w. work)
BSC Corby: 261180 (GB, shed)/291280 (GB, shed)/ 210181 (GB, shed)/ 080481 (GB)/ 290481 (GB)/ 060881/ 130881 (wkg, shunting wagons)/ 150881 (GB).
Not seen 270881.
BSC Corby (Pen Green Workshops): 190981/ 091081 (immaculate condition)/ 230182/ 130382/ 160382/ 210582/ 080682/ 250882/ 271082 (last day used)

Liveries and numbers:

D9537 to xx/xx (not seen 11/01/69, but recorded as being allocated 32), 32 from xx/xx to 10/74, 52 from 10/74.

BR two-tone green livery, black/yellow chevrons on nose-end, yellow buffer beams initially.
Subsequently all Sherwood green replaced by dark green.

Detail Differences:

Twin spotlights mounted on bonnet ends (Corby modification).
Two flashing lights on cab roof (towards 'A' end) (Corby modification).
Fitted with buffer-beam lifting lugs, safety chains and coupling-stick clips (Corby modifications).

Note:

1. 17/05/80, "Farewell to Corby" railtour, Gretton Brook to Wakerley and return, with D9529 (61). (IRS291)

D9538

D9538, Swindon Works ('A' Shop), 1970.
(Transport Topics)

D9538 (160), BSC Ebbw Vale, 6 February 1973.
(Rail-Photoprints)

Shell Haven No.: -

BSC No.: 160
Plant No.: -

Movements:
Despatched from 86A Cardiff Canton: xx/xx/70.
Arrived Shell Haven Refineries, Thames Haven, Stanford-le-Hope, Essex: xx/04/70.
To BR Swindon Works: by 05/08/70.
Returned Shell Haven Refineries, Thames Haven, Stanford-le-Hope, Essex: See transfer Sightings below.
Resold to British Steel Corporation: xx/xx/xx.
Arrived BSC Strip Mills Division (Tinplate), Ebbw Vale, Monmouthshire: 22/02/71.
Arrived BSC Tubes Division, Corby Quarries, Northamptonshire: by 25/04/76 (for spares only).
To BSC Steelworks Disposal Site, Corby (for storage): xx/12/80 (probably 29/12/80).
At BSC Steelworks Disposal Site: Scrapped by Shanks & McEwan Ltd, Corby: xx/09/82.

Sightings:
Shell Haven Refineries, Thames Haven, Stanford-le-Hope, Essex: Nil.
Swindon Works: 290770/050870 ('A' Shop)/ 220870 ('A'Shop)/ 171070/ 311070
Swindon Cocklebury Yard: 281070
Transfer: Swindon Works-Stanford-le-Hope: 281070 (8A43 16.55 Severn Tunnel Junction-Acton freight)
Shell Haven Refineries, Thames Haven, Stanford-le-Hope, Essex: Nil.

Reading Yard: 290171 (en-route BSC Ebbw Vale)
BSC Ebbw Vale Strip Mills Division (Tinplate), Monmouthshire: 230871/ 06-090672/ 060273 (in shed)/ 120573/ 300574 (finished, not to be repaired)/ 270375 (being prepared for further use)/ 250475/ 200975 (in store, wtg transfer)

BSC Corby: 160476 (arrived "two weeks earlier")/ 010576 (GB, shed, tyres badly worn)/ 100776 (GB, shed)/ 300477 (OOU)
BSC Gretton Brook Dump (outside): 291277/ 050278/ 060478/ 270778/ 180279/ 180479/ 120679/ 030879/ 230879/ 291279/ 160480/ 170580/ 010680/ 080680/ 180780/ 160880/ 220880/ 190980/ 121080/ 291080
BSC Steelworks Disposal Site, Corby: 291280 (inside)/ 210181 (inside)/ 090581 (inside)/ 010881/ 190981 (inside)/ 171181 (outside))/ 230182 (outside, minus engine parts & some bodywork)/ 070282 (minus engine)/ 190582/ 080682/ 250882 (whole)

Liveries and numbers:
The number D9538 was retained until at least the July-October 1970 Swindon Works visit, and possibly throughout its time with Shell Haven Refineries.

Renumbered 160 (in the BSC Ebbw Vale series) in 1971 (by 06/02/73) which it carried through to final disposal.

Photograph dated 25/05/75 appears to show D9538 (160) in all-over dark green livery with black/yellow chevrons.

Detail Differences:
No external modifications.

Note:
1. Never used at Corby.

D9539

D9539 (51), BSC Corby, 18 April 1979. (Anthony Sayer)

D9539 (51) and D9553 (54), BSC Corby Steelworks Disposal Site, 17 November 1981. This one managed to escape the carnage and talk of a move to Turkey was suggested; however, in the event, both locomotives moved into preservation at the Gloucestershire & Warwickshire Railway on 23 February 1983. (Martin Shill [IRS])

S&L/BSC Nos.: 30 and **51**
S&L Plant No.: 8311/30

Movements:
Despatched from 50B Hull Dairycoates: xx/10/68.
Arrived S&L(M), Corby Quarries, Northamptonshire: xx/10/68.
To BSC Steelworks Disposal Site, Corby: 29/12/80.
To Gloucestershire & Warwickshire Railway (for preservation): 23/02/83.

Sightings:
S&L/BSC Corby: 110169/241069/ 080370/ 060870/ 070871 (GB, Repair Shop)/ 130172 (GB, Repair Shop)/ 200173 (GB)/ 230673 (GB, shed)/ 250973 (wkg)/ 080974 (GB)/ 220275 GB)/ 070575/ 020176 (wkg)/ 010576 (wkg)/ 100776 (wkg)/ 071076 (wkg)/ 300477/ 050278/ 280378 (wkg)/ 150778 (GB, stopped awaiting reps)/ 270778 (GB, shed, waiting reps)/ 180479 (GB, running shed)/ 120679 (GB, wkg)/ 030879 (wkg)/ 230879/ 291279 (GB, Repair Shop)/ 160480 (GB, shed)/ 080680 (GB, shed)/ 220880 (GB, in shed)/ 090980 (GB, Repair Shop)/ 291080 (GB, shed)/ 261180 (GB, shed)
BSC Steelworks Disposal Site, Corby: 291280 (inside)/ 210181 (inside)/ 090581 (inside)/ 010881/ 270881/ 190981 (inside)/ 171181 (outside)/ 230182 (complete)/ 260182 (outside)/ 070282 (complete)/ 230282/ 120482/ 190582/ 080682/ 250882 (set aside for possible re-sale)/ 201182/ 190283

Liveries and numbers:
D9539 to xx/xx (noted numbered 30 on 11/01/69), 30 from xx/xx to 10/74, 51 from 10/74.

BR two-tone green livery, black/yellow chevrons on nose-end, yellow buffer beams initially.
Subsequently all Sherwood green replaced by dark green.

Detail Differences:
Twin spotlights mounted on bonnet ends (Corby modification).
Two flashing lights on cab roof (towards 'A' end) (Corby modification).
Fitted with buffer-beam lifting lugs, safety chains and coupling-stick clips (Corby modifications).

Note:
1. First arrival at Corby.

D9540

D9540 (508), NCB Philadelphia (Grassmoor), 1 May 1971. (G. Smith [IRS])

NCB Nos.: 508, No.36
Plant Registry No.: 2233/508

Movements:
Despatched from 50B Hull Dairycoates: 29/11/68.
Arrived NCB Philadelphia Loco Shed, Lambton Railway, Co. Durham: xx/xx/68 (official NCB records show 02/12/68).
To NCB Burradon: 25/11/71 (exchanged with ex-BR Class 11 12084).
To NCB Ashington: xx/06/72 (by 19/06/72) (IRLNC/8BRD), or, to Ashington CW: xx/06/72 (for repainting) (IRR142).
To NCB Ashington: xx/08/72 (IRR142).
To NCB Burradon: 09/09/72 (IRLNC/IRR142 only), or, by 04/74 (8BRD).
To NCB Weetslade CPP: 03/01/76 (8BRD), or, 12/01/76 (IRR142), or, xx/01/76 (IRLNC).
To NCB Ashington: 24/04/81.
At NCB Ashington: Never used at Ashington due to poor condition, Withdrawn 11/83.
At NCB Ashington: Scrapped by D. Short Ltd, North Shields: 10-11/01/84.

D9540 (No.36), NCB Weetslade, 15 June 1976. (Anthony Sayer)

Sightings:

NCB Philadelphia: 010269 (shed)/080269 (shed yard)/ 100269 (wkg, Herrington)/ 150269 (outside shed)/ 140369 (wkg)/ 150669/ 251069/ 210870/ 101270 (reps)/ 160471 (repair shop)/ 010571 (wkg)/ 260771 (wkg)/ 290771 (wkg)/ 251071

NCB Burradon: Nil.

NCB Ashington: 250572 (for ACW)/190672 (shed, for ACW)

Ashington Central Workshops: 270772 (recorded as 508) 290772/ 140872 (recorded as 508)

NCB Ashington: Nil.

NCB Burradon: 050673 (wkg, Hazlerigg Jct)/ 120673 (shed)/ 150873/ 050973 (shed)/ 231173/ 260374 (shed)/ 120774 (Weetslade)/ 240774 (shed)/ 280974/ 281074/ 141175 (wkg)/ 091275 (wkg Burradon-Backworth & return)

NCB Weetslade: 150676 (shed)/160776 (wkg)/ 280277 (wkg)

BR South Gosforth: 240777 (tyre-turning)

NCB Weetslade: 131177/230278 (wkg)/ 210378/ 050478 (shed, spare)/ 180778 (wkg)/ 080978 (wkg)/ 291078/ 170479 (wkg)/ 260679 (shed, spare)/ 090480 (wkg)/ 300680/ 040780 (shed)/ 051180 (wkg)/ 150381 (shed)

NCB Ashington: Arrived 240481 (from Killingworth Exchange Sdgs via BR, with D9502/25)/ 130681 ('scrap-line')/ 180681 ('scrap-line', no rods, OOU)/ 190681 ('scrap-line', no rods)/ 140881 ('scrap-line', rods off)/ 090981 (no engine oil pressure, new cylinder head required, turbo-blower /prop-shaft to be sent away)/ 120981 ('scrap-line')/ 051181 ('scrap-line')/ 161281 (scrap, for spares)/ 040182 (scrap, for spares)/ 160282 (scrap, for spares)/ 140482 ('scrap-line')/ 010782 ('scrap-line')/ 070782 ('scrap-line')/ 160882 (OOU)/ 011082 (OOU)/ 081182 (OOU)/ 291282 ('scrap-line')/ 200383/ 120583 (OOU)/ 170683 ('scrap-line')/ 260683 ('scrap-line')/ 220783 ('scrap-line')/ 280783 (OOU)/ 050883 ('scrap-line')/ 100983 ('scrap-line')/ 251083 ('scrap-line')/ 081183 (scrap, fitters taking parts off)/ 301183 ('scrap-line')/ 021283 (stored wtg disposal)/ 231283 (scrap)/ 060184 (scrap)/ 110184 ('scrap-line', cut-up 10-110184)

Liveries and Numbers:
Re-numbered 508 xx/08/69.

Repainted in Lambton emerald green with yellow buffer beams and black/yellow chevrons on the bonnet ends (BR dimensions); date unknown. Allocated Plant Registry No. not carried externally with this livery.

Repainted in Ashington blue livery (with black/yellow chevrons on nose-end <u>including</u> headcode box glass (BR dimensions)) and re-numbered No.36 at Ashington CW in 06-08/72. Carried until withdrawal/disposal.

NCB
Nº36
2233/508

Detail Differences:
Buffer-beam coupling-stick clips
Sealed-beam headlights presumed to have been fitted at NCB Philadelphia as D9504 (506) and D9525 (507), although no photographic evidence has been found to substantiate this. Photograph dated 1 May 1971 above shows painted over headcode glass.
Roof-mounted flashing lights (x2) (Weetslade modification). Noted 05/11/80, plus 14/08/81 after transfer to Ashington. Subsequently removed.

Notes:
1. Appears to have never visited LEW.
2. Believed to be one of three NCB North East locomotives never to have worked at Ashington, with the *possible* exception of 'running-in' turns in August/September 1972 after repairs at Ashington CW.
3. Ashington Periodic Reports.
   • Status, 24/11/81: OOU. Engine blower. Prop-shaft. Heat exchangers. Leak on head, Oil pressure nil.
   • Status, 08/03/82: Engine no oil pressure. Blower in need of repair. Prop-shaft to repair and leaks on heat exchangers. Tyres.

D9541

D9541 (No.26), BSC Harlaxton, 19 June 1971. Casthorpe Junction. Wirral Railway Circle 'Harlaxton 95' tour. Modified cab roof profile. Note Sherwood green cab, but with panel below side cab window repainted dark green and 'No.26' applied. Additional footplate brackets clearly visible. (Transport Treasury [John Tolson])

D9541 (66), BSC Corby, 18 April 1979. Gretton Brook shed. Single large headlight removed, but the mounting remains on the nose-end. 66 is believed to have never worked at Corby; the Corby-standard lifting lugs, safety chains and shunting-pole brackets were never fitted. (Anthony Sayer)

S&L/BSC Nos.: No.26 and **66**
S&L Plant No.: 8411/26

Movements:
Despatched from 50B Hull Dairycoates: xx/11/68. Booked transfer: 11/11/68.
Arrived S&L(M), Harlaxton Quarries, Lincolnshire: xx/11/68.
To BSC Tubes Division, Corby Quarries, Northamptonshire: 04/08/74.
To BSC Steelworks Disposal Site, Corby: 29/12/80.
At BSC Steelworks Disposal Site, Corby: Scrapped by Shanks & McEwan, Corby: xx/08/82.

Sightings:
S&L/BSC Harlaxton: 221168/180569/ 270969/ 080370/ 060770 (shed)/ 150571 (shed)/ 190671 (Wirral Railway Circle "Harlaxton 95" enthusiast tour)/ 130971 (wkg branch to BR Casthorpe)/ 060772 (wkg Casthorpe-Harlaxton incline)/ 210972 (wkg)/ 160473 (shed, non-active due to strike at Stanton Ironworks)/ 260973 (wkg, Harlaxton-Casthorpe Jct & return)/ 160174 (shed, OOU)/ 030374 (wkg, tracklifting)/ 190374 (shed)/ 240474 (shed) / Departed for Corby 010874
BSC Corby: 080974 (GB)/ 220275 (GB)/ 010576 (GB, shed)/ 100776 (GB, shed)/ 071076 (GB, shed)/ 300477/ 050278/ 060478/ 150778 (GB, supplying parts for useable locos)/ 270778 (GB, shed, waiting reps and/ or supplying parts)/ 180479 (GB)/ 120679 (GB, shed)/ 140779 (GB, shed)/ 030879 (GB, stored in shed, dsm)/ 230879/ 291279 (GB, shed, OOU)/ 160480 (GB, shed)/ 080680 (GB, shed)/ 180780 (GB, shed)/ 160880 (GB, shed)/ 220880 (GB, shed)/ 291080 (GB, shed)/ 261180 (GB, shed)
BSC Steelworks Disposal Site, Corby: 291280 (inside)/ 210181 (inside)/ 090581 (inside)/ 010881/ 270881/ 190981 (inside)/ 171181 (outside)/ 230182 (outside, minus engine parts)/ 260182 (outside)/ 070282 (part-stripped)/ 230282 (outside)/ 120482/ 190582/ 080682

Liveries and numbers:
D9541 to 06/70, No.26 from 06/70 to 10/74, 66 from 10/74.

BR two-tone green livery, black/yellow chevrons on nose-end, yellow buffer beams initially.
Panel below side cab window repainted dark green and 'No.26' applied 06/70.
Subsequently all Sherwood green replaced by dark green.

Detail Differences:
Cut-down roof profile (Harlaxton modification, retained at Corby).
Footplate brackets ('A' end) (Harlaxton modification)
Large spotlight mounted on bonnet ends (Harlaxton modification, retained at Corby).
No flashing lights on cab roof.
No buffer-beam lifting lugs, safety chains or coupling-stick clips fitted after arrival at Corby.

Notes:
1. D9503/41/8: "They will go away by road [from Harlaxton to Corby] as the tyres are not in good enough condition to travel by BR." (IRS171).
2. Lack of Corby modifications suggest D9541 (66) was never used at Corby.

D9542

D9542 (48), BSC Corby, 18 April 1979. (Anthony Sayer)

S&L/BSC Nos.: 27 and 48
S&L Plant No.: 8311/27

Movements:
Despatched from 50B Hull Dairycoates: xx/12/68.
Arrived S&L(M), Corby Quarries, Northamptonshire: xx/12/68.
To BSC Steelworks Disposal Site, Corby: 29/12/80.
At BSC Steelworks Disposal Site, Corby: Scrapped by Shanks & McEwan Ltd, Corby: xx/08/82.

Sightings:
S&L/BSC Corby: 110169/241069/ 080370/ 060870/ 070871 (GB)/ 200173 (GB)/ 250973 (Pen Green Workshops)/ 080974 (GB)/ 220275 (GB)/ 070575/ 010576 (GB, shed)/ 100776/ 300477/ 050278/ 150778 (GB, stopped wtg reps)/ 270778 (GB, shed, wtg reps and/or supplying parts)/ 180479 (GB, running shed)/ 120679 (GB, shed)/ 140779 (GB, shed)/ 030879 (GB, stored in shed, dsm)/ 230879/ 291279 (GB, shed, OOU)/ 160480 (GB, shed)/ 080680 (GB, shed)/ 180780 (GB, shed)/ 160880 (GB, shed)/ 220880 (GB, shed)/ 121080 (GB)/ 291080 (GB, shed)/ 261180 (GB, shed)
BSC Steelworks Disposal Site, Corby: 291280 (inside)/ 210181 (inside)/ 090581 (inside)/ 010881/ 270881/ 190981 (inside)/ 171181 (outside)/ 230182 (outside, minus parts of engine)/ 260182 (outside)/ 070282 (part-stripped)/ 230282 (outside)/ 120482/ 190582/ 080682

Liveries and numbers:
D9542 to xx/xx (noted numbered 27 on 11/01/69), 27 from xx/xx to 10/74, 48 from 10/74.
BR two-tone green livery, black/yellow chevrons on nose-end, yellow buffer beams initially.
Subsequently all Sherwood green replaced by dark green.

Detail Differences:
Twin spotlights mounted on bonnet ends (Corby modification).
No flashing lights on cab roof.
Fitted with buffer-beam lifting lugs, safety chains and coupling-stick clips (Corby modifications).

D9544

D9544, BSC Corby (Gretton Brook), 10 October 1976. The original Corby purchase documents did not mention D9544, but they did include D9512. Events as they unfolded in 1968 saw D9512 going to Buckminster for spares provision, and similarly D9544 to Corby, indicating the transposition of delivery arrangements for these two locomotives relative to the original plans. (RCTS Archive)

S&L/BSC Nos.: (31) and (53)
S&L Plant No.: 8311/31

Movements:
Despatched from 50B Hull Dairycoates: xx/11/68. Noted Newark 02/11/68.
Arrived S&L(M), Corby Quarries, Northamptonshire: 02/11/68.
At BSC, Corby Quarries: Progressively dismantled and used for spares during the 1970s.
At BSC, Corby (Gretton Brook): Remains scrapped: xx/09/80 (by 24/09/80).

**D9544, BSC Corby,
18 April 1979.** Gretton
Brook shed yard.
(Anthony Sayer)

Sightings:

S&L/BSC Corby: 110169 (shed)/241069 (for spares)/ 080370 (for spares)

BSC Gretton Brook Dump (outside): 060870 (no engine, wheels removed)/ 281071/ 110272/ 200173/ 250973/ 080974/ 220275/ 161175/ 020176/ 010576/ 100776/ 071076/ 101076/ 300477/ 200977/ 291277/ 050278/ 060478/ 150778/ 220978/ 180279/ 180479/ 120679/ 030879/ 230879/ 291279/ 160480/ 170580/ 270580/ 080680/ 180780/ 160880/ 220880/ Scrapped by 240980

Liveries and numbers:

BR two-tone livery and number D9544 retained until disposal in 1980. The lion and wheel emblem was over-painted in black, suggesting the application of a BSC number; however, allocated numbers (31 and 53) were never carried.

Detail Differences:

Fitted with buffer-beam lifting lugs (Corby modification).

Notes:

1. Bought as a source of spares.
2. "The 'spares' loco D9544 has been reduced to a mere shell dumped behind the shed; she has no engine, and the wheels have been sent to Harlaxton to enable them to assemble a complete loco from their 'spare'." (IRS118).

D9545

D9545, NCB Ashington MPD, 7 May 1969.
Less than one month after arrival and already sidelined. Forward-facing BR-style lamp-irons reflecting its recent life at Hull. (George Woods)

NCB No.: -
Plant Registry No.: -

Movements:
Despatched from 50B Hull Dairycoates: xx/xx/69. Sighted Tyne Yard: 13/04/69.
Arrived NCB Ashington: 15/04/69.
At NCB Ashington : Bought for spares and progressively dismantled; wheelsets to D9527 09/77, and cab to D9536 01/78.
At NCB Ashington: Remains scrapped, early 07/79. See sightings below.

Sightings:
NCB Ashington: 070569 (shed yard)/250569/ 140669 (shed)/ 290669 (OOU)/ 200769/ 080869/ 171069/ 161169 (shed, engine out)/ 300370/ 240570/ 220970 (shed)/ 011070 (shed)

NCB Ashington (Old Boiler Plant Sidings): 290771 (derelict)/ 251071/ 020572/ 190672/ 270772 (dsm)/ 040872 (dsm)/ 221072 (dsm)/ 180873 (dsm)/ 230174/ 120674/ 150774/ 240774 (dsm)/ 040675/ 250875/

D9545, NCB Ashington, 4 June 1975. Six years later and showing the effects of heavy cannibalisation. The wheelsets and cab would also find further use on D9527 and D9536 respectively over the coming years. (Anthony Sayer)

150576/ 150676/ 280676/ 210577 (dsm)/ 190977 (dsm)/ 131177/ 250178 (dsm)/ 210378 (dsm)/ 050478 (dsm)/ 180778 (rems)/ 291078 (rems)/ 240279 (rems)/ 170479 (dsm)/ 190579 (dsm)/ 310579 (dsm)/ 300779 (frames only)/ 230979 (derelict). Not listed 281279.

Liveries and Numbers:
BR two-tone livery (including lion & wheel roundels) and number D9545 retained until cab removed.

Detail Differences:
No external modifications.

Notes:
1. Bought as a source of spares.
2. "At Ashington the dismantled ex-BR locos (D9511 and D9545) used for spares have now been written-off and are for disposal." (IRS277, 02/80)

D9547

D9547 (28), BSC Corby, 23 June 1973. Steps on third side door. (Author's Collection)

D9547 (49), BSC Corby, 18 April 1979. (Anthony Sayer)

S&L/BSC Nos.: 28 and 49
S&L Plant No.: 8311/28

Movements:
Despatched from 50B Hull Dairycoates: xx/12/68.
Arrived S&L(M), Corby Quarries, Northamptonshire: xx/12/68.
To BSC Steelworks Disposal Site, Corby: 29/12/80.
At BSC Steelworks Disposal Site, Corby: Scrapped by Shanks & McEwan Ltd, Corby: xx/08/82 (ILoBBN/8BRD), or, xx/09/82 (IQ6).

Sightings:
S&L/BSC Corby: 110169 (GB, shed yard)/241069/ 060870/ 070871 (GB, Repair Shop)/ 130172 (GB, shed)/ 200173 (GB)/ 230673 (assisting steam railtour to Wakerley)/ 250973 (wkg)/ 080974 (GB)/ 220275 (GB)/ 070575/ 161175 (wkg)/ 010576 (wkg)/ 100776/ 300477/ 200977 (GB, shed)/ 050278/ 150778 (GB, stopped wtg reps)/ 270778 (GB, shed, part dsm)/ 180479 (GB, running shed)/ 120679 (GB, shed)/ 140779 (GB, shed)/ 030879 (GB, stored in shed, dsm)/ 230879/ 291279 (GB, shed, OOU)/ 160480 (GB, shed)/ 080680 (GB, shed)/ 180780 (GB, shed)/ 160880 (GB, shed)/ 220880 (GB, shed)/ 291080 (GB, shed)/ 261180 (GB, shed)
BSC Steelworks Disposal Site, Corby: 291280 (inside)/ 210181 (inside)/ 090581 (inside)/ 010881/ 270881/ 190981 (inside)/ 171181 (outside)/ 230182 (outside, minus engine parts & some bodywork)/ 260182 (outside)/ 070282 (engine stripped)/ 230282/ 120482/ 190582/ 080682

Liveries and numbers:
D9547 to xx/xx (noted numbered 28 on 11/01/69), 28 from xx/xx to 10/74, 49 from 10/74.

BR two-tone green livery, black/yellow chevrons on nose-end, yellow buffer beams initially.
Subsequently all Sherwood green replaced by dark green.

Detail Differences:
Twin spotlights mounted on bonnet ends (Corby modification).
Two flashing lights on cab roof (towards 'A' end) (Corby modification).
Fitted with buffer-beam lifting lugs, safety chains and coupling-stick clips (Corby modifications).

Note:
1. Steam railtour, 23/06/73. Gretton Brook-Wakerley Tipping Dock and return. D9547 operated at the rear of the train to prevent any possibility of a runaway; the crew were apparrently instructed not to assist unless specifically called upon to do so.

D9548

D9548, BSC Harlaxton, 27 September 1969. Modified roof. Engine removed, which led to some incorrect suggestions at the time that this locomotive was being used as a source of spares for D9503/41. (John Gardner [IRS])

D9548 (67), BSC Corby, 18 April 1979. (Anthony Sayer)

S&L/BSC Nos.: No.27 and 67
S&L Plant No.: 8411/27

Movements:
Despatched from 50B Hull Dairycoates: xx/11/68. Booked transfer: 11/11/68.
Arrived S&L(M), Harlaxton Quarries, Lincolnshire: xx/11/68.
To BSC Tubes Division, Corby Quarries, Northamptonshire: 04/08/74.
To BSC Steelworks Disposal Site, Corby: 29/12/80.
To Hunslet Engine Co. Ltd, Leeds: 19/11/81.
Subsequently exported to Spain (see Section 9).

Sightings:
S&L/BSC Harlaxton: 221168/011268 (outside shed, and, Casthorpe Sdgs)/ 180569/ 270769 (undergoing overhaul, minus engine)/ 270969 (shed yard, engine out)/ 080370/ 060770 (wkg, Harlaxton sdgs)/ 150571 (shed)/ 190671 (wkg)/ 060772 (spare in yard)/ 210972 (shed yard)/ 160473 (shed, non-active due to strike at Stanton Ironworks)/ 260973 (shed)/ 160174 (wkg)/ 190374 (shed)/ 240474 (shed)/ Departed for Corby 040874

BSC Corby: 080974 (GB)/220275 (GB)/ 070575/ 010576 (wkg)/ 100776 (shed)/ 250876 (wkg Broomfield Cottage)/ 300477 (wkg)/ 060478/ 150778 (workable)/ 270778 (by Sinter Plant, wkg)/ 160878 (wkg, Oakley Quarry)/ 260279 (wkg)/ 180479 (wkg)/ 120679 (wkg)/ 140779 (wkg)/ 030879 (wkg)/ 230879/ 031179 (wkg)/ 291279 (GB, workable)/ 040180 (wkg, Harringworth Lodge (last day))/ 160480 (GB, shed)/ 170580 (GB, shed yard)/ 080680 (GB, shed)/ 180780 (GB, shed)/ 160880 (GB, shed)/ 220880 (GB, shed)/ 090980 (GB, shed)/ 121080 (GB)/ 291080 (GB, shed)/ 261180 (GB, shed)
BSC Steelworks Disposal Site, Corby: 291280 (inside)/ 210181 (inside)/ 090581 (inside)/ 010881/ 270881/ 190981 (inside)/ 171181 (outside, being shunted by D9515 (62) onto low-loader for movement to Leeds)/ Departed 191181 to Hunslet, Leeds

Liveries and numbers:
D9548 to 06/70, No.27 from 06/70 to 10/74, 67 from 10/74.

BR two-tone green livery, black/yellow chevrons on nose-end, yellow buffer beams initially.
Panel below side cab window repainted dark green and 'No.27' applied 06/70.
Subsequently all Sherwood green replaced by dark green.

Detail Differences:
Cut-down roof profile (Harlaxton modification, retained at Corby).
Footplate brackets ('A' end) (Harlaxton modification)
Large spotlight mounted on bonnet ends (Harlaxton modification, retained at Corby).
Two flashing lights on cab roof (towards 'A' end) (Corby modification).
Fitted with buffer-beam lifting lugs, safety chains and coupling-stick clips after arrival at Corby.

Notes:
1. Harlaxton, 27/09/69: "D9548 is used as a source of spares for the other two of the class here." (IRS112)
2. "D9512/44/8.....are to be used to provide spare parts for the others." (RO0570)
   N.B. D9548 subsequently rebuilt.
3. Corby, 06/08/70: "The 'spares' loco D9544 has been reduced to a mere shell dumped behind the shed; she has no engine, and the wheels have been sent to Harlaxton to enable them to assemble a complete loco from their 'spare'." (IRS118)
4. D9503/41/8: "They will go away by road [from Harlaxton to Corby] as the tyres are not in good enough condition to travel by BR." (IRS171)

D9549

D9549 (33), BSC Corby, Undated. (Geoffrey Starmer [IRS])

D9549 (64), BSC Corby, 18 April 1979. Back on shed following my footplate ride from Harringworth Lodge quarry to Corby. (Anthony Sayer)

S&L/BSC Nos.: 33 and 64
S&L Plant No.: 8311/33

Movements:
Despatched from 50B Hull Dairycoates: xx/11/68.
D9546 sighted passing Toton on 18/11/68 (with D9553) (RO0169); this is a recording error, believed to have been D9549.
Arrived S&L(M), Corby Quarries, Northamptonshire: xx/11/68.
To BSC Glendon East Quarries: 08/10/73.
To BSC Corby Quarries: 26/06/74 (exchanged for 'Steelman' 20).
To BSC Tube Works, Corby: xx/09/80.
To Hunslet Engine Co. Ltd, Leeds: 14/11/81.
Subsequently exported to Spain (see Section 9).

Sightings:
S&L/BSC Corby: 110169/241069/080370/060870/070871 (GB)/200173 (GB)/250973 (GB)
BSC Glendon East: Nil.
BSC Corby: 210874 (wkg, Park Lodge Quarry)/080974 (GB)/220275 (GB)/070575/020176 (GB, shed)/010576 (wkg)/100776/300477 (wkg)/220877 (Pen Green Workshops, heavy reps)/050278/060478/120678 (GB, outside shed)/150778 (GB, Repair Shop)/270778 (wkg)/180479 (wkg)/120679 (GB, shed)/270679 (GB, shed yard, under repair)/030879 (wkg)/230879 (wkg)/211279 (wkg, Wakerley Quarry)/291279 (GB, workable)/160480 (wkg, Priors Hall tracklifting)/190480 (GB, shed)
BSC Corby (Works): 130580 (wkg, track-lifting)/170580 (GB, shed)/270580 (wkg, track-lifting)/080680 (GB, shed)/180780 (GB, shed, see Note 1)/160880 (GB, shed)/090980 (wkg, track-lifting)
BSC Corby (Tube Works): 240980 (wkg)/291080/311080/091280/291280/210181 (outside Tube Works shed)
BSC Steelworks Disposal Site, Corby: 090581 (inside)/010881/270881/190981 (inside)/ Departed 141181 to Hunslet, Leeds

Liveries and numbers:
D9549 to xx/xx (noted numbered 33 on 11/01/69), 33 from xx/xx to 10/74, 64 from 10/74.

BR two-tone green livery, black/yellow chevrons on nose-end, yellow buffer beams initially.
Subsequently all Sherwood green replaced by dark green.

Detail Differences:
Twin spotlights mounted on bonnet ends (Corby modification).
Two flashing lights on cab roof (towards 'A' end) (Corby modification).
Fitted with buffer-beam lifting lugs, safety chains and coupling-stick clips (Corby modifications).

Note:
1. BSC Corby, 18/07/80. "61 and 64 [D9529 and D9549] are.....working in the steelworks, solo, but return to Gretton Brook shed after duty." (IRS292)

D9551

D9551 (50), BSC Corby, 10 July 1976. Single-tone green livery. Rolls-Royce '32' here was one of several which carried duplicate numbers at Corby; D9537 carried the same number between October 1970 and when it was re-numbered 52 in October 1974.
(Tony Skinner)

D9551 (50), BSC Corby (Gretton Brook), 10 October 1976. Two-tone green livery retained.
(RCTS Archive)

S&L/BSC Nos.: 29 and **50**
S&L Plant No.: 8311/29

Movements:
Despatched from 50B Hull Dairycoates: xx/12/68.
Arrived S&L(M), Corby Quarries, Northamptonshire: xx/12/68.
To BSC Tube Works, Corby: xx/07/80.
To West Somerset Railway (for preservation): 05/06/81.

Sightings:
S&L/BSC Corby: (110169)/241069/ 060870 (GB, shed)/ 070871 (GB)/ 130172 (GB, shed)/ 200173 (GB)/ 250973 (wkg, Wakerley)/ 080974 (GB)/ 220275 (GB)/ 070575/ 020176/ 010576 (GB, shed)/ 100776 (GB, shed)/ 101076 (GB, shed yard)/ 300477/ 050278/ 150778 (GB, Repair Shop)/ 270778 (GB, Repair Shop)/ 180479 (GB, Repair Shed)/ 120679 (GB, shed)/ 270679 (GB, shed yard, under reps)/ 030879 (GB, workable)/ 230879/ 291279 (GB, workable)/ 040180 (wkg, North Bank ramp, last day)/ 160480 (GB, shed)/ 080680 (GB, shed)
BSC Corby (Tube Works): 180780/220880 (Steelworks shed yard)/ 140980 (Steelworks shed yard)/ 241080 (assisting coil train from BR/BSC Exchange Sidings to Tube Works)/ 291080/ 311080/ 091280/ 291280/ 210181 (wkg)
BSC Steelworks Disposal Site, Corby: 090581 (inside).
XX: 050681 ("going south on Motorway")

Liveries and numbers:
D9551 to xx/xx (not seen on 11/01/69, but recorded as being allocated 29), 29 from xx/xx to 10/74, 50 from 10/74. Noted numbered 29 and 50 on opposite cab sides on 27/06/79.

BR two-tone green livery, black/yellow chevrons on nose-end, yellow buffer beams initially.
Subsequently all Sherwood green replaced by dark green.

Detail Differences:
Twin spotlights mounted on bonnet ends (Corby modification).
Two flashing lights on cab roof (towards 'A' end) (Corby modification).
Fitted with buffer-beam lifting lugs, safety chains and coupling-stick clips (Corby modifications).

Note:
1. D9510 transferred to Tube Works, Corby, 07/80, for conversion to brake-tender to work with D9551 (50), but project abandoned.

D9552

**D9552 (21), BSC
Buckminster, 1970.**
(Transport Topics)

**D9552 (59), BSC Corby,
18 April 1979.** (Anthony
Sayer)

S&L/BSC Nos.: 21 and 59
S&L Plant No.: 8411/21

Movements:
Despatched from 50B Hull Dairycoates: xx/09/68.
Arrived S&L(M), Buckminster Quarries, Lincolnshire: xx/09/68.
BR Grantham station: 31/08/72 (8BRD, see Sightings and Note 2).
To BSC Tubes Division, Corby Quarries, Northamptonshire: 06/09/72.
At BSC Corby (Gretton Brook): Scrapped on site: xx/09/80 (by 24/09/80).

Sightings:
S&L/BSC Buckminster: 180469 (shed)/280969 (IRS enthusiast special)/ 270170 (shed, minor reps; normally works Market Overton traffic)/ 080370 (shed)/ 140971 (wkg)/ 230971 (shed)/ 120172 (shed)/ 250272 (shed)/ 050472 (shed)/ Departed for Corby 130672
BR Grantham (in transit to Corby): 310872 (with D9512/5/29/52)
BSC Corby: 200173 (GB, OOU)/250973 (GB)/ 080974 (GB)/ 221074 (GB, for spares)/ 220275 (GB)/ 070575/ 010576 (GB, shed, OOU)/ 100776/ 071076 (GB, shed, dsm)/ 300477
BSC Gretton Brook Dump (outside): 291277/ 050278/ 060478/ 150778/ 290878/ 180279/ 180479/ 120679/ 030879/ 230879/ 291279/ 160480/ 170580/ 270580/ 080680/ 180780/ 160880/ 220880/ Scrapped by 240980

Liveries and numbers:
D9552 to 09/69, 21 from 09/69 to 10/74, 59 from 10/74.

BR two-tone green livery, black/yellow chevrons on nose-end, yellow buffer beams initially.

Panel below side cab window repainted dark green and '21' applied 09/69; also 'S&L' noted on cabside on 28/09/69 (later removed).

Subsequently all Sherwood green replaced by dark green.

Detail Differences:
Footplate brackets ('A' end) (Buckminster modification)
No large spotlights on bonnet ends.
No flashing lights on cab roof.
No buffer-beam lifting lugs, safety chains or coupling-stick clips fitted after arrival at Corby.

Notes:
1. Buckminster Railtour, 28/09/69. Stainby to Market Overton (including reversals at Buckminster and Pain's Sidings on the ex-BR line), and return, then Stainby to Stainby Warren quarry and return.
2. D9510/52 possibly moved to Corby in 06/72.
   - E.S. Tonks notes: 24/06/72: D9512 in yard, D9515/29 (20/22) in shed, D9510/52 (21/23) to Corby ("2-3 weeks ago").
   - IQM6/8 (E.S. Tonks): D9510/52 to Gretton Brook, Corby 6/1972, D9512/5/29 to Gretton Brook, Corby 9/1972.
   - IRS148: Undated report (but 'surrounding' reports related to 06-07/72): "David Needham noted at Gretton Brook shed 21 and 23 from Buckminster."
3. Lack of modifications suggest that D9552 (59) was never used at Corby.

D9553

D9553 (54), BSC Corby, 27 July 1978. (Peter Wilcox)

S&L/BSC Nos.: 34 and 54
S&L Plant No.: 8311/34

Movements:
Despatched from 50B Hull Dairycoates: xx/11/68. Sighted passing Toton on 18/11/68 (with D9537/49).
Arrived S&L(M), Corby Quarries, Northamptonshire: xx/11/68.
To BSC Steelworks Disposal Site, Corby: 29/12/80.
To Gloucestershire & Warwickshire Railway (for preservation): 23/02/83.

Sightings:
S&L/BSC Corby: 110169/241069/ 080370/ 060870/ 140870 (wkg, Cowthick)/ 070871 (GB)/ 281071/ 130172 (GB, Repair Bay)/ 200173 (GB)/ 230673 (GB, shed)/ 080974 (GB)/ 220275 (GB)/ 161175 (wkg)/ 010576 (GB, Repair Bay)/ 100776 (wkg)/ 071076 (wkg)/ 300477/ 050278/ 060478/ 150778 (GB, stopped awaiting reps)/ 270778 (GB, shed, waiting reps and/or supplying parts)/ 120679 (wkg)/ 030879 (wkg)/ 150879 (wkg, Priors Hall Quarry)/ 230879/ 101179 (wkg)/ 291279 (GB, workable)/ 160480 (GB, shed)/ 080680 (GB, shed)/ 180780 (GB, shed)/ 220880 (GB, shed)/ 291080 (GB, shed)/ 261180 (GB, shed)
BSC Steelworks Disposal Site, Corby: 291280 (inside)/ 210181 (inside)/ 090581 (inside)/ 010881/ 270881/ 190981 (inside)/ 171181 (outside)/ 230182 (complete)/ 260182 (outside)/ 070282 (complete)/ 230282/ 120482/ 190582/ 080682/ 250882 (set aside for possible re-sale)/ 201182

Liveries and numbers:
D9553 to xx/xx (noted numbered 34 on 11/01/69), 34 from xx/xx to 10/74, 54 from 10/74.
BR two-tone green livery, black/yellow chevrons on nose-end, yellow buffer beams initially.
Subsequently all Sherwood green replaced by dark green.

Detail Differences:
Twin spotlights mounted on bonnet ends (Corby modification).
Two flashing lights on cab roof (towards 'A' end) (Corby modification).
Fitted with buffer-beam lifting lugs, safety chains and coupling-stick clips (Corby modifications).

D9554

D9554 (58) and D9507 (55), BSC Corby, 27 July 1978. Looking in a sorry state! Accident damage to cab. Part way through overhaul? (Pete Wilcox)

D9554 (58), BSC Corby, 18 April 1979. Back to health again, with two new sets of lights fitted. Disappearing into Gretton Brook shed at end of shift. (Anthony Sayer)

S&L/BSC Nos.: 38 and 58
S&L Plant No.: 8311/38

Movements:
Despatched from 50B Hull Dairycoates: xx/11/68.
Arrived S&L(M), Corby Quarries, Northamptonshire: xx/11/68.
To BSC Steelworks Disposal Site, Corby: 29/12/80.
At BSC Steelworks Disposal Site, Corby: Scrapped by Shanks & McEwan Ltd, Corby: xx/08/82.

Sightings:
S&L/BSC Corby: 110169/241069/ 080370/ 060870/ 070871 (GB)/ 130172 (GB, Repair Shop)/ 200173 (GB, Repair Shop)/ 250973 (wkg)/ 180774 (wkg, Wakerley)/ 080974 (GB)/ 220275 (GB)/ 180475 (wkg)/ 070575/ 230376 (Pen Green Workshops, for reps)/ 010576 (Pen Green Workshops, undergoing complete overhaul)/ 100776 (GB, shed))/ 300477/ 200977 (GB, shed)/ 050278/ 060478/ 150778 (GB, supplying parts for useable locos)/ 270778 (GB, Repair Shop)/ 180479 (wkg) / 120679 (wkg)/ 030879 (wkg)/ 150879 (wkg, Harringworth Lodge Quarry)/ 230879 (wkg) / 291279 (GB, workable)/ 020180 (wkg)/ 040180 (wkg, Park Lodge, (last day)/ 160480 (GB, shed)/ 080680 (GB, shed)/ 220880 (GB, shed)/ 090980 (GB, Repair Shop)/ 291080 (GB, shed)/ 261180 (GB, shed)
BSC Steelworks Disposal Site, Corby: 291280 (inside)/ 210181 (inside)/ 090581 (inside)/ 010881/ 270881/ 190981 (inside)/ 230182 (outside, minus engine)/ 260182 (outside)/ 070282 (engine stripped)/ 120482/ 190582/ 080682/ 190283

Liveries and numbers:
D9554 to xx/xx (noted numbered 38 on 11/01/69), 38 from xx/xx to 10/74, 58 from 10/74.

BR two-tone green livery, black/yellow chevrons on nose-end, yellow buffer beams initially.
Subsequently all Sherwood green replaced by dark green.

Detail Differences:
Twin spotlights mounted on bonnet ends (Corby modification).
Two flashing lights on cab roof (towards 'A' end) (Corby modification).
Fitted with buffer-beam lifting lugs, safety chains and coupling-stick clips (Corby modifications).

D9555

D9555, NCB Backworth, Undated. Are there enough shunting poles!?
(John Reay [Mike Richardson Collection])

NCB No.: D9555
Plant Registry No.: 9107/57

Movements:
Despatched from 86A Cardiff Canton: 04/03/70.
Noted Tyne Yard 05/03/70.
Arrived NCB Burradon: 05/03/70.
To Ashington CW: xx/09/74 (for repairs) (IRR142 only).
To BR South Gosforth: xx/02/75 (tyre-turning) (IRR142 only). Sightings indicate Gosforth visited before
    Ashington CW.
To NCB Ashington: 07/02/75 (IRLNC/8BRD), or, 18/03/75 (IRR142).
To NCB Burradon: xx/03/75 (8BRD only).
To NCB Ashington: by 21/11/75 (8BRD only).
To NCB Backworth: 03/12/75 (8BRD), or, 08/12/75 (IRR142), or, 31/12/75 (IRLNC).
To NCB Weetslade CPP: xx/01/76 (IRR142 only).
To NCB Backworth: circa 05/76 (IRR142 only).
To NCB Ashington: 15/08/80.
To LEW Philadelphia: 11/11/81 (for overhaul and repaint) (IRR142), or, 12/02/82 (IRLNC). No 8BRD date.
To NCB Ashington: 10/03/82 (IRR142), or, 29/03/82 (IRLNC). No 8BRD date.
At NCB Ashington: Withdrawn from service 22/11/85 after derailment at Lynemouth (IRR142 only).
To Rutland Railway Museum, Cottesmore (for preservation): 24/09/87, arrived 25/09/87.

D9555 (9101/57) and D9518 (No.7), NCB Ashington, 7 March 1987. Their industrial career at an end, the Class 14s stand amongst the carnage at Ashington with the demolition of the railway system already well underway. However, a new career in preservation awaits.
(Anthony Sayer)

Sightings:
NCB Burradon: 300370/030470 (wkg)/ 230570/ 240570 (shed)/ 020770 (wkg)/ 180770 (shed)/ 070870 (Weetslade)/ 150870 (shed)/ 210870 (wkg)/ 030970 (Brenkley Drift)/ 150970/ 180970/ 111170 (wkg)/ 181170 (Burradon-Weetslade)/ 050371/ 240771/ 010971 (wkg)/ 051071/ 251071 (shed)/ 190572/ 250572/ 140772 (shed)/ 050673 (wkg, (Hazlerigg Jct)/ 120673 (shed)/ 150873/ 050973 (shed)/ 280973/ 231173/ 240174 (wkg)/ 260374 (shed)/ 250474/ 120674 (wkg, Seaton Burn)/ 240774 (shed). Not listed 281074 (moved to Ashington CW)
BR South Gosforth: 170874 (side-rods removed)
Ashington CW: Nil.
NCB Ashington: 040675
NCB Backworth (Eccles): Arrived by 091275/150576/ 150676 (shed)/ 170876 (wkg, Weetslade)/ 131177/ 230278 (wkg)/ 050478 (wkg)/ 291078 (shed)/ 030779 (spare)/ 090480 (wkg)
NCB Ashington: 060980 (shed)/061280/ 040181 (shed)/ 290381/ 100481 (Ly)/ 180681 (Ly)/ 190681 (Ly)/ 140881 ('scrap-line')/ 240881 (standing for engine)/ 120981 ('scrap-line')/ 051181 ('scrap-line')/ 111181 (sent to LEW)
LEW Philadelphia: 040182/010282/ 080382 (ex-Works)
NCB Ashington: 140482 (wkg, No.3 Ldg loco, ex-Work)/ 010782 (wkg, No.3 Ldg loco)/ 070782 (shed yard)/

13-160782 (wkg)/ 16-200882 (wkg)/ 06-100982 ((wkg)/ 27-290982 (wkg)/ 19-211082 (reps)/ 01-021182 (wkg)/ 291282 (wkg)/ 200383/ 120583 (wkg, No.3 Ldg loco, including shunting D9500 [No.1] and D9502 onto/off low-loader resp)/ 14-170683 (wtg spares)/ 20-240683 (wtg for spares)/ 260683 (shed)/ 270683 (wtg for spares)/ 29-300683 (wkg)/ 11-150783 (wkg)/ 220783/ 15-190883 (Ly)/ 230883 (reps)/ 06-090983 (wkg/spare)/ 100983 (spare)/ 12-160983 (Ly)/ 19-230983 (Ly)/ 251083 (Ly)/ 071183-111183 (Ly)/ 15-171183 (reps)/ 21-251183 (Ly)/ 301183 (Ly)/ 021283 (Ly)/ 12-161283 (Ly)/ 19-231283 (Ly)/ 04-060184 (reps)/ 10-120184 (reps, new turbo-blower)/ 16-190184 (spare)/ 23-270184 (Ly)/ 30-310184 (Ly)/ 130284 (Ly)/ 070784 (Ly)/ 030585 (Ly)/ 290885 (Ly)/ 16-190985 (Ly)/ 200985 (compressor fault)/ 23-270985 (Ly)/ 051085 (Ly)/ 07-111085 (Ly)/ 161085 (collision with 38, repaired at Ly)/ 28-311085 (Ly)/ 021185 (Ly)/ 18-211185 (Ly)/ 221185 (**derailed at Ly**, recovered by BR breakdown-crane)/ 241185 (Ly)/ 011285 (Ly)/ 161285 (Ly, derailment-damage, OOU)/ 06-100186 (Ly, OOU)/ 120186 (Ly, broken sand-box, no handbrake)/ 210286 (Ly, OOU)/ 110386 (too costly to repair, held for spares)/ 170386/ 200386 (wheels to crack-test on 250386)/ 010486 (wheels crack-tested, ready to move to

Ashington)/ 050486 (Ly, OOU)/ 080486 (parts donor for D9502)/ 020586 (Ly, OOU)/ 150586 (Ly, OOU)/ 270686 (Ly, OOU, wtg movement to Ashington)/ 170986 (Ly, OOU)/ 190986 (Ly, wtg decision)/ 291186 (Ashington 'scrap-line', wtg scrapping, transferred from Ly just prior to visit)/ 121286 ('scrap-line')/ 181286 (wtg scrap)/ 301286 ('scrap-line')/ 050187 ('scrap-line')/ 230187 ('scrap-line', wtg scrap)/ 280187 ('scrap-line')/ 300187/ 050287 (dumped between w/b and shed)/ 130287 (near w/b)/ 200287 (outside shed)/ 260287 (shed yard)/ 280287 (outside shed)/ 010387 (shed yard)/ 070387 (shed yard east)/ 130387 (siding near w/b)/ 150387 (shed yard)/ 110487 (shed yard)/ 200487 (dumped, shed yard)/ 170587 (shed)/ 130687/ 030887 (shed)/ 100987

Liveries and Numbers:
Retained BR two-tone green livery (including lion & wheel roundels) and numbered D9555 until sent to LEW, Philadephia, in 11/81.

Repainted in North-East Area dark-blue livery including bonnet fronts (with red handrails, red coupling rods, black/yellow striped buffer beams (/ / / configuration) and renumbered 9107/57 at LEW, Philadelphia (completed 03/82). Cabside details:

   NCB
North East Area
Plant Nº 9107/57
Serial Nº D9555

Detail Differences:
Buffer-beam coupling-stick clips.

Notes:
1. "NCB Backworth finished steam working on approx 13/12/75 with the arrival of two ex-BR D95xx. D9555 had arrived by 9/12, but not in use immediately, whilst a second one (*subsequently identified as D9525*) arrived on 13/12." (IRS Archive)
2. Incident at Lynemouth, November 1985.
   Ashington Daily Reports:
   - 22/11/85 (D9555). "After exam and report on work to be done, Loco Engineer (Team Valley), Mr. B. Pickering told me to scrap this loco." (AshDR)
   - 19/03/86 (D9502). "To be repaired with parts off D9555." (AshDR)
   - 16/04/86 (D9502). "Spare parts only." (AshDR)
   IRS Archive reports:
   - Lynemouth, 16/12/85 (parked-up in yard). "D9555 had been involved in an over-zealous shunting mishap at New Moor a couple of weeks earlier."
   - "On Friday 22/11/85 9107/57 (ex D9555) was derailed at Lynemouth and although damage was not thought to be serious, mainly brake gear, sandboxes, etc., the loco is to be..... stripped for spares. A replacement Hunslet is expected from Durham wc 25/11/85 (*AB514*)."
   - Ashington, 29/11/86. D9555 "transferred from Lynemouth just prior to my arrival".
   - Ashington, 23/01/87. D9555: "the wheels have been crack tested for BR's benefit, but it is OOU and for scrap. The fitter informed us that it is the last of the Paxmans to have alloy heads. All of the others have cast-iron ones which are far superior."
3. Ashington Periodic Reports:
   - Status, 24/08/81: Standing for engine.
   - Status, 24/11/81: Engine. Prop-shaft. Heat exchangers. Engine at Philadelphia Works, sent 11/11/81.
   - Status, 16/04/86: Spare parts only.
   - Status, 13/02/87: Damaged beyond repair. Replacement parts needed. Brake gear and sanders smashed. Possible transmission damage. Wheels crack detected and OK. Alloy cylinder heads.

Chapter 3

NATIONAL COAL BOARD: OPENCAST EXECUTIVE

3.1 General.

The NCB Opencast Executive (NCBOE) sites at British Oak (Crigglestone) and Bowers Row (Astley) were operated on their behalf by Hargreaves (West Riding) Ltd (subsequently Hargreaves Industrial Services Ltd from October 1974).

Both sites had previously been 'full-blown' colliery operations, but coal preparation facilities were retained after closure of the pits, operated by the NCB Opencast Executive. Work undertaken at the two sites included receipt of coal from local opencast sites, coal preparation (screening) and despatch to local power stations.

Two Class 14s were purchased by Hargreaves to replace steam, one each for use at British Oak and Bowers Row. Both were initially delivered to British Oak for commissioning work to be undertaken.

3.2 NCBOE British Oak Disposal Point, Calder Grove, Crigglestone.

The British Oak Disposal Point at Crigglestone was located on the west side of the Wakefield-Barnsley BR line near Calder Grove and was accessed by the Flockton Exchange Sidings. Coal preparation work was undertaken on the site of the closed Caphouse Colliery.

Coal was received from local opencast extraction sites, prepared, and despatched to power stations predominantly by rail and barge (the latter also owned and operated by Hargreaves). Destinations included Thornhill (near Ravensthorpe), Ferrybridge 'B' and 'C' power stations (all by barge, via the Calder and Hebble Navigation canal), and Elland and Eggborough power stations (by rail).

British Oak underwent a full programme of modernisation and re-equipment during late-1968/early-1969 including a new canal staithe, diesel locomotives and wagons. An official ceremony was held on 29 January 1969, involving Hargreaves, NCBOE and British Waterways. Both Class 14s were repainted into the distinctive Hargreaves black/orange livery in readiness for this ceremony with D9513 and D9531 renumbered D1/9513 and D2/9531 respectively at the same time.

D9513 and D9531 arrived from Arnott Young's scrap yard Parkgate & Rawmarsh in November 1968. The plan was for these two locomotives to be commissioned at British Oak with one subsequently forwarded to the Bowers Row facility at Astley. This is indeed what happened but the commissioning work took considerably longer than originally anticipated.

It had been expected that the ex-LMS 'Jinty' 47445 at British Oak would work its last train on 26 January 1969, after which the 650hp diesels would take over. In the event the IRS *Bulletin* No.108 reported:

- Fire dropped on 47445 on 27/01/69.
- D1/9513 started work on 28/01/69.
- D1/9513 and D2/9531 part of the Staithe Re-Opening ceremony on 29/01/69.
- D1/9513 failed on 30/01/69 (loss of oil pressure, clogged filters [containing metal]).
- 47445 lit up once again on 31/01/69 after three days of retirement.

Reliability and availability problems with the two Class 14s meant that the services of 47445 would be

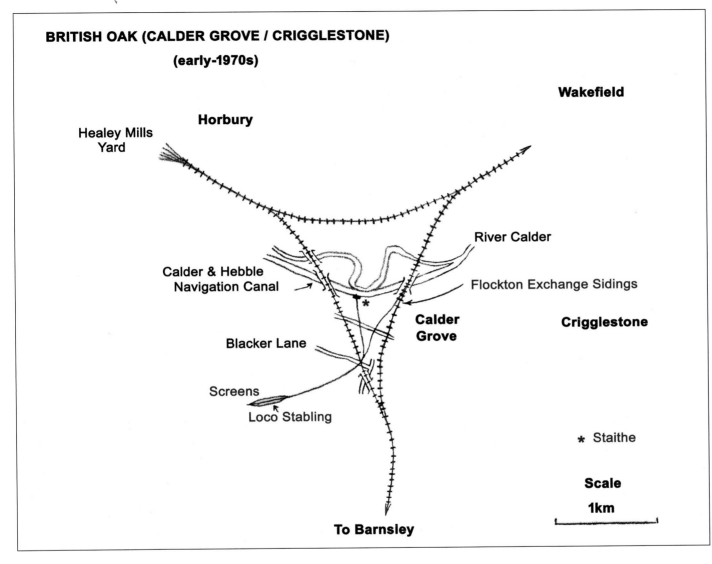

BRITISH OAK (CALDER GROVE / CRIGGLESTONE)

(early-1970s)

Wakefield

Horbury

Healey Mills Yard

River Calder

Calder & Hebble Navigation Canal

Flockton Exchange Sidings

Calder Grove

Crigglestone

Blacker Lane

* Staithe

Screens

Loco Stabling

Scale

1km

To Barnsley

required for many more months. In April 1969, it was reported that both diesels were in 'poor condition and unlikely to work for some time'; this was further exacerbated by the fact that 'considerable difficulty is being experienced by the fitting staff in carrying out repairs owing to the lack of lifting equipment and in-workshop facilities.' Assistance was brought in from Hunslet Engine Co. (albeit with only limited

gearbox experience) and BR Healey Mills fitters (who were not trained on Class 14s)!

By 24 July it was recorded that D2/9531 was working, with D1/9513 dismantled undergoing contract repairs. The plan was that once repairs had been completed on D1/9513, then D2/9531 would be overhauled in turn, and then when D2/9531 was completed D1/9513 could be released to go

to Bowers Row. In reality, D9513 went to Bowers Row immediately after completion of its overhaul and running-in on 5 September 1969, necessitating the continued use of 47445 while D2/9531 was repaired.

During the August-November 1969 period D2/9531 underwent its overhaul with 47445 continuing hard at work. On 23 November, however, '47445 was…being shunted by [a] diesel into its final

D9513 (D1/9513), NCBOE British Oak, Crigglestone, 18 August 1969. Roger Monk has kindly provided the following commentary: 'My notes say it [D1/9513] was bringing empty wagons from the BR exchange sidings to the opencast screens. I am fairly certain it was propelling the wagons from the exchange sidings across the Blacker Lane level crossing towards the screens which were around the curve to the right ...The railway bridge over the NCBOE line is the Crigglestone Junction to Horbury Fork Junction spur of the former Lancashire & Yorkshire Railway, which enabled trains from Barnsley to join the Calder Valley line towards Healey Mills Yard. The level crossing here was quite dangerous as visibility for road users was limited by the bridge abutments. In steam days a redundant loco was parked at the buffer stops you can see in the picture; this deliberately gave the impression to road users that it was actually on the crossing with the hope they would slow down. The line running due north from Blacker Lane crossing served the staithe on the Calder Canal. The NCB line on which the train is running was the former Caphouse Colliery Railway.' (Roger Monk [IRS])

resting place outside the offices. Now that the diesel works OK they will get rid of the steam'. 47445 then became the spare locomotive until it finally departed to Derby for preservation on 11 July 1970.

D9531 stayed on at British Oak until sold to NCB North East Area, departing for Northumberland on 11 October 1973.

The Disposal Point at Crigglestone closed in May 1993, nearly twenty years after the departure of D9531. In the intervening period several ex-BR Class 03, 08 and 11 locomotives were operated at the site alongside other industrial shunters.

D9513 (D1/9513) and ex-LMS 'Jinty' 3F 47445, NCBOE British Oak, Crigglestone, 10 March 1969. The somewhat derelict shed here is believed to have been demolished soon after this picture was taken, with locomotives stabled in the open thereafter. Coal screens to the right with a 16t mineral wagon being loaded. The 'Jinty' remained at Crigglestone until July 1970 having seen plenty of service in the intervening period while the Class 14s were brought up to a satisfactory standard. (Cliff Shepherd [IRS])

D9513 and D9531, NCBOE, British Oak, Crigglestone, 1969. (Kevin Lane)

3.3 NCBOE Bowers Row Disposal Point, Astley.

The 1¼ mile 'branch' to Bowers Row ran west from the BR Castleford to Garforth line from Bower's Allerton Colliery Junction (about ½ mile south of Kippax station). The section of line north of this junction to Garforth East Junction closed in July 1969 , and, as a consequence, all traffic access to Bowers Row during the time of the Class 14s' period of operation was from the south. About ½ mile along the branch was the BR/ NCB exchanges sidings, with the remaining ¾ mile operated by the NCB. The Disposal Point at Bowers Row was situated on the site of the former Lowther Pit

D9513 arrived at Bowers Row on 5 September 1969. A repeat of the situation previously experienced at Crigglestone was clearly not expected, and the resident steam locomotive, *Pepper* (RSH 7164), was immediately cut up for scrap. This was an expensive mistake as by 2 October 1969 D1/9513 had broken down with an auxiliary generator defect; it was still out of use on 30 October but was noted in use again on 20 November.

D9513 remained at Bowers Row until October 1973 when it was sent to Allerton Bywater Central Workshop for repairs, prior to movement to NCB Ashington Colliery in January 1974.

Rail operations at Bowers Row ceased in the late-1980s, but in the period following D9513's departure several ex-BR Class 03 and Class 11 shunters were used at the site.

3.4 Class 14 Suitability.

The site maps for both Crigglestone and Bowers Row illustrate the limited geographical size of both operations. The use of 650hp Class 14 trip-freight locomotives, in hindsight at least, seemed somewhat excessive both operationally and financially and it is, perhaps, not surprising that they were sold on to the NCB North East Area for further use and replaced by eminently more suitable 200/350hp shunters.

Bowers Row (early-1970s)

To Leeds — Garforth — To Church Fenton — Closed 1969 — Swillington — Scale 1km — Kippax — Great Preston — Astley — Ledston — Bowers Row — Exchange Sidings — Allerton Bywater Colliery & Central Workshops — Castleford — Castleford — To Leeds — To Pontefract

Bowers Row Disposal Site, Astley.

Chapter 4

NATIONAL COAL BOARD: DURHAM/ NORTHUMBERLAND

4.1 NCB North-East Organisation.

It is worth describing the organizational structure of the National Coal Board (NCB) following Nationalisation in 1947, well before the arrival of the Class 14s in 1969, as this helps to inform:

- the initial allocation of diesel locomotives generally, and the Class 14s specifically, via the so-called 'Co-ordinated Locomotive Policy',
- the numbering systems deployed on locomotives following their arrival in the North East,
- the liveries and styles of lettering carried,
- the Works selected to carry out heavy maintenance,
- the changes to areas of operation over the Class 14s eighteen- year history in the area.

On Nationalisation of the UK coal industry on 1 January 1947, collieries in Durham, Northumberland and Cumberland were organized within the **Northern Division**, sub-divided into ten Areas. With effect from 1 January 1950 the Northern Division was split into the **Durham Division** and the **Northern (Northumberland and Cumberland) Division**, retaining the ten geographical area as before, as follows:

Durham Division

No.1 Area	North-East Durham
No.2 Area	Mid-East Durham
No.3 Area	South-East Durham
No.4 Area	South-West Durham
No.5 Area	Mid-West Durham
No.6 Area	North-West Durham

Northern (Northumberland & Cumberland) Division

No.1 Area	South Northumberland
No.2 Area	Mid-Northumberland
No.3 Area	North Northumberland
No.4 Area	Cumberland

On 1 January 1962, Nos.1 & 2 Areas in Northumberland were combined to form No.1/2 Area, and on 1 January 1963 the former No.5 Area in Durham was divided between Nos.4 and 6 Areas, the latter becoming No.5. In addition, on 1 July 1963 the Northern Division No.4 Area (Cumberland) was transferred over to the North Western Division.

On 1 January 1964, the two remaining Northumberland Areas were combined with what had become five Areas in Co. Durham to form the **Northumberland & Durham Division**. The five Durham Areas retained their former numbers, but the two in Northumberland became simply South Northumberland and North Northumberland. In June 1965, the former No.2 area in Durham was divided between Nos.1 and 3 Areas.

On 26 March 1967, the Divisional organisational tier was abolished and replaced by an up-graded Area structure. Thus, in Durham, Nos. 1 and 5 Areas combined to form the **North Durham Area** and Nos. 3 and 4 Areas combined to form the **South Durham Area**. In Northumberland the two Areas (South and North Northumberland) combined to form the **Northumberland Area**. In addition, the Area Workshops were transferred to a new Workshops Division.

Following the introduction of the new Area organisation, a new Northumberland Area 'Internal Railways' Management Committee was set up in recognition of the need to control and integrate internal railway operations in the newly created Area following the elimination of the Divisional level of management. Meetings were usually chaired by the Area Chief Engineer. Meetings were attended by the Traffic Managers of Ashington, Bates and Burradon Collieries and the Divisional Transport Officer. The first meeting was held in October 1967, and subsequent meetings were initially held at six-weekly intervals increasing later to three-monthly. Meeting minutes covering most of the period between October 1967 and December 1973 have been perused (courtesy of Trevor Scott) and they have provided a very useful insight into NCB traffic decisions during this crucial transition period. References will be made to these meetings over the ensuing pages.

On 1 April 1974, the Northumberland, North Durham and South Durham Areas were combined to form the **North East Area**. This arrangement lasted for fifteen years when, on 31 December 1988 and after the demise of the Class 14s, the North East Area was abolished and replaced by the **North East Group**.

4.2 'Co-ordinated Locomotive Policy'.

At the Northumberland Area 'Internal Railways' Committee Meeting on 24 April 1969 Mr. Watson [Area Chief Engineer] stated that 'the policy … was to fit up one place at a time with the necessary size diesels according to requirements'.

In Northumberland the policy manifested itself in terms of:

- A logical transitioning of collieries from steam to diesel. In the case of the collieries which ultimately deployed Class 14s this was Ashington, Bates, Burradon and Backworth (in order). This explains why Backworth, with Shilbottle/Whittle, became the last collieries deploying steam power; with respect to Backworth, the 18 May 1972 'Internal Railways' meeting minutes stated 'Future requirements were to be left until all other standardisation within the Area was completed.'
- The aim 'to standardise on 'Paxman' and 350hp locomotives'.

4.3 Plant Registry Numbers and Plant Pool.

The period 1950 to 1964 was a period of relative organisational stability and it was during this time, in 1956, that the NCB introduced nationally the Plant Numbering System under which every significant item of plant was allocated a Plant Registry number. This number began with the identification of the place where the plant was located. Initially this was a four figure number, in which the first was the number of the Division, followed by the number of the Area and ending with a two digit location/colliery code. So, for example, 2233 was 2 (Durham Division), 2 (No.2 Area- Mid-East Durham) and 33 (Philadelphia). Following these digits was an identifying number for each piece of kit concerned. Thus, in railway terms, all locomotives, wagons, guards vans, brake-tenders, etc., were uniquely identified.

Despite several re-organisations after 1956, including the major 1967 re-organisation where the Divisions were abolished, the numbering of new locomotives continued to be based on the 1950 Division and Area structure. Thus, with the introduction of the Class 14s at Ashington in 1969, the locomotives were given Plant Registry numbers commencing 9312 (see table on pages 131 and 132). Even when D9513/31 arrived in the North-East in 1973/74 the Divisional first digit was being used, although the second Area digit did recognise the June 1965 Durham Area boundary changes!

The Plant Registry numbers were used for asset management and engineering control purposes, including Planned Preventative Maintenance (PPM). Closely associated with the Plant Registry was the Plant Pool process, which controlled a wide range of mining equipment, such as coal cutters, fans, conveyor drives, etc., including 'hiring' them out to user collieries, and managing repairs. With the formation of the North East Area in 1974, the Plant Pool took over ownership of all diesel locomotives over 50hp. This change ultimately led to a full Area-wide system for PPM work and major overhauls, and progressively facilitated the concentration of certain types of equipment, including locomotives, at designated locations.

The Plant Pool control system resulted in Plant numbers being applied externally to locomotives following overhaul with the apparent intention for local (i.e. pre-North East Area) numbers to be superseded. Old habits died hard, however, and many locomotives, including a number of Class 14s, had their old pre-1974 numbers re-applied (in addition to their Plant Nos.) following return to site after Works attention.

The Plant Pool system was abolished from February 1988 and Plant Registry followed in March 1988, one year after the demise of the Class 14s.

4.4 'Local' Locomotive Numbering.

With the arrival of new diesel locomotives in 1965, the Northumberland & Durham Division began a new numbering scheme, which was continued by North Durham Area after the Divisional structure was abolished in 1967. Diesels were therefore numbered upwards from 500, with D9504/25/40 acquiring the numbers 506-8 respectively; these three Class 14s were subsequently followed by D9513 and D9531 as 523 and 524 (but, for these two, only as part of their Plant Registry number).

Similarly, the new Northumberland Area embarked on revised number ranges for new and second-hand diesels. When the Class 14s began to arrive at Ashington they were numbered backwards from 100, preceded by the Plant Registry number (see table below).

At the Northumberland Area 'Internal Railways Committee Meeting on 24 April 1969, Mr. Butters (Mechanical Services Engineer] was asked to 'prepare a suitable schedule for the re-numbering of locos throughout the Area, allocating certain groups of numbers to the various collieries, and also [to] revise the present list of locos within the Area.' Minutes of the 9 September Meeting recorded that Butters had prepared the list and was actioned that this list 'be kept up to date and when all the changes were made, following closure of Rising Sun [closed 24/04/69] and Mill [18/07/69], re-numbering of all the locos would be done.'

In May 1972, the revised 'local' numbering system was introduced with the Ashington system allocated 1-20, Bates 21-30, and the Backworth and Burradon Group 31-50. This had not been fully implemented when the Northumberland Area was merged into the North East Area in 1974.

Details of the Plant Registry and 'Local' numbers carried by the nineteen north-east Class 14s are given below:

Class 14 - NCB Durham and Northumberland - Plant Registry Nos. and 'Local' Nos..

NB Plant Registry No.	NCB 'Local' No(s). Carried	Ex-BR No.	Despatched Ex-BR	Delivered NCB	First Delivery Point(s)
2233/506	506	D9504	50B 27/11/68	02/12/68*	Philadelphia, Co. Durham
2233/507	507	D9525	50B 28/11/68	02/12/68*	Philadelphia, Co. Durham
2233/508	508, No.36	D9540	50B 29/11/68	02/12/68*	Philadelphia, Co. Durham
–	–	D9545	50B xx/xx/69	14 or 15/04/69	Ashington, Northumberland (purchased for spares)
9312/100	No.2	D9528	86A 06/03/69	14/03/69	Ashington, Northumberland
9312/99	No.9	D9508	86A 06/03/69	14/03/69	Ashington, Northumberland
9312/98	–	D9511	50B xx/xx/xx	07/01/69	Ashington, then Bates (04/69), Burradon (05/69)
(9312/97)	–	D9502	86A 30/06/69	19/07/69	Ashington, Northumberland, then Burradon (by 09/69)
9312/96	No.4	D9514	86A 30/06/69	19/07/69	Ashington, Northumberland
9312/95	No.7	D9518	86A 30/06/69	19/07/69	Ashington, Northumberland
9312/94	No.6	D9527	86A 30/06/69	19/07/69	Ashington, Northumberland

NB Plant Registry No.	NCB 'Local' No(s). Carried	Ex-BR No.	Despatched Ex-BR	Delivered NCB	First Delivery Point(s)
9312/93	No.8	D9517	86A 17/11/69	25/11/69	Ashington, Northumberland
9312/92	No.1	D9500	86A 17/11/69	25/11/69	Ashington, Northumberland
9312/91	No.5	D9536	86A 04/03/70	06/03/70	Ashington, Northumberland
9312/90	No.3	D9521	86A 04/03/70	06/03/70	Ashington, Northumberland
9107/57	D9555	D9555	86A 04/03/70	05/03/70	Burradon, Northumberland
9312/59	37	D9535	86A 09/11/70	xx/11/70	Ashington, Northumberland (11/70), then Burradon (01/71), or, Burradon (11/70)
2100/523	D2/9531, No.31	D9531	BO 11/10/73	19/10/73	Ashington, ex-Hargreaves, NCBOE British Oak (BO), Crigglestone
2100/524	D1/9513, 38	D9513	AB xx/01/74	21/01/74	Ashington, then Backworth (06/74, for repaint), Burradon (07/74 Ex-Hargreaves, NCBOE Bowers Row (via Allerton Bywater CW (AB))

Notes:

1. Plant Registry code descriptions:
   2233 Durham Division, No.2 Mid-East Durham Area, Philadelphia Loco Shed.
   9312 Northumberland Division, North Northumberland Area, Ashington Loco Shed.
   9107 Northumberland Division, South Northumberland Area, Burradon.
   2100 Durham Division, No.1 North-East Durham Area (which included the northern half of No.2 Mid-East Durham Area from 28 June 1965, including the Lambton Railway and Philadelphia Loco Shed).
2. The four digit 'prefix' of the Plant Registry code specified the *first* intended operational location for the locomotives; in the main this was retained throughout their lives with the NCB irrespective of subsequent movements to other collieries or railway systems.
3. Bracketed Plant Registry numbers indicate locomotives where the numbers were not carried externally.
4. The allocation of the 2100 Plant Registry prefix to D9513/31, after their arrival from Yorkshire, possibly suggests that they were originally destined for use in the North Durham Area, even though they were actually delivered for use in the Northumberland Area.
5. Ashington: Initial Plant Registry based numbering.
   Numbered downwards from 9312/100, with 9312/98, 99 and 100 renumbered during the last two weeks of March 1969.
6. Subsequent 'Local' Numbering:
   Nos. 1-9   Within the Ashington 1-20 number series
   No.36, 37, 38 Within the Burradon/Backworth Group 31-50 number series.
   506-8   Within the North Durham Area 500+ number series.
7. Despatched/Delivered ex-BR.
   Despatched: Date despatched from BR depot (or NCB Yorkshire sites where highlighted in red).
   Delivered: Date delivered to specified NCB Colliery.
8. Asterisked **Delivered** dates for D9504/25/40 are the NCB official dates. D9504 was actually sighted at Philadelphia on 29/11/68 and D9525/40 may also have arrived slightly earlier.
9. D9513 was variously referred to as 2100/525 and 9312/513 in the Ashington Loco Shed Daily Reports during 1985/86, although it was only ever recorded as 2100/524 by the IRS. In practice, no 2100 or 9312 number was ever carried externally by D9513.

4.5 Workshops.

As already mentioned, Workshops were transferred from the relevant local Divisions to a new centralised Workshops Division in 1967.

Extensive rationalisation followed as a result and revised engineering practices were introduced. With the creation of North East Area in 1974, it was decided that from

April 1975 all repairs to the Area's underground diesel fleet would be concentrated at Ashington Central Workshops (Northumberland), with Philadelphia Central Workshops

(Co. Durham, now Tyne & Wear) handling all repairs to surface diesels and underground battery electric locomotives for the entire Area. The Philadelphia Workshops were more usually referred to as Lambton Engine Works. This 'co-ordinated locomotive policy' may have represented the least-cost option overall but will inevitably have resulted in increased overhaul costs for the Ashington fleet specifically.

Battery electric locomotive repairs were progressively transferred to Ashington from July 1985. Lambton Engine Works ceased all locomotive work in May 1987, soon after the demise of the Class 14 fleet, although the last Class 14 repaired at Philadelphia took place much earlier in 1984. All remaining locomotive repair work was transferred back to Ashington Central Workshops. Philadelphia closed completely in December 1989 and Ashington in April 1994.

4.6 Class 14 Purchase Cost from BR.

The Class 14s were supposedly purchased for £4,000 each, although, unlike the locomotives purchased by Stewarts & Lloyds (see Section 6), this has never been confirmed via official documentation.

4.7 Class 14 Operational Areas.

Such was the intensity of coal operations in the south of Northumberland and the north of County Durham, that 'full-blown' railway systems had progressively developed in the century leading up to the nationalisation of the coal industry, to integrate several collieries with local coal preparation plants (for coal washing, screening, etc.), coke ovens, waste disposal

points and staithes on the Rivers Blyth, Tyne and Wear (where coal was loaded into vessels for sea-borne movement to London).

These 'internal' NCB railway systems were extensive operations by any standards (reaching up to 10 miles in length), and were supported to varying degree by BR via suitably positioned NCB/BR exchange sidings. 'Running rights' by NCB on BR lines, and vice versa, were commonplace, frequently necessitating the deployment of block signalling. This 'set-up' was very different from the 'isolated' colliery operations which typified South Wales, Derbyshire, Nottinghamshire and Yorkshire, where local NCB shunting was heavily supported by major BR servicing arrangements for the movement of coal away from the collieries to processing plants and customers.

To a very significant extent this situation explains why the Class 14s (together with other large 'industrial' locomotives) gravitated to the North-East where their 650hp rating, combined with trip-working characteristics, made them eminently suited to the prevailing integrated and geographically spread railway systems. In the same way, redundant 200/350hp BR shunters (and other small 'industrials') were more operationally and financially suited to the confined operations which typified collieries further south and in South Wales.

The major railway systems of Durham and Northumberland were, however, already in a state of decline when the Class 14s moved north in 1969. In a replication of circumstances already suffered during their time on BR, the Class 14s watched their world

progressively fall apart again during their time with the NCB. Collieries progressively closed as a consequence of:

- seams being worked out or becoming geologically compromised,
- collieries being joined together underground to reduce the number of points where coal and spoil were brought to the surface,
- the use of drift mines to enable the 'drawing' of coal to the surface by conveyor belts straight to coal preparation plants (without the need for rail transportation), and,
- perhaps most significant of all, the national economics of coal extraction and usage which favoured the coalfields of Derbyshire, Nottinghamshire and Yorkshire.

These factors in combination had an adverse impact on the volume of coal mined from North East collieries and the proportion transported by rail, and inevitably resulted in the North East railway systems being severely truncated during the 1960s, particularly the NCB 'internal main line' routes to riverside staithes.

The pace of decline for the Class 14s in the North East was slower than when working for BR, and hence they survived at Philadelphia (Lambton) until 1975 (when 350hp ex-BR Class 11s were deemed sufficient for the remaining tasks), at Backworth until 1980, at Weetslade until 1981, and at Ashington until 1987.

One further aspect of the North East railway systems needs to be mentioned. Many publications list the Class 14s as being located at Ashington, Backworth, Burradon, Weetslade or Philadelphia Collieries, but by the very nature of the railway *systems* this was not strictly accurate; whilst it is true that they were *allocated* to the Locomotive Sheds at these locations, the locomotives actually worked over a significantly wider geographical area, serving several collieries or facilities in the area.

There were several other railways systems in the North East which never enjoyed the services of the Class 14s (e.g. Bowes, Derwenthaugh, etc.). Maybe if the British Steel Corporation had not been so quick in' buying twenty-three locomotives from Hull for use in the ironstone fields of Lincolnshire and Northamptonshire, then maybe the 'Paxmans' could have worked on these systems as well.

Summaries of the systems in the North East which deployed the Class 14s are given below.

4.7.1 Lambton Railway.
Loco Shed: **Philadelphia.**

Organisational structure covering period of Class 14 usage:

- North Durham Area initially, then, North East Area from 1/4/1974.

Plant Registry code (based on the 1950 Durham Division/Area structure): 2233.

In the mid-1960s, the main NCB section of this railway ran from Herrington Colliery to Penshaw Sidings, east of the BR Sunderland to Durham line alongside Penshaw station. Served en route were:

- Houghton Colliery (via a 1m branch from Houghton Junction),
- Lambton 'D Colliery, Lambton 'D' Coal Preparation Plant and Lambton Coking Plant (both via a ½m branch from Burnmoor Junction),
- Lumley Sixth Colliery (via another branch (1m) from Burnmoor Junction),
- Harraton Colliery (on a 4m BR branch from Penshaw on which the NCB had running rights).

Also on this section were the Philadelphia Loco Shed and Lambton Engine Works (subsequently Philadelphia Central Workshops).

From Penshaw, Lambton Railway locomotives had running powers over the BR Durham-Sunderland line for 4¾m to Lambton Staithes, Sunderland, which were reached via a branch (1m) from a junction ½m east of Pallion station. Running rights were also exercised onwards to Sunderland South Dock.

From Herrington Colliery to the Lambton Staithes on the River Wear was distance of approximately 9¼m.

Even before the arrival of the Class 14s, significant sections of the Lambton Railway system, as operated by NCB locomotives, had ceased. Lambton 'D' Colliery closed in February 1965, followed by Harraton Colliery in May 1965 and Lumley Sixth Colliery in January 1966. The loss of these collieries severely reduced the tonnage being handled by Lambton Staithes, and on 6 January 1967 these closed too, thereby ending all running over BR tracks. The giving up of running powers beyond Penshaw to Sunderland reduced the end-to-end mileage of the Lambton Railway by roughly 50 per cent.

Class 14s at Philadelphia.
D9504/25/40 arrived from BR in December 1968 according the official NCB records. The Railway's steam locomotives were officially replaced by diesels on 16 February 1969, although one or two steam locomotives were apparently maintained as substitutes to cover for diesel failures. Other early diesels in the Lambton fleet included ex-BR Class 11s, 12119 and 12120.

By early-1969, IRS *Bulletin* No.108 (April 1969) reported that 'Six diesels (inc D9504/25/40) with 17 men now work all the remaining system.'

At Houghton Colliery, rail traffic was replaced by road haulage in February 1975; closure followed on 2 October 1981. The use of road transport probably precipitated the removal of the final Class 14 from the Lambton system in March 1975. From that date, and as part of the Area 'co-ordinated locomotive policy, lower powered diesel-electric shunters (including BR Class 08s, 10s and 11s, plus other industrials) were considered sufficient on the massively diminished Lambton Railway until final closure of the system in 1985.

At Herrington Colliery, rail traffic was similarly replaced by road in March 1984 with the colliery closing in November 1985. Rail traffic to the Lambton Engine Works also ceased in March 1984. The use of locomotives from the Philadelphia Loco Shed finally ceased in July 1985, ten years after departure of the last Class 14.

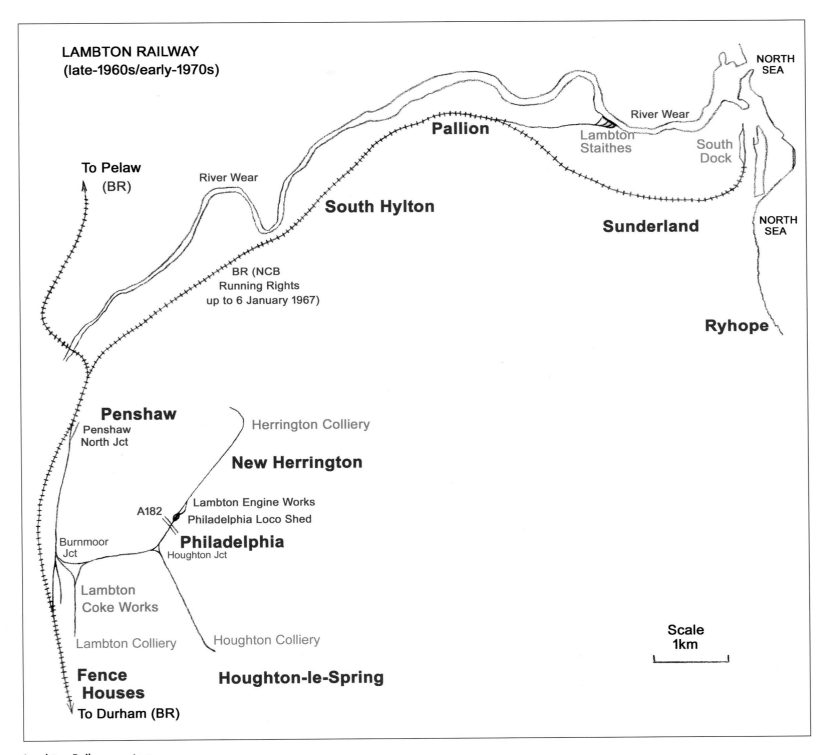

LAMBTON RAILWAY
(late-1960s/early-1970s)

NORTH SEA

River Wear

Pallion

Lambton
Staithes

South
Dock

To Pelaw
(BR)

River Wear

South Hylton

Sunderland

NORTH
SEA

BR (NCB
Running Rights
up to 6 January 1967)

Ryhope

Penshaw

Herrington Colliery

Penshaw
North Jct

New Herrington

Lambton Engine Works

A182

Philadelphia Loco Shed

Philadelphia

Houghton Jct

Burnmoor
Jct

Lambton
Coke Works

Lambton Colliery

Houghton Colliery

Fence
Houses

Houghton-le-Spring

To Durham (BR)

Scale
1km

Lambton Railway system.

Summary: Class 14 locomotives which operated from Philadelphia:

	Local NCB No.	From (per NCB records)	To
D9504	506	02/12/68 (ex BR Hull)	21/08/73 (to Bolden)
D9525	507	02/12/68 (ex BR Hull)	14/03/75 (to Ashington)
D9540	508	02/12/68 (ex BR Hull)	25/11/71 (to Burradon)

Notes:
1. All of the Philadelphia Class 14s were repainted into 'emerald' green. The black/yellow chevron panels and yellow buffer-beams were retained.
    D9525 was repainted by 15/02/69 (see I.S. Carr photo, SLS *Journal*, July 1969). IRS member Douglas Capewell subsequently recorded on 1 August 1969: 'Two diesels recently repainted, but they grind away on the longer trips' a comment seemingly applicable to Class 14s (*D9504/40?*) rather than the Class 11s.
2. C.E. Mountford & D. Holroyde's book *The Industrial Railways & Locomotives of County Durham* (Part 2) record all three Class 14s being re-numbered in the 5xx series in August 1969.
3. D9504 (506) and D9525 (507) received a pair of sealed-beam headlights fitted behind the headcode glass panels. It is possible that D9540 (508) also received this modification although no photographic evidence has been found of this locomotive so modified.

Right: **D9540, with D9504/25, NCB Philadelphia, 8 February 1969.**
(Rail-Photoprints)

Below: **D9504, NCB Philadelphia Loco Shed, 11 February 1969.**
(Author's Collection)

D9525(507) and 12098(513), NCB Philadelphia, 30 August 1972. Sealed-beam headlights still to be fitted. (Trevor Scott Collection)

4.7.2 Ashington Railway System.
Loco Shed: **Ashington.**

Organizational structure covering period of Class 14 usage:

- Northumberland Area initially, then, North East Area from 1/4/1974.

Plant Registry code (based on the 1950 Northern (Northumberland & Cumberland) Division/Area structure): 9312.

The Ashington System.
By the mid-1960s a roughly circular route of nearly 9 miles in length, together with several branches, formed the Ashington system. To all intents and purposes, Ashington, Linton, Ellington, Lynemouth and Woodhorn Collieries were on the main circuit (in clockwise order), with Coneygarth Drift, Pegswood Colliery, Longhirst Drift, and Newbiggin Colliery on branches of varying length. However, between 1965 and 1969, prior to the Class 14s taking over:

- Coneygarth Drift, and, Pegswood and Woodhorn Collieries were linked underground to Ashington;
- Linton Colliery, Longhirst Drift and Newbiggin Colliery were closed; and,
- the coal output from Ellington and Lynemouth Collieries was 're-routed' to the surface via Bewick Drift with a direct conveyor belt connection to the Lynemouth Washery.

As a consequence of these changes the route between Linton and Ellington (2 miles) became redundant and was ultimately lifted. The line between Ellington and Lynemouth (2 miles), whilst disused for through traffic, was used for a period as a siding for wagons awaiting use at Lynemouth. The route between Ashington (north of the A1068 road and the New Moor Stocking Site) and Linton (2½ miles) also became disused (although this was rebuilt in 1978 to allow BR access to the Butterwell opencast site).

In addition:

- the section of line between Hirst Junction (just east of Ashington) to Lynemouth was up-graded and transferred to BR control; NCB retained running rights however (a complete reversal of arrangements hitherto), but the change necessitated the use of guards vans on all NCB

Ashington Railway system.

trains due to the unfitted wagon stock involved. This change was as a logical consequence of the increased traffic flows secured by BR at this time (including all sale coal from Lynemouth and the traffic associated with the Lynemouth aluminium smelter), and,

- a new link was installed at Hirst Junction enabling direct

access from Ashington to Lynemouth without the need for a reversal at New Moor (opened 3 August 1970).

Thus, by the time of the arrival of the Class 14s in 1969, the system was already something of a shadow of its former self, with the core route being Ashington to Lynemouth (3½ miles, much of it now traversable by the NCB on the basis of running

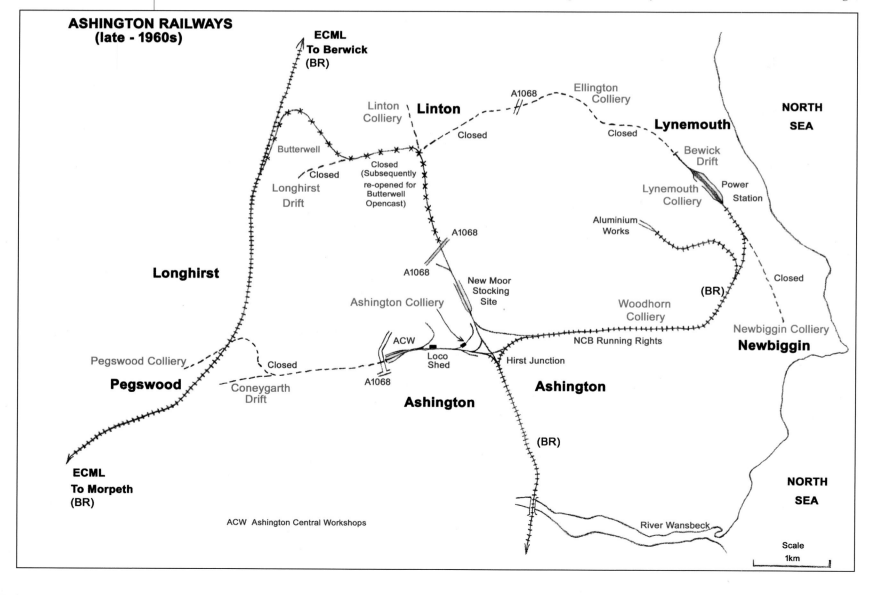

ASHINGTON RAILWAYS (late - 1960s)

ACW Ashington Central Workshops

rights), together with an NCB branch to the New Moor coal stocking site (midway between Ashington and the closed Linton site); this traffic, alongside shunting at Ashington (Colliery, Washery and exchange sidings) and at Lynemouth was, however, sufficient to require seven locomotives in traffic in 1969 and well into the 1980s.

Over the years all of the Northumberland and Durham Class 14s gravitated to Ashington as a consequence of:

- the reduction of other systems to the point where the more powerful trip locomotives were no longer needed (e.g. Philadelphia), or,
- colliery or system closures (e.g. Backworth in July 1980 and Weetslade in 1981), combined with:
- the deliberate policy to concentrate the Class 14s at progressively fewer sites, ultimately Ashington only.

Whilst all locomotives on the Ashington system were allocated to Ashington Loco Shed, two were normally resident at Lynemouth for extended periods being changed around for maintenance and repairs as required.

With the small remaining output from Ashington Colliery coming to the surface via a 'drift' by the mid-1980s and the closure of the Ashington Washery in December 1986 virtually all of the NCB trackwork west of Hirst Junction become redundant, with the exception of the access route to the Loco Shed, and as a consequence track-lifting commenced in early 1987.

The transfer of coal from Lynemouth to the New Moor

stocking site, via a reversal at Hirst Junction continued up to 27 March 1987, still utilising Class 14s (supported by BR Class 08s when necessary), but after this date traffic ceased and there was no further requirement for a railway system at Ashington. The remaining lines, together with the Shed and adjacent signalbox/control centre, were closed.

Ashington Colliery itself closed in January 1988 outliving the 'Paxmans' by 10 months.

The Ashington Fleet.
D9511 was the first Class 14 to arrive at Ashington, from Hull Dairycoates, on 7 January 1969. Apart from D9545, secured from Hull for spare parts only, all subsequent arrivals at Ashington during 1969 and 1970 were from the Western Region (specifically, 86A Cardiff Canton).

D9508/28 arrived at Ashington in March 1969, followed by D9502/14/8/27 in June, and D9500/17 in November. D9521/36 turned up in March 1970, with D9535 finally arriving in November.

D9502/11/35 all departed very soon after arriving in Ashington, with D9511 moving onto Bates Colliery for trials (see Section 4.7.6) and subsequently to the Burradon system (along with D9502/35, see Section 4.7.3).

Ashington was therefore left with D9500/8/17/21/4/8/27/8/36 to form the core fleet of nine locomotives, with D9545 for spares, making ten in total. The operational nine, plus D9502/11/35, all received Ashington Plant Registry 9312/xx numbers due to Ashington being their initial point of delivery.

The nine 'core' Ashington Class 14s (plus D9511 before it departed to Bates) had their Plant

D9521 (9312/90), NCB Ashington, 27 July 1970. (Billy Embleton)

Registry numbers painted on their cabsides on a black 'patch' applied over their old BR numbers. Operationally, the locomotives were referred to on the basis of their final two unique numbers, or, three numbers in the case of D9528 ('100').

Reflecting their running rights on BR metals between Ashington and Lynemouth line, the Ashington Class 14s were fitted with metal plates reading 'Registered by the Railway Executive 1953', with a serial number; D9500 (9312/92) was allocated serial No. 1433, for example. It will be noted that the date of registration was eleven years before the locomotives were built and sixteen years prior to being deployed by the NCB!

Insights from the NCB Northumberland Area 'Internal Railways' Committee Meetings (1969/70).
The following comments have been extracted from the 'Internal Railways' meeting miutes:

Meeting 16/10/68: 'It was reported that Mr. Sewell [Area Mechanical Engineer] had viewed some BR diesel shunting locomotives which were available for disposal at Hull. Arrangements had been made to have one of these locomotives … on trial to see how it worked on the Lynemouth/Ashington run.'

Meeting 08/01/69: 'Mr. Sewell confirmed that one diesel had been received [D9511]. Mr. Sewell and Mr. Thompson [Rail Transport Officer (North)] to determine suitability of loco after test results.'

Meeting 05/03/69: 'Two further 650hp diesel locomotives were now en route to Ashington [D9508/28]. These locomotives will haul a load of 400tons. Mr. Thompson thought this load could be increased by using a brake-tender in the train. Mr. G. Clarke [Regional Transport Manager] agreed to check with BR to see if they had a minerals brake van which we could convert into a small brake-tender.'

Meeting 24/04/69: 'Three locomotives had been delivered and these appear to have been a good buy. Mr. Thompson drew attention to the braking power of these, which limited sets to 15 loaded 20ton wagons. Mr. Butters [Mechanical Service Engineer] was asked to investigate and arrange trials in conjunction with Mr. Thompson.
'Mr. Watson said money was budgeted for a further two locomotives and a third would probably be acquired. Mr. Butters to arrange a visit to inspect surplus BR diesel locomotives.'

Meeting 09/07/69: 'Mr. Butters … reported on the arrival of 4 650hp diesel locomotives [D9502/14/8/27] one of which would go to Burradon relieving a 311hp [loco] for Bates. Mr. Butters also reported on one trial made at Ashington of the braking power of these big diesels. It was agreed Messrs. Butters and Thompson carry out further tests. This problem did not arise at Havannah where sets of 24 wagons were normal.'

Meeting 11/09/69: 'Further braking tests had proved satisfactory in dry conditions and the use of brake-wagons improved the braking potentials. Agreed to watch for any surplus BR brake-wagons for this purpose.'

Meeting 30/10/69: 'A further two 650hp diesels had been authorised and would be delivered to Ashington.'

Meeting 18/12/69. Minutes not seen but the arrival of D9500/17 may have been mentioned.

Meeting 23/04/70. No mention made of the delivery of D9521/36 the previous month.

Meeting 29/10/70: 'Another 650hp Paxman was on order for Burradon [D9535].' (*Pencilled in as arrived*)

Clayton Class 17s for Ashington?
Trevor Scott recalls that his uncle, an NCB employee, visited BR St. Rollox Works in Glasgow in 1971/72 to inspect the stored Class 17 locomotives there with a view to buying up to four for the main line Leading Locomotive duties at Ashington, i.e. two in traffic, one spare and one for spares. The objective was to try to secure locomotives with a greater haulage capacity and with better braking characteristics than the Class 14s. In the event the idea was not progressed because of the poor condition of the locomotives seen.

Re-Painting and Re-numbering the Ashington Class 14s.
During the summer of 1972 the nine 'core' Ashington Class 14s were re-painted into a mid-blue livery with inverted 'V' chevrons on the bonnet ends and yellow buffer-beams; locomotives were re-numbered, within the allocated Ashington fleet number range (Nos.1-20), at the same time, as follows:

BR No.	Plant No. (Old No.)	New No.	Last date seen (Old No.)	First date seen (New No.)	IRR142 Notes (Trevor Scott)	RO1172 (27/07/72) Re-No. (Y/N)
D9500	9312/92	No.1	19/03/72	16/06/72	Done by 07/06/72	Y
D9528	9312/100	No.2	10/05/72	13/06/72	Done by 07/06/72	Y
D9521	9312/90	No.3	05/06/72	13/06/72	Done by 07/06/72	–
D9514	9312/96	No.4	10/05/72	10/07/72	Done by 19/06/72	–
D9536	9312/91	No.5	20/05/72	01/08/72	During 06/72	Y
D9527	9312/94	No.6	08/07/72	17/08/72		N
D9518	9312/95	No.7	11/07/72	21/08/72		N
D9517	9312/93	No.8	14/08/72	29/08/72		N
D9508	9312/99	No.9	25/08/72	25/09/72		N

Sources:
N.C.B. Traffic Working at Lynemouth Colliery (17/09/71-29/08/72), N.C.B. Traffic Working at Ashington Colliery (25/09/72-24/04/73), Industrial Railway Record and *Railway Observer*.

Additional Class 14s.
By the end of 1970 a total of fourteen locomotives had been purchased by the NCB for the Northumberland Area, with ten of these at Ashington (the 'core' nine, plus spares D9545) plus four at Burradon (D9502/11/35/55).

Over the period 1971 to 1974 a further five locomotives were obtained for use in the Northumberland Area, three from the NCB North Durham Area (D9504/25/40) and two from Hargreaves (West Riding) Ltd, Yorkshire (D9513/31).

The NCB Northumberland Area 'Internal Railways' Committee Minutes over the 1972/73 period highlighted the policy to standardise on Class 14s at Ashington and Burradon and their desire to secure additional 'Paxmans':

Meeting 18/05/72: 'Ashington standing with nine Paxmans, also one Yorkshire and one North British. Future requirements are ten Paxman (eight operating and two standby). Budget requirements: two Paxmans to replace Yorkshire and North British locomotives; no major overhauls to be done to the latter two locomotives.'

Meeting 14/09/72: 'Another two Paxman locomotives to be purchased. One for Ashington, one for Burradon.'

Meeting 14/12/72: 'Holdings were 9 Paxman, 2 North British, 1 Yorkshire. Agreed that the two North British be scrapped when they became unserviceable … The next Paxman delivered to be held at Ashington.'

Meeting 19/09/73: 'Two new Paxman diesels were to be delivered week-ending 24 September 1973 and it was agreed to distribute one to Burradon and one to Ashington.'

Meeting 20/12/73: 'One of the two Paxmans expected had been received and another was expected to be delivered 11th January, 1974; these were being put through ACW [Ashington Central Workshops] for examination prior to use.'

By the end of 1981, the nineteen locomotives operating in the North East Area had all gravitated to Ashington (variously from Burradon, Backworth and Weetslade); the additional nine locomotives arrived in a multitude of different liveries, as listed below:

BR No.	Local NCB No.	Livery	Ashington (N.B. Final arrival only)	Date
D9511	9312/98	BR two-tone green	From Burradon (received after fire damage, subsequently scrapped)	Circa 10/72 (after 07/72)
D9531	D2/9531	Hargreaves black/orange	From NCBOE British Oak (via Ashington CW, or, Burradon)	By 03/74
D9513	38	Backworth Blue	From Weetslade (via LEW)	14/02/77
D9555	–	BR two-tone green	From Backworth (on closure)	15/08/80
D9535	37	Backworth Blue	From Backworth (on closure)	15/08/80, or, by 06 or 13/09/80
D9502	–	BR two-tone green	From Weetslade (on closure)	24/04/81
D9525	507	Philadelphia green	From Weetslade (on closure)	24/04/81
D9540	No.36	Ashington Blue	From Weetslade (on closure)	24/04/81
D9504	506	Philadelphia green	From Weetslade (on closure, via LEW)	11 or 16/09/81

Notes:
1. D9511 and D9540 never worked at Ashington after arrival from Burradon and Weetslade respectively.
2. D9535 (very probably) never worked at Ashington after arrival from Backworth.

Further Repaints.
During the period 1979-82 four Ashington-based Class 14s were repainted in the NE Area dark-blue livery at Lambton Engine Works as follows:

BR. No.	NCB No. Pre-LEW	Date released from LEW, Philadelphia	NCB No. Post LEW	Comments
D9500	No.1	14/08/79	9312/92	'No.1' subsequently replaced
D9521	No.3	30/06/82	9312/90	'No.3' subsequently replaced
D9531	D2/9531	27/10/81	2100/523	'No.31' subsequently added
D9555	–	10 or 29/03/82	9107/57+D9555	

Detail Differences.
Detail differences between locomotives which operated on the Ashington system were few and far between.

Ashington locomotives never carried headlights, although D9502/4/25/40 are known to have arrived from Weetslade with roof-mounted flashing lights. This equipment was removed soon after arrival, leaving some 'tell-tale' residual wiring on the roof gutter-line area as evidence.

The only other known difference was the lamp-iron arrangement, although, as far as is known, lamp-irons were never used at Ashington and the differences were a residual feature from their time with BR. Thus D9511/45 had forward-facing lamp-irons reflecting their time at Hull, whilst the remainder had sideways-facing WR-style lamp-irons.

Operations.

Trevor Scott in his article 'Northumberland Paxmans' in the IRS *Industrial Railway Record* (No.142, September 1995) provided considerable insights into the operation of the Class 14s at Ashington. By kind permission I have been able to reproduce significant extracts, as follows:

'The following locomotive requirements were instituted from 16th March 1969:

Locomotive Roster, Ashington.

Location	Duty	No. of Shifts	Shifts Operated
Ashington	No.1 Pit Loco	3	2400-0800, 0800-1600, 1600-2400
	No.2 Pit Loco	3	2300-0700, 0700-1500, 1500-2300
	No.1 Leading Loco	3	2400-0800, 0800-1600, 1600-2400
	No.2 Leading Loco	3	2400-0800, 0800-1600, 1600-2400
	No.3 Leading Loco	3	2400-0800, 0800-1600, 1600-2400
Lynemouth	No.1 Loco	3	2300-0700, 0700-1500, 1500-2300
	No.2 Loco	3	2300-0700, 0700-1500, 1500-2300

Generally speaking the five Ashington duties included the following work:

- No.1 Colliery Loco: moving wagons from the Colliery screens over the weighbridge and into the loaded sidings.
- No.2 Colliery Loco: working the Duke Street battery serving Duke Street coal depot and the tippler for inward loaded wagons for washing and blending.
- No.1 Leading Loco: working to Lynemouth Colliery with exchange traffic (i.e. coal from Lynemouth to New Moor for stocking, stone from Ashington to Lynemouth for dumping at sea).
- No.2 Leading Loco: shunting the New Moor stocking grounds.
- No.3 Leading Loco: working as required.

The two at Lynemouth were outstationed from Ashington, with one each working the north and south ends of the Colliery.

Scott continued:

'These shift patterns remained almost unchanged until 1981, except for the withdrawal of the 2300 to 0700 shift on the Ashington No.2 Loco on 28th April 1969 …

'From the time dieselisation was completed, it was normal to have a Paxman locomotive rostered to all of the duties, except for the Ashington No.1 Pit job which would be entrusted to Ashington's Yorkshire Janus 2708 or North British 27766. This situation lasted until the 10th December 1974 when Yorkshire 2708 was transferred away to Bates Pit and North British 27766 had been scrapped. For nearly three years after that date, the Paxmans were the only standard gauge locomotives at Ashington. It was not until the arrival of Andrew Barclay 613 from Dawdon Colliery in November 1977 that the situation changed. A second Barclay, 623, arrived direct from the manufacturer on the 23rd March 1978 and from then on, it was normal to have both Ashington Pit duties covered by the Barclays with the Paxmans working at Lynemouth and on the three leading turns. During March 1981 613 was moved to Whittle and consequently the No.2 Pit job was returned to a Paxman.

'With production decreasing, the decision was taken to reduce Ashington Washery to two shift working and this was introduced with effect from 22nd June 1981. At the same time, the railway operations were also cut back to two shifts. The 1600-2400 shift on the No.1 Pit and all three Leading locomotive duties were withdrawn, only the Lynemouth workings being retained on three shifts.

65

ASHINGTON LOCO SHED   8 NOV 1983

TO MR A. BELL UNIT MECH ENGINEER
FROM T PURDY

ASHINGTON LOCOS
NO 7   PLANT NO 9312/95
NO 1   PLANT NO 9312/92
NO 502 PLANT NO D 9502
NO 38 PLANT NO 9312/513
NO 613 PLANT NO 20·110 107

SPARE LOCOS
NO 5   PLANT NO 9312/91
NO 3   PLANT NO 9312/90
NO   PLANT NO

LYNEMOUTH LOCOS
NO 555 PLANT NO 9701/57
NO 506 PLANT NO D 9504

LOCOS O · O · N
NO 8 PLANT NO SCRAP   NO 36 PLANT NO SCRAP
NO 9 PLANT NO SCRAP   NO 37 PLANT NO SCRAP
PLEASE NOTE MECHS TAKEING PARTS OFF
LOCOS AT PHILLY FOR OVERHAUL
NO 507 PLANT NO 2233/507

LOCOS STANDING TO BE SENT TO PHILLY
NO 6 PLANT NO 9312/94 STANDING FOR COMPLETE OVERHAUL

WORK   DONE   IN   SHED
NO 31 PLANT NO 2100/523 STANDING FOR NEW ENGINE.
NO 38 BRAKES SET UP OIL PUT IN COOLING FAN
502 LEFT SIDE B. END SAND VALVE REPAIRED
4 WAY VALVES REPAIRED FOR SPARES

NCB Ashington Loco Shed Daily Report for 8 November 1983. (Courtesy Trevor Scott)
Points of note:
1. Four 'Paxmans' (D9500 [No.1], D9502, D9513 [38] and D9518 [No.7]) and a Andrew Barclay locomotive (613) on the Ashington turns, with two further 'Paxmans' at Lynemouth (D9525 [507] and D9555 [9107/57 (incorrectly shown as 9701/57).
   Two spare 'Paxmans' at Ashington Shed (D9521 [No.3] and D9536 [No.5].
   Light repairs being undertaken at Ashington Shed on D9502 and D9513 (38) between duties.
   D9531 (No.31) stopped awaiting new engine.
   D9525 (507) away at Lambton Engine Works, Philadelphia, for overhaul.
2. D9527 (No.6) shown as 'standing for complete overhaul' (which in fact it never received). On the Daily Report for 28 November 1983 (see next page) No.6 is shown as 'Scrap'.
3. D9508 (No.9), D9517 (No.8), D9535 (37) and D9540 (No.36) all shown as scrap with fitters removing parts prior to scrapping in January 1984 (with, as it turned out, D9527 (No.6) as well).
4. Note how D9502, 38 (D9513) and D9555 were referred to as 502, 513 and 555; the Plant Nos. for these three locomotives were regularly reported as such even though they never officially or physically carried these numbers.

After this change, increased demand on the Washery capacity occasionally led to a requirement for overtime and this was arranged as necessary.

'Gradually production fell back even further and ultimately it was decided to reduce the Washery to a single shift as from 17th February 1986 [with the reduced amount of stone waste sent to Lynemouth by road]. At the same time, the Ashington Nos.1 and 2 locomotive hours were reduced to 0800 to 1800.

'The rundown continued with the total closure of the Washery at Ashington on 19th December 1986 with the last BR load departing sometime after that. The last BR empties were removed on the 22nd December and after that the colliery was closed to BR traffic. The only rail traffic left was stock coal from Lynemouth to New Moor.

'When work started up again after the Christmas break, there was only a requirement for the two locomotives working at Ashington on 2400 to 0800 and 0800 to 1600 shifts. One locomotive shunted at New Moor and the other hauled coal trains between Lynemouth and New Moor. Poor availability of the Paxmans led to a Class 08 being provided at Lynemouth and this normally worked between Lynemouth and New Moor with the Paxman retained to shunt the colliery as necessary. The Lynemouth requirement was still for two locomotives around the clock but the provision of rapid loading facilities had much reduced the work load.

79

ASHINGTON LOCO SHED   MON 28 NOV 1983

TO MR A. BELL UNIT MECH ENGINEER

FROM T. PURDY

ASHINGTON LOCOS

NO 1 PLANT NO 9312-92

NO 7 PLANT NO 9312-95

NO 38 PLANT NO 9312-525

NO 502 PLANT NO 9312-97

NO 613 PLANT NO 20-110-109

SPARE

NO 3 PLANT NO 9312-90

NO 5 PLANT NO 9312-91

LYNEMOUTH LOCOS

NO 506 PLANT NO 2233-506

NO 555 PLANT NO 9701-57

SCRAP LOCOS

6, 8, 9, 36, 37,

LOCOS UNDER REPAIRS

NO 507 PLANT NO 2233-507   AT PHILLY

NO 31 PLANT NO 2100/523   NEW ENGINE TO FIT

WORK DONE AT ASHINGTON

NO 4 PLANT NO 9312-96 ENGINE STANDING FOR COMPLETE OVERHAUL.

NO 506 PLANT NO 2233-506 TRANSMISSION COUPLING NOT FITTED RIGHT

BY FIRM NEW TRANS/SHAFT REQUIRED

NCB Ashington Loco Shed Daily Report for 28 November 1983. (Courtesy Trevor Scott)
Points of note:
1. D9527 (No.6) now awaiting scrapping, with D9514 (No.4) shown as 'standing for complete overhaul' instead. Like No.6, No.4 never received the required overhaul and was ultimately scrapped in November/December 1985.
2. Same two Class 14s at Lynemouth indicative of the long periods that locomotives were out-stationed away from Ashington.
3. Note that the Plant No. for D9513 (38) has now 'changed' to 9312/525. In later years D9513 was also recorded as 2100/524. The IRS *Northumberland Coalfield* book indicates that Bates Colliery's D3038 was the official 2100/525.

'From the 2nd February 1987 the two Paxmans at Ashington were replaced by two hired Class [BR] 08's, leaving only a single Paxman working at Lynemouth. During March this locomotive was swapped with Andrew Barclay 488 from Ashington shed and an era had ended. The final duties took place during week commencing 30th March 1987 on the 0800 to 1600 shift; a hired Class 08 being used to marshal wagons for scrap or transfer away.'

After the closure of Ashington Washery all coal produced at Ashington Colliery was moved by road to the Lynemouth Washery, until closure in January 1988.

Despite the closure of Ashington Loco Shed in March 1987 and the demise of the Class 14s, two locomotives were still required to shunt Lynemouth Colliery. Two Andrew Barclay shunters were deployed to fulfil this work, with minor maintenance undertaken locally at Lynemouth. The New Moor stocking ground also continued in use for a short period while stocks were cleared; all movements were undertaken by road.

In terms of infrastructure, after the closure of Ashington Washery track was rapidly ripped up. On 23 January 1987 Trevor Scott reported that 'Contractors have lifted the yard beside the shed and at the start of this week moved over to the west end of the yard. There is just one line left to the shed, and the sidings beside it. Next they will start on the Washery and Duke St. sidings'. On 5 February Scott reported: 'All track-work in the colliery yard with the exception of the road into the workshops and the loco shed and out to New Moor has been lifted'. By the end of 1987 all that was left was a single-line route from the site of the old Hirst Crossing northwards past New Moor up to the Butterwell Opencast site.

Examples of the daily locomotive works sheets as produced by Tommy Purdy, the Head Fitter at Ashington Loco Shed are illustrated on the previous page and above.

Locomotive Performance.
It apparently took two days to get D9511 started after it arrived on 7 January 1969 and it suffered a number of initial teething problems,

and as a consequence locomotive crews were somewhat unimpressed. However, by March 1969, D9511 was reported as 'performing with moderate success'.

An enthusiast visiting Ashington on 16 November 1969 reported 'Much difficulty experienced with diesels in cold weather and starting particularly bad. The ex-BR 0-6-0DH are not very well liked and said to be 'a bit rough'. Their starter motors are virtually useless.'

The minutes of the Northumberland Area 'Internal Railways' Committee made a number of references to performance issues with the Class 14s and these are listed below:

Meeting 29/10/70: 'There had been a number of cracked cylinder heads on the Lynemouth Paxmans. Mr Butters to investigate further.'

Meeting 14/12/72: Ashington Locomotives. 'Trouble with the locomotive cylinder heads were being experienced due to valve seats (phosphor-bronze) working loose in the alloy head. Workshops were proposing to carry out a 'locktite' method of securing - to be followed up.'

Meeting 21/03/73: Ashington Locomotives. 'The cylinder head trouble had been overcome.'

A submission by Keith Severn to the IRS in July 1980 reported:

'The use of the ex-BR 0-6-0DH's is dependent upon the state of the tyres. Since running over BR metals is included in the trip work to Lynemouth … only

locos with a good set of tyres are used. The spares situation for these locos is becoming critical with condition of the tyres determining whether locos are …cannibalised for spares.'

'Paxmans' v. 'Barclays'.
From 1983 North East Area management attempted to wind down the Class 14 fleet and to standardise on 400hp Andrew Barclay locomotives. At twenty years since construction, many Class 14s were reaching the point where major overhauls were required. The Western Region policy of component exchange had been continued by the NCB but only D9500/21/31/55 had received General body repairs since new.

Given that the cost of overhauling a Class 14 Paxman engine was stated, at £20,000, to be three times that of a Barclay locomotive, NCB management were looking to phase out the 'Paxmans' when major repairs became necessary. Added to the cost factor, significant numbers of surplus Barclay locomotives and other motive power were accumulating in the North East Area with the general contraction of colliery operations

Various Barclays locomotives were trialled at Ashington on the Leading duties and at Lynemouth Colliery. The local crews much preferred their Class 14s (how times had changed since 1969!) and trials seemed to be doomed to failure despite determined senior management efforts. Somewhat ironically, overheating of the Barclays seemed to be the prevailing problem!

Trials are understood to have continued right up to 1986, but

ultimately the Ashington Traffic Manager and the locomotive crews had their way and the Class 14s worked virtually to the end of operations in March 1987, although some support from BR Class 08s was ultimately required.

An enthusiast visiting Ashington in February 1986, undoubtedly with some artistic license, reported: 'Paxmans … are superb machines for an industrial railway, powerful and extremely capable, well liked by the crews and used hard, especially the locos stationed at Lynemouth. The Barclays are looked upon as just 'shunting engines' and not 'Leading engines' as are the Paxmans and they will not be taking over any Paxman duties before they are withdrawn.'

One other reason for crew's preference for Class 14s was the provision of seating and the ability to put their feet up on the driving console between duties!

Works and Depot Attention.
Major overhauls of the 'Paxmans' were carried out at Ashington Central Workshops until March 1975, at which point the work was taken over by Lambton Engine Works, Philadelphia, although the power units were apparently still sent back to Ashington for attention! D9518 (No.7) appears to have been the first Class 14 repaired at Philadelphia arriving in May 1975.

During the early 1980s, colliery closures and the rationalisation of railway systems generally across the North-East led to a significant surplus of motive power. As a consequence the decision was taken to halt Class 14 Works repairs during 1984. This decision was made primarily on cost grounds compared with the more basic Andrew Barclay machines.

Trevor Scott visited Ashington on 11 January 1984 and gleaned the following information: 'Colliery sources suggest that 507 would be returning from Philadelphia 16th or 17th January and 506 would be going for attention. Nos. 4 and 31 were then due overhauls and after these were completed no further overhauls to Paxmans would be carried out at Philadelphia.'

Such was the drive to reduce costs that D9531 (No.31) was repaired at Ashington Loco Shed and D9514 (No.4) was never repaired and consigned to the scrap-heap. Whether D9504 (506) visited Philadelphia after D9525 (507) is unclear; the Ashington Daily Report as late as 1 February 1984 was showing 'standing for new transmission to be fitted at Philadelphia' but by 13 February the status had changed to 'receiving new transmission' suggesting fitment at Ashington. Unfortunately no Daily Reports or sightings for the next five months have been seen. D9525 was, probably, the last Class 14 to visit Philadelphia, with D9504 (506) just a possibility.

The decision to discontinue Works repairs did not receive widespread support from the Ashington and Lynemouth locomotive men; as already mentioned, the crews considered the alternative Andrew Barclay motive power to be totally unsuitable especially on the Leading jobs.

Without Works repairs and the fleet now in steady decline,

only the Herculean efforts of the Ashington Traffic Manager and the Shed fitters kept the locomotives running, largely on a 'rob Peter to pay Paul' basis, supported by only basic facilities to allow engine and transmission changes. When necessary, external contractors were used for some component refurbishment and repair work, for example:

- British Engines Ltd (Newcastle) for engine refurbishment work, with engine swapping at Ashington; this company was extensively involved with engine low pressure issues on D9525 (507) in 1986, and,
- somewhat ironically, Andrew Barclay (Kilmarnock); prop-shaft repairs to D9504 (506) during 1985/86.

Even as late as February 1987, repair work was being undertaken to keep at least the minimum number of Class 14s in traffic, with, for example, D9525 (507) having a new turbo-charger bracket fitted, a not insignificant job involving the removal of the bonnet top and other components. The Class 14s suffered this problem in BR days and was clearly never fully resolved!

General locomotive condition and spare parts shortages ultimately led to the hire of BR shunters from Blyth Cambois and Gateshead depots in 1987 to supplement the ailing 'Paxmans'.

Tyre-Turning.
With no tyre-turning facilities available at Ashington, locomotives with wheelset problems were initially sent to the BR depot at

South Gosforth for attention. However, when this depot was taken over by the Tyne & Wear Metro in 1978, locomotives were sent to BR Thornaby (Teesside). Coupling rods were removed from locomotives at Ashington prior to movement off-site and re-fitted on return.

Wind-Down.
Although all nineteen Class 14s which operated in the North-East could be found at Ashington over the years, they were never all there at one time. Locomotives progressively fell by the wayside as major components failed or when general works attention was required. Thin or out-of-profile tyres were also a common problem which resulted in locomotives being removed from traffic following examinations by BR inspectors; the Class 14s undertook significant mileages on BR tracks and, whilst they had running rights, strict tyre profile and thickness regulations were applied for the privilege of doing so. Full wheelset changes on the Class 14s were a complicated and expensive process.

As effectively surplus locomotives arrived from Burradon, Backworth and Weetslade the pace of locomotives being removed from traffic increased dramatically. Details of the demise and disposal of the nineteen locomotives over the period 1979 to 1987 are given in Section 4.8.

The final locomotives in working order were D9500/4/21/5 with D9504 (506) and D9521 (No.3) known to have worked at Lynemouth over the final few days of operation before final closure in March 1987.

Ashington Railway System, Northumberland.

D9517 (No.8), NCB Ashington, 28 June 1976. Looking east; depot in left distance, with the elevated Control Office and Weighbridge behind. Colliery winding gear in far distance.
(Anthony Sayer)

D9518 (No.7), NCB Ashington 5 April 1986. Depot in background. Control office and weigh cabin to right.
(Anthony Sayer)

D9518 (No.7), NCB
Ashington, 5 April
1986. (Anthony Sayer)

D9518 (No.7), NCB Ashington, 22 February 1983. Ashington Central Workshops in background. (Mike Richardson)

D9514 (No.4), NCB Ashington, 19 June 1981. (Pete Wilcox)

D9518 (No.7), NCB
Ashington, 23 January
1974. (Anthony Sayer)

D9531 (D2/9531), NCB
Ashington, 10 June
1975. (Anthony Sayer)

D9531 (2100/523), Lynemouth to Ashington, 14 April 1982. No 1 Leading turn. (Trevor Scott)

D9555 (9107/57), New Moor to Ashington, 14 April 1982. No 3 Leading turn with coal ex-stock. (Trevor Scott)

Unidentified Class 14, NCB Ashington, Undated. (John Reay [Mike Richardson Collection])

D9502, Hirst Junction, Ashington, 29 November 1983. Alcan aluminium smelter and Lynemouth power station visible in the distance. (Mike Richardson)

Right: **D9531(No.31), NCB Ashington, 12 August 1985.** En route from Lynemouth to Ashington, engine and van, at Hirst Junction. (David Ford)

Below: **NCB Ashington, 7 January 1987.** D9521 (No3), following collision with van, and D9500 (No1, to right, in attendance). According to Adrian Freeman: "The incident took place just to the east of Ashington. A van was heading south along the road (i.e. left to right in the photo) towards the level crossing as No. 3 was heading east, light engine. The van did not stop at the crossing and the loco struck the front corner of the van, spinning it round. The loco came to a stop a short distance down the line. In the photograph the fire brigade have arrived, as has No. 1 with brake-van from the east. I don't think the van driver was seriously injured, and I suspect that No. 3 suffered negligible damage; it was seen running again later in the day." (Adrian Freeman)

Ashington Loco Shed

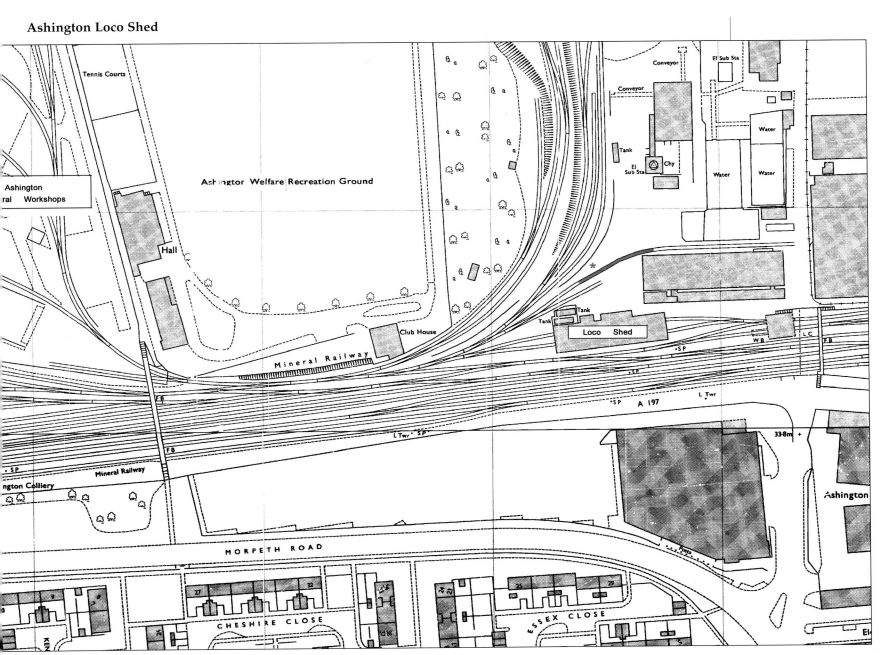

Ashington Loco Shed area, west of Ashington Colliery. Note the two footbridges which afforded excellent opportunities for photographing the Class 14s. The red asterisk denotes where D9545 was dumped, and the red line shows the location of the 'scrap-line' (see Section 4.8). (© Crown Copyright and Landmark Information Group Ltd 2020 (www.Old-Maps.co.uk Ref. 450282995))

Transition at Ashington Loco Shed, 29 June 1969. (Brian Webb [IRS])

D9521 (No.3) and D9536 (No.5), NCB Ashington, 15 June 1976. (Anthony Sayer)

D9521 (No.3), NCB Ashington, 28 February 1987. The identity of the Class 14 on the left was unspecified but given the \\\ buffer-beam stripes and the 'white' bonnet-top handrails this must be D9500. Note the buffer-beam stripes slanting in the opposite direction on D9521 (No.3). (Bruce Galloway)

D9521 (No.3), NCB Ashington, 28 February 1987. Coupling-pole hooks clearly apparent at the top of the buffer beam. (Bruce Galloway)

D9525 (507) and D9513 (38), NCB Ashington, 28 February 1987. With respect to D9513, note the red buffer-beam and the vacuum pipe still fitted. Coupling-pole clips in differing positions. Note the differing buffer-beam profiles (bottom edge). (Bruce Galloway)

D9531 (No.31), NCB Ashington, 26 August 1986. (Douglas Johnson)

D9521(No.3) and
D9504 (506), NCB
Ashington, 26 August
1986. (Douglas Johnson)

To BR for Tyre-Turning.

D9540 (No.36), BR South
Gosforth, 24 July 1977.
(Derek Elston)

**D9513 (38), 51L
Thornaby, 26 July 1981.**
(John Carter)

**D9500 (9312/92),
Thornaby, 18 May
1982.** Not '9531' as
suggested on the fuel
tank! Tyre-turning
completed. (Transport
Topics)

Brake-Tender Usage.

D9500 (No.1) and brake-tender 9300/2, NCB Ashington, 4 June 1975. During the period 1970-76 three brake-tenders were used with the 'Paxmans'. The tenders were constructed from vacuum-fitted open wagons, half filled with concrete, and were used on Leading Loco duties between Ashington and Lynemouth. (Anthony Sayer)

D9527 (No.6) and brake-tender 9300/2, NCB Ashington, 15 June 1976. Note the wire from the bonnet roof of the 'Paxman' across to the brake-tender to the receptacle on the front (top left) of the wagon, presumably a marker light. (Anthony Sayer)

D9500 at Lynemouth.

D9500 (No.1), NCB Lynemouth, 28 June 1976. Ashington blue livery. (Anthony Sayer)

D9500 (9312/92), NCB Lynemouth, 13 March 1982. North East Area blue repaint with the Plant Registry number only. The 'No.1' local identifier was re-applied later by Ashington staff. A similar situation occurred with D9521 (No.3) and D9531 (No.31). (Douglas Johnson)

4.7.3 Burradon.
Loco Shed: Burradon.

Organisational structure covering period of Class 14 usage:

- Northumberland Area initially, then North East Area from 1/4/1974.

Plant Registry code (based on the 1950 Northern (Northumberland & Cumberland) Division/Area structure): 9107.

Although never officially called the Burradon Railway, the Loco Shed at Burradon Colliery in the mid-1960s acted as the focal point of the system, extending from Hazlerigg Colliery in the west to Burradon Colliery in the east a distance of approximately 3½ miles). Branches from Havannah Drift (¾ mile), Seaton Burn Colliery (1¼ mile) and Weetslade Colliery (¼ mile) also joined the main route. Locomotives also worked eastwards from Burradon to the Backworth 'C' stone disposal point at the north end of the Backworth Railway and the NCB/BR exchange sidings at Holywell Junction on the BR Blyth & Tyne route (2 miles).

By the time of arrival of the Class 14s in 1969, Hazlerigg, Seaton Burn and Weetslade Collieries had already closed (April 1964, August 1963, and September 1966 respectively). However, the Seaton Burn screens were retained to handle coal from Brenkley Drift (via a narrow-gauge railway) and the Coal Preparation Plant (CPP) at Weetslade also remained open.

Burradon Colliery closed in November 1975 and the Loco Shed followed on 3 January 1976 with remaining duties transferred to a new depot at Weetslade effective from 5 January 1976.

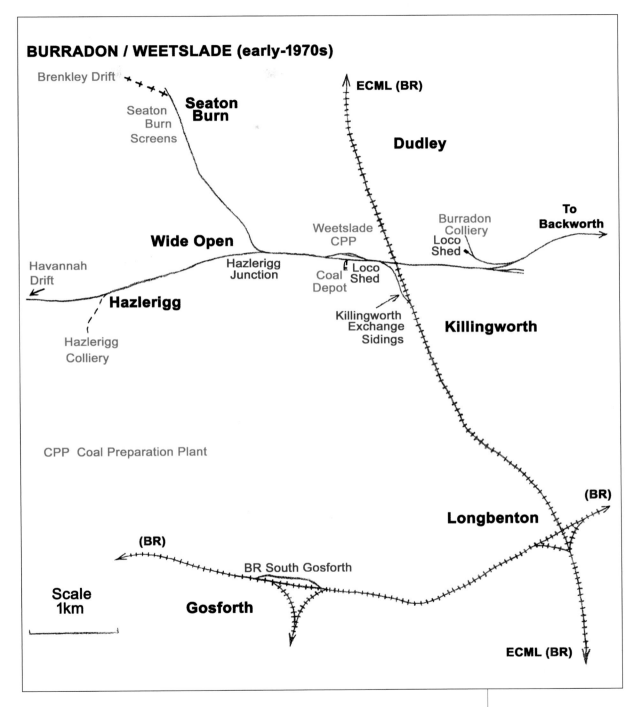

Burradon/Weetslade system.

Class 14s at Burradon.
Class 14 locomotives which operated from Burradon were:

	Local NCB No.	From	To
D9502	–	06/09/69 (ex-Ashington)	xx/01/76 (to Weetslade)
D9504	506	17/12/74 (ex-Bolden)	03/01/76 (to Weetslade)
D9511	–	05/05/69 (ex-Bates)	Circa 10/72 (after xx/07/72) (to Ashington)
D9513	38	xx/07/74 (by 12/07/74) (ex-Backworth)	03/01/76 (to Backworth)
D9525	507	07/03/75 (ex-Philadelphia)	14/03/75 (to Ashington) (see Note 2)
D9531	D2/9531	10 or 19/10/73 (ex-NCBOE British Oak)	By xx/03/74 (to Ashington) (see Note 3)
D9535	37	12/11/70 (ex-BR Cardiff Canton), or, xx/01/71 (ex-Ashington)	03/01/76 (to Weetslade)
D9540	No.36	25/11/71 (ex-Philadelphia)	03 or 12/01/76 (to Weetslade)
D9555	–	05/03/70 (ex-BR Cardiff Canton)	by 21/11/75 (to Ashington), then, xx/12/75 (to Backworth)

Notes:
1. The period of Class 14 activity at Burradon was from May 1969 to January 1976 (Loco Shed closure). D9502/4/13/35/40 were allocated to Burradon at the time of closure of the system. D9513 was subsequently transferred to Backworth and D9502/4/35/40 to Weetslade.
2. It is possible that D9525 was transferred direct from Philadelphia to Ashington and, therefore, never visited Burradon. N.B. No known Burradon sightings.
3. It is also possible that D9531 was transferred direct from NCBOE British Oak to Ashington CW in October 1973 and then staying at Ashington following repairs. If this was the case, D9531 never visited Burradon. N.B. No known Burradon sightings.
4. NCB Northumberland Area 'Internal Railways' Committee. Relevant entries:

Meeting 18/05/72: Burradon Locomotives. 'The present holding is five Paxman [D9502/11/35/40/55] and three Ruston, one of the latter requiring major overhaul. The agreed requirements were six Paxman and two others.'

Meeting 14/09/72: Ashington Locomotives. 'Another two Paxman locomotives to be purchased. One for Ashington, one for Burradon.'

Meeting 14/12/72: Burradon Locomotives. 'Present holding: 4 Paxman [D9502/35/40/55], 4 Ruston &Hornsby.'

Meeting 20/06/73: Burradon Locomotives. 'Holding: 4 Paxman (1 under repair), 3 Ruston & Hornsby, 1 Ruston & Hornsby for scrap. A steamer had been borrowed from Eccles to help out while the Paxman was being repaired and extra stockpiling was being carried out during Summer months.'

Meeting 19/09/73: Burradon Locomotives: '5 diesels (4 Burradon, 1 Dudley). D9535 overhaul at Area Central Workshops to be completed by 21.9.73. D9512 (*sic* D9502) going into ACW for general overhaul.
   Backworth Locomotives. '3 steamers in use, 3 other steamers (in use at Burradon while diesels were under repair).'

Meeting 20/12/73: Burradon/Dudley Locomotives: '3 Paxman, 2 Ruston & Hornsby, 1 steamer (from Backworth). A diesel was at Ashington [sic, Backworth] for repair and painting (*D9535*).'
   Backworth Locomotives. '1 steamer being used at Burradon while diesels under repair and being painted.'

Burradon fleet repaints.

The Burradon fleet always exhibited a variety of liveries. Some progress was made in sprucing up the fleet with D9540 painted at Ashington in August 1972, D9535 at Backworth in November 1973 and D9513 at Backworth in July 1974; these three were renumbered No.36, 37 and 38 respectively at the time of re-painting. D9504 (506), plus D9525 (507) at Backworth, were next in line for repainting and renumbering to 39 and 40 (not necessarily respectively, being dependent on the order of 'shopping'), although this work was never undertaken.

Operations.

IRS Archive comments made by enthusiasts visiting Burradon during 1970 regarding the Class 14s included:

'The shed foreman was bemoaning the fact that he had to obtain spares of various parts of these engines – the engine, transmission, gearbox, electrical, etc. – from no less than six different sources.'

'Apparently spares and maintenance instructions are almost unobtainable for the Swindon-built diesels.'

Trevor Scott quoted some maximum loadings over the Burradon system in his *Industrial Railway Record* (No.142) article:

Burradon to Weetslade	25x20ton hoppers, empty or loaded
Weetslade to Burradon	30x20ton empty or 20x20ton loaded hoppers
Weetslade to Brenkley	30x20ton empty hoppers
Brenkley to Weetslade	25x20ton loaded hoppers
Weetslade to Havannah	30x20ton empty hoppers
Havannah to Weetslade	20x20ton loaded hoppers
Burradon to Backworth	15x20ton loaded or 30x20ton empty hoppers
Backworth to Burradon	10x20ton loaded or 20x20ton empty hoppers

Fire on D9511.

D9511 sustained severe damage at Havannah Drift in July 1972. The Northumberland Area 'Internal Railways' Committee minutes referred to the fire on two separate occasions:

Meeting 14/09/72: 'Fire on 650hp Paxman locomotive at Havannah. This had piped CO_2 fire-fighting equipment installed which did not operate when glass was broken and wire pulled. Notices to be displayed in Paxman cabs that safety pins in the fire-fighting equipment should be in the release position when locomotives are in service.'

Meeting 14/12/72: 'It was agreed that the fire-damaged Paxman locomotive would not be repaired but cannibalised for spares. Reported that three Paxman locomotives had been refitted with fire-fighting cylinders, but the drivers must ensure that pins were removed when locomotive was put in operation.'

D9502, NCB Burradon, Undated. Still in condition as delivered from the Western Region. (Rail-Online)

D9511 (9312/98), NCB Burradon, 9 May 1969. (George Woods)

D9540 (No.36), NCB Burradon, 5 June 1973. Backworth's 44 (RSH7760 of 1953) meets Burradon's 'Paxman' No.36 (D9540 of 1965). The Class 14 is about to pass Hazelrigg Junction Signal Box west of Weetslade. Steam locomotive 44, along with two other steam locomotives, were loaned from Backworth to Burradon in 1973 to cover for D9502/35 away at Ashington Central Workshops for major repairs. (Michael Urquhart)

D9555, NCB Burradon, 5 June 1973. Passing Hazlerigg Junction signal box. (Michael Urquhart)

D9504(506), Havannah Drift branch, Undated. Seems to be high Summer given the state of the undergrowth! Note the roof-mounted flashing light. (Trevor Scott)

4.7.4 Backworth Railways.
Loco Shed: **Backworth (Eccles).**

Organisational structure covering period of Class 14 usage:

• Northumberland Area initially, then North East Area from 1/4/1974.

This system ran roughly in a north-west to south-east direction and by the 1960s ran from the site of the disused Backworth 'C' Colliery (at this time used as a stone disposal point) to staithes on the River Tyne at Whitehill Point, a distance of about 5½ miles. The line directly served Eccles Colliery (formerly Backworth 'A') en route. In addition a 1½ mile branch from Fenwick Colliery joined the 'main line' at Backworth. Further south another 1½ mile branch from Algernon Colliery also joined the 'main line' at Murton Row. Links to the BR Blyth & Tyne line were available at both Earsdon Junction and Holywell Junction. Backworth-based locomotives also took trains of coal over the Burradon branch to the Washery and Coal Preparation Plant at Weetslade, via a curve at Fisher's Lane Crossing, a distance of approximately 3 miles.

For clarity, it should be noted that Backworth Loco Shed was located adjacent to Eccles Colliery.

Relative to the Ashington and Burradon systems, the Class 14s arrived at Backworth fairly late, with the first arriving from Burradon and Ashington in late-1975. By this time Algernon and Fenwick Collieries had closed

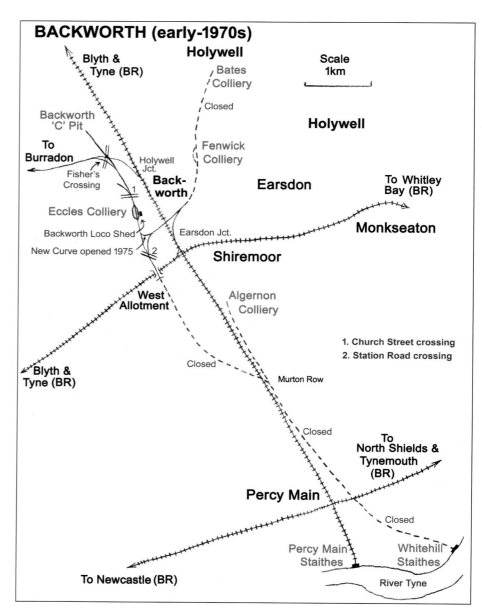

Backworth system.

(in February 1966 and August 1973 respectively), and traffic to the Whitehill Point staithes had ceased in August 1969 with the line closed completely south of West Allotment. As a consequence the residual traffic for the Class 14s was restricted to:

• Sale coal from Eccles via the BR/NCB exchanges sidings,
• Coal to the Weetslade Coal Preparation Plant (for processing) and the Distribution Depot, and,
• Stone waste to the Backworth 'C' Pit site.

As part of the North-East Area 'co-ordinated locomotive policy', Backworth Loco Shed became the last in the NCB North East Area to use steam locomotives; steam officially ended on 13 December 1975, although there were examples of steam deputising for failed diesels into January 1976.

BR traffic between Weetslade and Holywell Junction officially ceased on 11 July 1977, though reduced numbers of NCB trains ran from Backworth to Weetslade until the 7 November 1977. As a consequence all coal was dispatched via Earsdon Junction on the BR Blyth & Tyne branch.

Eccles Colliery ceased production in May 1980, with rail traffic ending on 17 July 1980.

Class 14s at Backworth.
Burradon Colliery closed on 22 November 1975 and this resulted in two of the Paxman diesels (D9502/13) becoming surplus to requirements. The opportunity was taken to transfer these two and two further spare locomotives from Ashington to Backworth (D9525/55), thus eliminating the last NCB steam locomotives in regular use in Northumberland.

Class 14 locomotives which operated from Backworth/Eccles were:

	Local NCB No.	From	To
D9502	–	xx/01/76 (by 17/02/76) (ex-Burradon)	xx/06/76 (after 02/06/76) (to Weetslade)
D9513	38	10/06/74 (ex-Ashington, for painting only)	After 04/07/74, by 12/07/74 (to Burradon)
		03/01/76 (ex-Burradon)	01 or 02/76 (to Weetslade)
		By 15/05/76) (ex-Weetslade)	By 13/11/76 (to Ashington, via LEW)
D9525	507	13 or 15/12/75 (ex-Ashington)	15/08/80 (to Ashington or Weetslade) (see Note 4)
D9535	37	By 24/10/73 (ex-Burradon, for painting only)	By 23/11/73 (to Burradon)
		Circa 05/76 (by 15/05/76) (ex-Weetslade)	By 06 or 13/09/80 (to Ashington)
D9555	–	xx/12/75 (ex-Ashington) (see Notes 3 & 5)	15/08/80 (to Ashington)

Notes:
1. NCB Northumberland Area 'Internal Railways' Committee. Relevant entries:

   Meeting 21/03/73: Backworth: 'It was agreed to continue at present with use of steamers at Fenwick/Eccles but to stop major repairs to steamers during next twelve months and to embark on a policy of changeover to diesel when these were available. In the meantime, a trial in use of a diesel to be made. Training for men in use of diesel, possibly at Ashington.'

   Meeting 20/12/73: Backworth Locomotives. 'One English Electric had now been delivered and this was earmarked for Backworth. The changeover to diesel engines was in abeyance until the training programme could be established after the lifting of the overtime ban. Three steamers in use, two steamers spare, one steamer being used at Burradon while diesel under repair and being painted.'

2. Excluding D9513 and D9535 in 1973/74 (both at Backworth for re-painting), the period of Class 14 revenue-earning activity at Backworth started from December 1975 and continued until August/September 1980, soon after the closure of Eccles Colliery.
3. Various dates have been quoted for D9555's arrival at Backworth, all December 1975.
4. D9525/35/55 were allocated to Backworth at the time of closure of the system in July 1980. D9535/55 were subsequently transferred to Ashington; as regards D9525 there is conflicting information with both Ashington and Weetslade suggested. Trevor Scott comments: 'The Paxman locomotives at Backworth were divided between Ashington and Burradon on closure, with two going to Ashington and the other to Burradon [sic].' Clearly not Burradon, as this depot closed in January 1976, but in Trevor's tables the transfer reads 'Moved to Weetslade during 8.80'.
5. D9555. 8BRD (only) indicates time spent at Weetslade between 01/76 and circa 05/76 although there are no sightings during this period to confirm this.

Liveries.
Like the Burradon fleet, the Backworth 'Paxmans' carried an assorted mix of colours. D9525 (507) was due for a repaint into blue livery (and re-numbering in the Burradon/Backworth range, either 39 or 40) but this was never completed.

Operations.
Trevor Scott, once again, provided very useful insights into Class 14 operations at Backworth in his 'Northumberland Paxmans' article as follows:

'When the Paxmans arrived at Backworth, there were only three locomotive duties. One locomotive worked 2400-0800 and 0800 to 1600, the second from 0800 to 1600 and a third locomotive was kept as a spare. This shift pattern remained until the colliery ceased production during May 1980. From then on until rail traffic finished on 17th July 1980, locomotives were normally only operated on the 0800 to 1600 shift for lifting coal from stock and transferring it to the exchange sidings at Earsdon

on the BR Blyth & Tyne branch. Very occasionally twelve hour working took place which gave 24-hour coverage but this was quite rare.'

Trevor also quoted some maximum loadings over the Backworth/Burradon link:

Burradon to Backworth	15x20ton loaded or 30x20ton empty hoppers
Backworth to Burradon	10x20ton loaded or 20x20ton empty hoppers

D9535 (37), NCB Backworth (Eccles), 1975. Outside Eccles Colliery locomotive shed, the servicing and maintenance facility for the Backworth Railway. Although the railway system was known as the Backworth Railway, it was centred on Eccles Colliery. The 'Backworth' name referred to the nearby village and also the fact that, prior to nationalisation of the coal industry in 1947, the owning company had been Backworth Collieries Ltd. (Martyn Hearson (Renown))

D9555 (left) and D9525(507), NCB Backworth Loco Shed, 9 April 1980. The washery to the left of the shed has been removed following a partial collapse, with screening and washing work subsequently taken over by Weetslade. (Trevor Scott)

D9555, D9513(38 D1/9513) and D9502, plus D9525 (507) on the left, NCB Eccles (Backworth), 15 June 1976. Beyond the door at the far end was the Eccles Workshop (where D9535 was repainted blue in late-1973) and the locomotive staff mess room. (Anthony Sayer)

D9513 (38) between D9502 (left) and D9555, NCB Backworth, 15 June 1976. (Anthony Sayer)

D9535 (37), NCB Eccles (Backworth), 16 May 1975. A sign of the future for Backworth. No. 48 rests in Eccles north yard while the driver enjoys some bait. 37, one of Burradon's 'Paxmans', traverses Church Road Level Crossing (north of Eccles Colliery) with empties from Burradon. The somewhat ornate washer of the old 'B' pit is visible between the locos. Note the dark red buffer beam on 37, indicative of its repaint at Backworth in 1973. (Michael Urquhart)

D9555, NCB Eccles (Backworth), 5 April 1978. (Trevor Scott Collection)

D9525 (507), NCB Backworth, 5 April 1978. D9525 is seen arriving at the yard to the south of Eccles Colliery with a rake of wagons from Earsdon Junction via the relatively new curve which was opened in October 1975; this connection eliminated the need for reversing movements across Station Road at the south end of the yard. (Trevor Scott)

D9555, NCB Backworth, Undated. View of the yard south of the Eccles Colliery, looking north.
(John Reay [Mike Richardson Collection])

Unidentified 'Paxman' (probably D9555), NCB Eccles (Backworth), Undated. On the west side of the Colliery very close to the site entrance from the B1322 road, looking north-west.
(John Reay [Mike Richardson Collection])

4.7.5 Weetslade.
Loco Shed: **Weetslade.**

Area organizational structure covering period of Class 14 usage:

- North East Area.

See map on page 163.

Locomotives based at the new Weetslade Loco Shed took over from where Burradon left off from 5 January 1976. The depot was located adjacent to the Weetslade Coal Preparation Plant (on the site of Weetslade Colliery which closed in September 1966).

Production at Havannah Drift ceased on 12 November 1976 and the mine closed in March 1977. This resulted in railway activity west of Weetslade being restricted to the Seaton Burn branch.

Locomotives from the Backworth colliery system continued to work to Weetslade with coal for treatment until 7 November 1977. Locomotives from Weetslade continued to work on to the Backworth railway via the link at Fisher's Lane Crossing with shale and stone for disposal at the Backworth 'C' Pit stone disposal point until this ceased in November 1977 and, as a consequence, the line east of Weetslade was closed (apart from the short trip to the NCB/BR Killingworth exchange sidings.

With the closure of Havannah Drift and the cessation of traffic to/from Backworth, the only locally extracted coal on the system came from Brenkley Drift via the Seaton Burn screens, with additional traffic for washing and screening coming via the BR link at Killingworth. The Weetslade system closed on 25 March 1981 and the Brenkley Drift coal was transferred to Ashington for washing until closure in October 1985.

Class 14s at Weetslade.
Class 14 locomotives which operated from Weetslade were:

	Local NCB No.	From	To
D9502	–	Circa 06/76 (ex Backworth)	24/04/81 (to Ashington)
D9504	506	03/01/76 (ex Burradon)	21/04/81 (to Ashington, via LEW, Philadelphia)
D9513	38	01 or 02/76 (ex-Backworth)	22/11/76 (to Ashington, via LEW, Philadelphia)
D9525	507	xx/08/80 (ex-Backworth)	24/04/81 (to Ashington)
D9535	37	xx/01/76 (ex-Burradon)	01 or 05/76 (by 15/05/76) (to Backworth)
D9540	No.36	xx/01/76 (ex-Burradon)	24/04/81 (to Ashington)

Notes:
1. The period of Class 14 activity at Weetslade was January 1976 to April 1981 (system closure).
2. D9502/4/25/40 were allocated to Weetslade at the time of closure of the system. At this point all four locomotives had been fitted with roof-mounted flashing lights, with D9502/4/40 receiving two each and D9525 receiving four. All were subsequently transferred to Ashington, D9502/25/40 direct and D9504 via Lambton Engine Works; the additional roof lights obviously did not render them out of gauge!
3. It will be noted that there was a high degree of similarity between the lists of locomotives which 'officially' operated from Backworth and Burradon/Weetslade. In all probability there will have been some 'unofficial' operational re-allocations between the systems given their inter-connected nature and overlapping traffic flows; indeed, the two railways were frequently referred as the Backworth and Burradon Group.
4. D9555. 8BRD (only) indicates time spent at Weetslade between 01/76 and circa 05/76 although there are no sightings during this period to confirm this.

42 (RH 384141) and D9540 (No.36),NCB Weetslade Loco Shed, 26 July 1979. New two-road shed which replaced Burradon in January 1976. (Trevor Scott)

Operations.
Trevor Scott again, regarding the workload for the Weetslade locomotive fleet after the closure of the Weetslade-Backworth link in 1977:

'Sufficient traffic could be found for two Paxmans, whilst one of the smaller locomotives shunted the coal depot on a single shift. The Paxmans worked two shifts, one locomotive operating between Brenkley and Weetslade, the other shunting the washery and Leading traffic to Killingworth Exchange Sidings. A third Paxman was retained as a spare. Traffic to the coal depot ceased during the summer of 1979.'

Such was the reduced demand for colliery locomotives, particularly the larger Class 14s, Weetslade effectively carried two spare locomotives (or, perhaps, more accurately, one spare and one surplus).

D9504 (506), NCB
Weetslade Washery,
26 June 1979. (Trevor Scott)

D9504 (506), NCB
Weetslade, 15 June
1976. (Anthony Sayer)

D9540(No 36), NCB Weetslade, 1974.
Photograph taken from the B1319 road crossing, east of Weetslade, looking east towards the new A189 road under construction. D9540 on the line from Burradon. (Trevor Scott)

D9540 (No36), NCB Weetslade, Undated.
En route from Weetslade Washery to Killingworth BR/NCB Exchange Sidings. Photograph taken from the A189 road bridge looking west; B1319 road in the middle distance. (John Reay [Mike Richardson Collection])

D9504 (506), NCB Weetslade, Undated. Same vantage point looking south-east towards Killingworth BR/ NCB Exchange Sidings. (John Reay [Mike Richardson Collection])

4.7.6 Bates (Blyth).
Loco Shed: **Bates.**

Area organizational structure covering period of Class 14 usage:

- Northumberland Area.

In the late 1960s this NCB system extended from the site of Isabella Colliery (closed February 1966) to Bates Colliery. Extensive sidings at Bates served staithes on the River Blyth at the east end of the Colliery. Access to BR was via the BR/NCB Exchange sidings at Isabella which connected into the Blyth & Tyne route further south at Isabella Colliery Junction north of Newsham.

Bates was a major colliery and survived until February 1986, but the history of Class 14s was very short indeed, little more than two weeks in fact! The issue was very sharp track curvature at Pumphouse Corner part way between Bates and Isabella, which required locomotives with a wheelbase shorter than that offered by the Class 14s. Ex-BR locomotives were subsequently involved in colliery operations in the form of 350hp Classes 08 and 11, as well as a sizeable number of industrial locomotives.

Class 14 at Bates.

	Local NCB No.	From	To
D9511	9312/98	18/04/69 (ex-Ashington)	05/05/69 (to Burradon)

4.7.7 Bolden.
Loco Shed: **Bolden.**

Organisational structure covering period of Class 14 usage:

- North Durham Area initially, then, North East Area from 1/4/1974.

Traffic from Bolden Colliery joined the BR Pontop-South Shields line (with NCB running rights, brake van required) from the colliery junction over the Pontop flat crossing near Boldon Colliery station (which crossed the BR Gateshead-Sunderland line) to Tyne Dock, Whitburn Junction, and Deans Sidings (NCB/BR exchange)

a distance of about 2 miles. Deans Sidings connected into the Harton Electric Railway.

Minor locomotive repairs were undertaken at Boldon, with more major work carried out at Westoe or Whitburn (although whether D9504 ever reached the latter is unknown).

Boldon Colliery closed on 26 June 1982.

Class 14 at Bolden.

	Local NCB No.	From	To
D9504	506	xx/02/74 (ex-Philadelphia)	17/12/74 (to Burradon via BR Cambois)

D9504 (506), NCB Westoe Colliery, 14 June 1974. 506 'under the wires' of the Harton Electric Railway. Bonnet roof and side doors removed at 'A' end. (Trevor Scott Collection)

4.8 Gradual Demise of the North-East Paxmans.

The Ashington 'Scrap-Line'.

The following visit reports predominantly cover locomotives dumped on the Ashington 'scrap-line' (for precise location, see map on page 155); other locations where Class 14s were dumped are also mentioned where applicable.

Date	Locomotives	Comments
29/07/71	D9545 (derelict)	
25/10/71	D9545 (OOU)	
02/05/72	D9545 (being cannibalised)	
19/06/72	D9545 (OOU)	
04/08/72	D9545 (dsm)	
22/10/72	D9545 (for spares)	
xx/12/72*	D9511 (9312/98) (A-B)	D9545 not listed.
24/07/73	D9511 (9312/98) (OOU, part dsm, for spares)	D9545 not listed.
18/08/73	D9511 (9312/98), D9545	
23/01/74	D9511 (9312/98), D9545	
12/06/74	D9511 (9312/98), D9545	
15/07/74	D9511 (9312/98), D9545 (both dsm)	
04/06/75*	D9511 (9312/98) (A-B), D9545	
25/08/75	D9511 (9312/98), D9545 (both for spares)	
15/05/76	D9511 (9312/98), D9545	
15/06/76*	D9545 (dsm, on wheels) (A-B)	D9511 (9312/98) not photographed.
28/06/76	D9511 (9312/98), D9545	
21/05/77	D9511 (9312/98), D9545 (both OOU/dsm))	
19/09/77	D9511 (9312/98), D9545 (both OOU/dsm))	
13/11/77	D9511 (9312/98), D9545	
25/01/78	D9511 (9312/98), D9545 (both derelict/dsm))	
05/04/78	D9511 (9312/98) (minus wheels), D9545 (very little remaining)	
	Also: D9528 (No.2) (exact location not specified)	
15/04/78	Nothing listed on 'Scrap-line'	D9511/45 not listed.
	Also: D9528 (No.2) (in shed, engine out)	
24/02/79* W-E	D9518 (No.7) (B-A, sub re-inst), D9528 (No.2) (B-A)	D9511/45 not photographed.
17/04/79	D9545 (dsm)	
	D9511 (9312/98), D9518 (No.7) (sub re-inst), D9528 (No.2)	
19/05/79	D9545 (no cab)	
	D9511 (9312/98), D9518 (No.7) (sub re-inst), D9528 (No.2)	
30/07/79	D9545 (frames only remaining)	
	D9511 (9312/98), D9518 (No.7) (sub re-inst), D9528 (No.2)	

Date			Locomotives	Comments
23/09/79*	W-E		**D9545** (dumped, off wheels)	
			D9511 (9312/98) (X-X, fire-dam), **D9518** (No.7) (B-A, sub re-inst), **D9528** (No.2) (B-A)	
28/12/79			**D9518** (No.7) (sub re-inst), **D9528** (No.2)	No evidence of **D9511/45**.
				D9511/45 C/U 07/79 (8BRD), or, c10-12/79
07/05/80			**D9518** (No.7) (sub re-inst), **D9528** (No.2)	
04/07/80*	W-E		**D9528** (No.2) (B-A), **D9518** (No.7, sub re-inst) (B-A)	
06/09/80			**D9528** (No.2), **D9535** (37) (sub re-inst?)	**D9518** (No.7) to LEW, Philadelphia
				D9535/55 ex-Backworth 08-09/80.
26/10/80*	W-E		**D9535** (37) (B-A, sub re-inst?), **D9528** (No.2) (B-A)	
06/12/80			**D9528** (No.2)	**D9535** (37) to BR Thornaby?
04/01/81			**D9528** (No.2), **D9535** (37)	**D9535** ex-BR Thornaby?
			Also: **D9508** (No.9) stabled near shed.	
23/01/81*	W-E		**D9536** (No.5) (A-B, sub re-inst), **D9528** (No.2) (B-A)	**D9508** not photographed.
				D9535 (37) to LEW Philadelphia?
29/03/81*	W-E		**D9535** (37) (A-B), **D9536** (No.5) (A-B, sub re-inst), **D9528** (No.2) (B-A)	**D9535** ex-LEW Philadelphia?
			Also: **D9508** (No.9) location not specified	
08/04/81			**D9528** (No.2), **D9535** (37), **D9536** (No.5) (sub re-inst)	D9508 (No.9) not listed.
10/04/81			**D9528** (No.2), **D9535** (37), **D9536** (No.5) (sub re-inst)	D9508 (No.9) not listed.
				D9502/25/40 ex-Weetslade 24/04/81
19/06/81*	W-E		**D9535** (37) (A-B), **D9536** (No.5) (A-B, sub re-inst), **D9528** (No.2) (B-A)	D9502 in shed operational
			Also: **D9508** (No.9) under Weighbridge.	
			Also: **D9525** (507) and **D9540** (No.36) (both no-rods) in Ashington Yard	
14/08/81			**D9528** (No.2), **D9535** (37), **D9536** (No.5) (sub re-inst), **D9555** (sub re-inst)	
			Also: **D9508** (No.9) under Weighbridge.	
			Also: **D9525** (507) and **D9540** (No.36) (both no-rods) in Ashington Yard	
				D9504 ex-Weetslade (via LEW) 11/09/81
12/09/81			**D9508** (No.9), **D9528** (No.2), **D9535** (37), **D9536** (No.5) (sub re-inst), **D9540** (No.36), **D9555** (sub re-inst)	
			Also: **D9525** in Shed (rods off for tyre-turning)	
				D9536 to LEW Philadelphia, 16/09/81
05/11/81*	W-E		**D9540** (No.36) (A-B), **D9555** (A-B, sub re-inst), **D95xx** (A-B)	D9508/28/35/6 not photographed.
				D9528 C/U 12/81
14/04/82			**D9508** (No.9), **D9517** (No.8), **D9535** (37), **D9540** (No.36)	
07/07/82			**D9508** (No.9), **D9517** (No.8), **D9535** (37), **D9540** (No.36)	
20/03/83			**D9508** (No.9), **D9517** (No.8), **D9525** (507), **D9540** (No.36) (location not specified)	**D9535** not listed.

Date		Locomotives	Comments
12/05/83		**D9508** (No.9), **D9517** (No.8), **D9525** (507) (sub re-inst), **D9535** (37), **D9540** (No.36) (all OOU)	
17/06/83		**D9517** (No.8), **D9525** (507) (sub re-inst), **D9540** (No.36)	
		Also: **D9508** (No.9) under Weighbridge	
		Also: **D9535** (in and and around shed)	
26/06/83*	W-E	**D9540** (No.36) (A-B), **D9525** (507) (A-B, sub re-inst), **D9517** (No.8) (B-A)	
		Also: **D9508** (No.9) under Weighbridge	
		Also: **D9535** (37) (A-B), **D9504** (506) (B-A, sub re-inst) near 'Scrap-line'	
			D9504/25 both re-instated.
22/07/83		**D9517** (No.8), **D9535** (37), **D9540** (No.36) (all OOU)	
		Also: **D9508** (No.9) under Weighbridge	
05/08/83*	W-E	**D9540** (No.36) (A-B), **D9535** (37) (A-B), **D9517** (No.8) (B-A)	D9508 (No.9) not photographed.
10/09/83		**D9517** (No.8), **D9535** (37), **D9540** (No.36)	
		Also: **D9508** (No.9) under Weighbridge	
25/10/83 (See Note 4)		**D9508** (No.9), **D9517** (No.8), **D9535** (37), **D9540** (No.36)	
		Also: **D9527** (No.6) half under Weighbridge	
30/11/83*	W-E	**D9540** (No.36) (A-B), **D9517** (No.8) (B-A), **D9535** (37) (A-B)	
		Also: **D9508** (No.9) shed yard and **D9527** (No.6) under Weighbridge being stripped	
02/12/83 (See Note 5)		**D9508** (No.9), **D9517** (No.8), **D9527** (No.6), **D9535** (37), **D9540** (No.36) (all stored awaiting disposal)	
			Tender by 14/12/83: **D9508/17/27/35/40**
11/01/84 (See Note 6)		**D9508** (No.9), **D9517** (No.8), **D9527** (No.6), **D9535** (37), **D9540** (No.36)	
15/01/84 (See Note 7)		**D9508** (No.9) part-cut.	N.B. Incomplete list of locos present.
			D9508/17/27/35/40 C/U 01/84
05/04/84		Shed Yard: **D9514** (No.4) ("all six wheels off track")	
07/07/84		**D9514** (No.4), **D9521** (No.3) (sub re-inst), **D9536** (No.5)	
03/05/85*	W-E	**D9502** (B-A), **D9536** (No.5) (B-A), **D9514** (No.4) (B-A)	
11/05/85		**D9502**, **D9525** (507) (sub re-inst), plus two others (presumably **D9514**/36)	
15/06/85	W-E	**D9525** (507) (sub re-inst), **D9502**, **D9536** (No.5), **D9514** (No.4)	In order listed.
29/08/85	W-E	**D9525** (507) (sub re-inst), **D9502**, **D9536** (No.5), **D9514** (No.4)	In order listed.
05/10/85	W-E	**D9525** (507) (sub re-inst), **D9502**, **D9536** (No.5), **D9514** (No.4)	In order listed.
14/10/85*	W-E	**D9525** (507) (B-A, sub re-inst), **D9502** (B-A), **D9536** (No.5) (B-A), **D9514** (No.4) (B-A)	

Date		Locomotives	Comments
20/10/85		D9502, D9514 (No.4), D9525 (507) (sub re-inst), D9536 (No.5)	
02/11/85*	W-E	D9525 (507) (B-A, sub re-inst), D9502 (B-A), D9536 (No.5) (B-A), D9514 (No.4) (B-A)	
			D9525 repaired at Ashington.
24/11/85		D9502, D9514 (No.4), D9536 (No.5)	
01/12/85	W-E	D9502, D9536 (No.5), D9514 (No.4) (all being stripped of parts)	In order listed.
16/12/85 (See Note 8)		D9502, D9536 (part-cut), D9514 (No.4) (part-cut)	
			D9514/36 C/U 05-12/12/85
12/01/86		D9502	
21/02/86		D9502	
05/04/86		D9502	
15/05/86		D9502	
27/06/86		D9502	
20/07/86		D9502	
26/08/86*	W-E	D9502 (B-A)	
27/09/86		D9502	
29/11/86		D9502, D9525 (507) (sub re-inst), D9555 (9107/57)	
30/12/86		D9502, D9525 (507) (sub re-inst), D9555 (9107/57)	
23/01/87		D9502, D9525 (507) (sub re-inst), D9555 (9107/57)	
28/01/87		D9502, D9555 (9107/57)	
05/02/87		D9502	
		Also: D9555 (9107/57) and D9518 (No.7) between Weighbridge and Shed.	
		Also: D9531 (No.31) under Control Office	
28/02/87*	W-E	D9502 (B-A)	
		Also: D9555 (9107/57) and D9518 (No.7) between Weighbridge and Shed.	
		Also: D9531 (No.31) under Control Office	
13/03/87		D9502	
		Also: D9555 (9107/57) and D9518 (No.7) between Weighbridge and Shed.	
		Also: D9531 (No.31) under Control Office	
20/04/87		D9502	
		Also: D9555 (9107/57) and D9518 (No.7) between Weighbridge and Shed.	
		Also: D9531 (No.31) under Control Office	
		Also: D9500 (No.1), D9504 (506), D9513 (38), D9521 (No.3), D9525 (507) inside shed	

Date	Locomotives	Comments
17/05/87	**D9502** Also: **D9500** (No.1), **D9504** (506), **D9513** (38), **D9518** (No.7), **D9521** (No.3), **D9525** (507), **D9531** (No.31), **D9555** inside shed	
03/08/87	**D9502** Also: **D9500** (No.1), **D9504** (506), **D9513** (38), **D9518** (No.7), **D9521** (No.3), **D9525** (507), **D9531** (No.31), **D9555** inside shed	Invitation to tender mid-08/87, closing date 02/09/87.

Notes:

1. Abbreviations:

W-E	West to East, to be read in conjunction with:
A-B	'A' end to West, 'B' end to East.
B-A	'B' end to West, 'A' end to East.

Dsm	Dismantled
OOU	Out of use
Sub re-inst	Re-instated to traffic subsequent to sighting.

2. Listings marked * were derived from photographs and were, therefore, frequently incomplete.

3. Re 25/10/83 visit:

   IRS Archive (John Wade, undated): Ashington, 25/10/83: 'Team Valley Headquarters had written and proclaimed that 5 Class 14s were to be withdrawn (notification had been received the previous week). The fitter here said that HQ had also given them a month to strip these of all useful spares and then they were going up for tender to scrap merchants. These were being marshalled together and dumped at the back of the shed.
   'These were: No.8 9312/93 (D9517), No.6 9312/94 (D9527), No.9 9312/99 (D9508), and 37 (D9535).'

   IRS Archive (John Wade, 08/11/83 in response to Bob Darvill comments 03/11/83**):** Ashington, 25/10/83: 'In shed: No.3 (D9521 …but when I arrived it was in use (at 13.00hrs) marshalling 37 (D9535) and No.8 (D9517), both withdrawn, from the shed to round the back of the shed to join No.36 (D9540) and No.9 (D9508) already dumped here for scrap…
   'Under the 'office arch': No.6 (D9527) (half-in, half-out) also withdrawn.'

4. Re 11/01/84 visit:

   IRS Archive (Trevor Scott, 11/01/84): 'Work has started on the cutting up of surplus locomotives on 10/1/84, beginning with No.36 ex-BR D9540 which was reduced to a pile of scrap by late afternoon 11/1; No.9 (D9508) will be next, followed by 37 (D9535), No.8 (D9517), and, finally, No.6 (D9527).'

5. Re 15/01/84 visit:

   IRS Archive (Trevor Scott, 19/01/84): 'The cutting up of the second locomotive, No.9, has taken longer not being completed until the 17th due to bad weather.'

6. Re 16/12/85 visit:

   IRS Archive (Paul Green, 16/12/85): 'No.4 9312/96 (D9514) and No.5 9312/91 (D9536) were in the final stages of scrapping. All that remained were the wheels and *skirting*(?).'

7. Re 29/11/86 visit:

   IRS Archive (Trevor Scott, 01/12/86): 'D9502 and 9107/57 (D9555) were behind the shed waiting scrapping, the latter having been transferred from Lynemouth just prior to my arrival.'

D9545, D4056 and D9511 (9312/98), NCB Ashington, 23 January 1974. (Anthony Sayer)

D9545, NCB Ashington, 15 June 1976. (Anthony Sayer)

D9511 (9312/98), D9518 (No.7), D9528 (No.2) and unidentified D95xx (left to right), NCB Ashington, 23 September 1979.
I believe that the 'wreck' of 'D9511' is actually D9545. The cab has been removed, and, it is in exactly the same location as my previous shot of D9545; in addition, the dirty marks on the buffer beam look identical. The unidentified D95xx is, in all probability, the true fire-damaged remains of D9511. Either way, both D9511 and D9545 lasted until September, two months later than previous information on disposals, although, of course, that might depend on people's personal definition of what constitutes 'disposal'! Although D9518 (No.7) was on the 'scrap-line, it was repaired and returned to traffic. (Brian Webb [IRS])

D9528 (No.2) with D9518 (No.7), NCB Ashington, 4 July 1980.
(MasonPhenix19 Collection)

**D9535(37),
D9536(No.5) and
D9528(No.2), NCB
Ashington, 29 March
1981.** (Douglas Johnson)

**D9540 (No.36), NCB
Ashington, 26 June
1983.** (Anthony Sayer)

D9525(507) and D9517 (No.8), NCB Ashington, 26 June 1983. (Anthony Sayer)

D9535 (37) and D9504 (506), NCB Ashington, 26 June 1983. (John Sayer)

**D9540 (No.36),
NCB Ashington,
30 November 1983.**
(John Carter)

**D9535 (37),
NCB Ashington,
30 November 1983.**
(John Carter)

D9517(No.8), with D9527 (No.6) under the Control Office, NCB Ashington, 30 November 1983. Both in the process of being stripped before final disposal. (John Carter)

D9525 (507), D9502, D9536 (No.5) and D9514(No.4), NCB Ashington, 2 November 1985. (Anthony Sayer)

D9502 and two part-cut Class 14s, NCB Ashington, Undated.
The part-cut locomotives were D9514 (No.4) and D9536 (No.5), cut-up during November 1985.
(both Ian [ijr65])

Disposal Summary.
Class 14 - NCB Disposal Details.

NB Plant Registry No.	NCB 'Local' No(s). Carried	Ex-BR No.	Disposal Details
–	–	D9545	Scrapped NCB Ashington, early 07/79 (see Note 1)
9312/98	–	D9511	Scrapped NCB Ashington, early 07/79 (see Note 1)
9312/100	No.2	D9528	Scrapped NCB Ashington early 12/81
2233/508	No.36	D9540	Scrapped NCB Ashington by D.Short, North Shields, 10-11/01/84
9312/99	No.9	D9508	Scrapped NCB Ashington by D.Short, North Shields, 17/01/84
9312/59	37	D9535	Scrapped NCB Ashington by D.Short, North Shields, 18-20/01/84
9312/94	No.6	D9527	Scrapped NCB Ashington by D.Short, North Shields, 20-23/01/84
9312/93	No.8	D9517	Scrapped NCB Ashington by D.Short, North Shields, 23-24/01/84
9312/96	No.4	D9514	Scrapped NCB Ashington by Robinson & Hannon Ltd, 05-16/12/85
9312/91	No.5	D9536	Scrapped NCB Ashington by Robinson & Hannon Ltd, 05-16/12/85
9107/57	D9555	D9555	Sold for preservation, departed Ashington 25/09/87
9312/92	No.1	D9500	Sold for preservation, departed Ashington 25/09/87
(9312/97)	–	D9502	Sold for preservation, departed Ashington 25/09/87

NB Plant Registry No.	NCB 'Local' No(s). Carried	Ex-BR No.	Disposal Details
2233/506	506	D9504	Sold for preservation, departed Ashington 26/09/87
9312/95	No.7	D9518	Sold for preservation, departed Ashington 26/09/87
2233/507	507	D9525	Sold for preservation, departed Ashington 29/09/87
2100/523	No.31	D9531	Sold to C.F. Booth, re-sold for preservation, departed Ashington 02/10/87
(2100/524)	38	D9513	Sold to C.F. Booth, re-sold for preservation, departed Ashington 12/10/87
9312/90	No.3	D9521	Sold to C.F. Booth, re-sold for preservation, departed Ashington 14/10/87

Notes:
1. Sightings and photographs suggest that the disposal of D9511/45 was later than July 1979, actually sometime between October and December 1979. At the time of final disposal both locomotives were heavily dismantled and there may have been some different interpretations of 'disposal' by various enthusiasts!
2. Invitation to tender for disposal of D9508/17/27/35/40 issued in late-1983 with a closing date of 14/12/83.
3. Invitation to tender for the disposal of last nine locomotives was distributed in August 1987 with a closing date for sealed bids set for 2 September.
4. Liveries of the last nine on departure from Ashington:

Class 14: Liveries of Last Nine Locos at Ashington.

NB Plant Registry No.	NCB 'Local' No(s). Carried	Ex-BR No.	Disposal Details
9107/57	D9555	D9555	NE Area dark-blue, RHR, / / / buffer-beam stripes
9312/92	No.1	D9500	NE Area dark-blue, WHR, \ \ \ buffer-beam stripes
(9312/97)	–	D9502	BR two-tone green, Λ chevrons, yellow buffer-beams
2233/506	506	D9504	Philadelphia green, Λ chevrons, yellow buffer-beams
9312/95	No.7	D9518	Ashington blue, Λ chevrons, yellow buffer-beams
2233/507	507	D9525	Philadelphia green, Λ chevrons, yellow buffer-beams
2100/523	No.31	D9531	NE Area dark-blue, RHR, / / / buffer-beam stripes
(2100/524)	D1/9513, 38	D9513	Backworth blue, Λ chevrons, red buffer beams
9312/90	No.3	D9521	NE Area dark-blue, RHR, / / / buffer-beam stripes

Abbreviations:
RHR   Red handrails.
WHR   White handrails.
/ / / \ \ \   Orientation of buffer-beam stripes.

4.9 Dereliction at Ashington.

D9502, NCB Ashington, 26 August 1986. (Douglas Johnson)

2268. D9513 (38, D1/9513) and D9521 (No.3), NCB Ashington, 10 October 1987. Ashington shed in the process of demolition. (Anthony Sayer)

D9518 (No.7), NCB Ashington, 28 February 1987. View from the Control Office. Engine repairs on D9518 were never completed; a job left for the preservationists.
(Bruce Galloway)

D9531 (No.31), D9555 (9107/57), D9518 (No.7), NCB Ashington, 28 February 1987. Control Office, signal box and weighbridge; D9531 underneath, and D9555 and D9518 beyond. (Bruce Galloway)

Chapter 5

NATIONAL COAL BOARD: SOUTH WALES

Mardy Colliery.

NCB Mardy.
Mardy Colliery was located at the head of the Rhondda Fach valley. The NCB railway ran north-west from the BR/NCB Exchange Sidings, immediately north-west of Maerdy station, to Mardy colliery a distance of approximately 1¼ miles.

Standard gauge rail traffic ceased in 1987 and the colliery closed on 20/12/90.

D9530 arrived at Mardy Colliery from Gulf Oil Refinery Ltd, Waterston, Dyfed (via BR Cardiff Canton) in October 1975, on hire from A.R. Adams & Son, Newport, Gwent. The locomotive appears to have seen only intermittent use with several visits made to BR Cardiff Canton and Ebbw Junction depots for repairs between 1976 and 1978. D9530 was scrapped on site at Mardy in April 1982 after a long period out of use.

D9530's livery was Gulf Oil light blue throughout its time at Mardy.

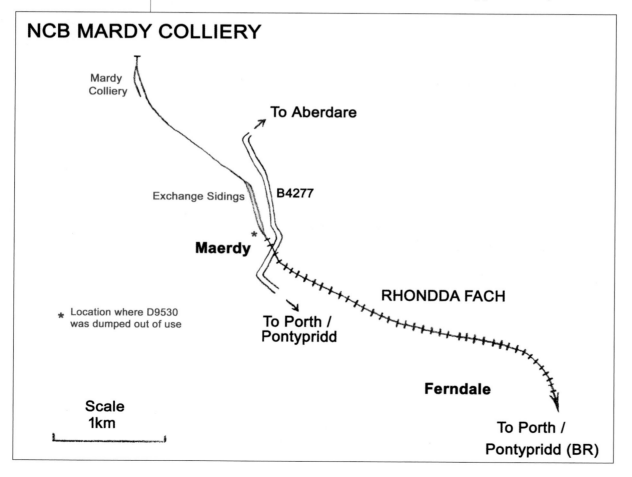

NCB MARDY COLLIERY

Mardy Colliery

To Aberdare

Exchange Sidings

B4277

Maerdy

* Location where D9530 was dumped out of use

To Porth / Pontypridd

RHONDDA FACH

Ferndale

To Porth / Pontypridd (BR)

Scale 1km

D9530, 86B Ebbw Junction, 25 July 1976. 'D9530' chalked on cab side. (Anthony Sayer)

D9530, NCB Mardy, 6 July 1980. Out of use and derelict. Dumped adjacent to the BR/NCB Exchange Sidings a short walk to the north of the B4277 Porth-Aberdare road crossing near the site of Maerdy station. It would be another 21 months before the final disposal of D9530. (Anthony Sayer)

Chapter 6

STEWARTS & LLOYDS/ BRITISH STEEL CORPORATION

6.1 S&L/BSC – General.

In November 1949, the quarrying operations of Stewarts & Lloyds Ltd were split from their iron and steel manufacturing operations and were administered separately as Stewarts and Lloyds (Minerals) Ltd (S&L(M)); this company took over all of the mineral workings under the control of S&L in one over-arching organization. This included the Corby area (operated by Lloyds Ironstone Co. Ltd as a subsidiary of S&L), plus quarries in Northamptonshire, Leicestershire, Rutland and Lincolnshire operated by Stanton Ironworks Co. Ltd, as well as several other smaller operations.

The British Steel Corporation was formed on 28 July 1967 following the nationalisation of the assets of fourteen former private companies including Stewarts & Lloyds. The operation of the pre-nationalisation companies was not formally taken over until 1 July 1968, with the Stewarts & Lloyds iron and steel activities organised under the BSC Northern & Tubes Group banner.

The quarries, however, continued to operate as Stewarts & Lloyds (Minerals) Ltd.

From 29 March 1970 BSC was re-organised into six Divisions on the basis of products: General Steels, Special Steels, Strip Mills, Tubes, Chemicals and Construction. As a consequence, the quarrying operations in Northamptonshire and Lincolnshire were positioned within BSC Tubes Division (Minerals), and Stewarts & Lloyds (Minerals) ceased to exist.

Although technically the Class 14 locomotives operated throughout under the nationalised British Steel Corporation, their first 15-18 months were operated under the Stewarts & Lloyds (Minerals) Ltd umbrella, whilst management sorted out the new organisational structure.

Four main quarry groupings were served by the Class 14s between 1968 and 1980, as follows:

- Buckminster (Lincolnshire) largely extracting iron-ore for use at the Scunthorpe Steelworks via the BSC/BR exchange sidings at Stainby,
- Harlaxton (Lincolnshire), supplying Stanton, Shelton and Beeston ironworks via the BSC/BR Casthorpe exchange sidings.
- Glendon East (Northamptonshire), feeding Corby, via the BSC/BR Glendon East exchange sidings, and,
- Corby (Northamptonshire) with iron-ore supplied to the Corby Steelworks by a substantial internal BSC railway system.

Each of these operations included several quarry workings integrated by substantial BSC railway operations involving local shunting work as well as trip-working from the quarries either to BSC/BR exchange sidings, or, in the case of Corby, directly to the steelworks; this work was ideally suited to the 650hp Class 14s. Similarities with the NCB Northumberland operations are very clear.

The first of the Class 14s to arrive in the ironstone fields of Lincolnshire and Northamptonshire was D9529 at Buckminster in August 1968. Why Buckminster first? Greg Evans, IRS member and researcher, offers the following potential explanation:

'It is said that the idea of buying them from BR came from the fact that North of the Welland Quarries Manager (the late Tim Barclay) espied some sort of national newspaper article that BR faced huge embarrassment having had all these locomotives built … with no work. This gave him the idea to purchase some of them to replace the steam locomotives in the North of the Welland quarries.'

At a guess the newspaper article concerned was the one in the 24 June 1968 edition of the *Daily Mail* (pages 160 and 161 in my previous book "Class 14: Their Life on British Railways").

All locomotives were allocated 'Plant Nos.' (or 'Card of Account Nos.') by S&L(M) for asset control purposes; small plastic plaques were carried externally (under one of the forward-facing cab windows at 'B'-end) on most Corby/Glendon locomotives (see example on page 55) and also inside the cab. An 8311 prefix was used for the Corby/Glendon locomotives and 8411 for the Buckminster/Harlaxton (North of Welland) locomotives. The Plant Nos. were never changed during their subsequent time with BSC, despite running number and location changes.

6.2 Buckminster Quarries.
Class 14s at Buckminster: D9510/5/29/52, plus D9512 for spares (5).
Period of Class 14 productive activity: August 1968 - January 1972 (locomotives departed by rail mid-1972).

Iron-ore extraction from the Buckminster area commenced as early as 1908, with the ore moved south to Buckminster Sidings on the Bourne to Saxby line for onward movement to customers. By 1916, traffic was also able to reach the national system to the north near the Great Northern station at Stainby on the Highdyke Branch (which joined the GN main line just south of Grantham). This development was an operationally and financially advantageous outlet for ore movements to the steelworks in Scunthorpe.

As is the nature of iron-ore mining, quarrying around Buckminster spread extensively as old quarries were worked out, only to be replaced by new quarries nearby, most with rail links of varying length to the main arterial route between Buckminster Sidings and Stainby Sidings (3½ miles). The quarries at Buckminster were given numbers in chronological order of their commencement of extraction, from No.1 to No.20.

Railway workshop and locomotive shed facilities were developed at Gunby approximately one mile south of Stainby, and the complex was frequently named Sewstern after the nearby village.

By the mid-1960s, a general reduction in the demand for iron-ore severely impacted Buckminster to the extent that only No.15 and No.16 quarries were operating, with only the latter utilising rail transportation. By December 1964 rail traffic was limited to the area north of Sewstern, with rail-borne ore only exiting the site via Stainby, and at very low levels. The nearby Market Overton quarry in Rutland was closed in September 1966 due to the slump in demand.

By 1967, something of an upturn was experienced as a consequence of supplying more ore to Scunthorpe's Normanby Park and Redbourn Works. As well as increasing output from Buckminster, the quarry at Market Overton was re-opened with ore extracted from the No.6 quarry here and dispatched 'internally' to Stainby for onward movement to Scunthorpe. This involved the movement of ore from Market Overton to the quarry's original exchange facility at Pains Sidings, then via the closed BR Saxby-South Witham-Bourne route to Buckminster Sidings, and finally northwards on the Stewarts & Lloyds route to Stainby via Sewstern. This resulted in operational and financial advantages to both BR and the steel companies given the more direct route to Scunthorpe via Grantham, rather than via Peterborough. Stewarts & Lloyds leased the track between Pains and Buckminster Sidings from BR, and traffic resumed on 2 October 1967. This 'long-distance' traffic was handled by Buckminster locomotives, and assuming that the local Market Overton shunters worked up to Pain Sidings, the run from there to Stainby for the Class 14s was approximately 4¼ miles.

From October 1967 the anticipated movement of ore to Scunthorpe was 15,000 tons per week, split roughly equally between Buckminster No.16 quarry (and subsequently Nos.17, 18 and 20) and Market Overton.

This set the scene for the arrival of the Class 14s in 1968 and for the next three years. D9529 arrived from Hull Dairycoates on 26 August 1968 for a two-month trial, with D9552 following in September immediately taking over the Market Overton trip. D9552 was able to handle 28-30 loaded wagons per trip, substantially more than the fourteen for a Rolls Royce 'Sentinel'. The trials were successful and

D9510/2/5 arrived in November, although D9512 was only purchased as a source of spares. Success at Buckminster was also the precursor to Class 14 operations at Harlaxton, Corby and Glendon East.

The usual roster for the four operational Class 14s was two on workings from Stainby to the local quarries, one to Market Overton, and one spare.

The operational four were renumbered 20 to 23 (D9529/52/15/10 in order) in September 1969; unlike the Harlaxton locomotives, no 'No.' prefix was carried. D9512 retained its BR number throughout its time dumped at Sewstern shed. Similarly, 20-23 were repainted from BR two-tone green livery to all-over Brunswick green, whilst D9512 retained its progressively deteriorating BR livery throughout.

In 1971, the demand for iron-ore slumped once more, and with the introduction of new steelmaking facilities at Scunthorpe deploying high-grade imported ores already on the horizon, the demise of Buckminster and Market Overton quarries was inevitable. Market Overton closed on 31 December 1971; Buckminster carried on for one more month and the last train-load of ore left Stainby on 27 January 1972.

Closure proved to be slightly premature when demand uplifted temporarily in 1972 but Harlaxton was able to cope with this short-lived 'spike' (see below) without resort to the temporary re-opening of Buckminster.

Dismantling started from Market Overton back to Stainby, and D9510 (23) is known to have assisted with the removal of scrap materials.

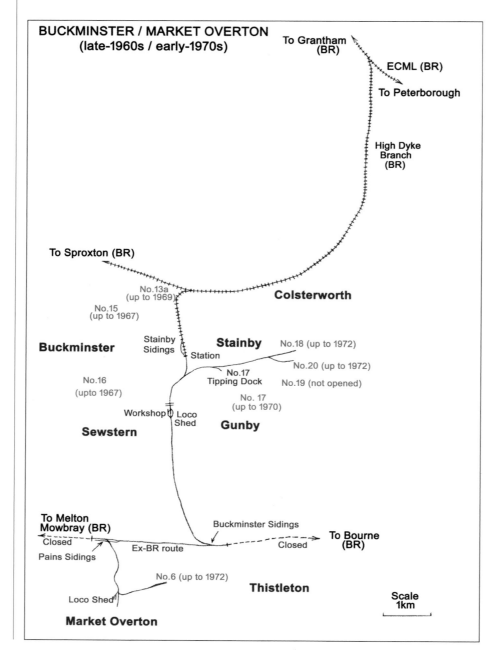

Buckminster & Market Overton Quarries.

E.S. Tonks in his book *The Ironstone Quarries of the Midlands (Part VIII South Lincolnshire)* quotes: 'Two of the Buckminster diesels [listed as D9510/52 in an accompanying table] left for Gretton Brook, Corby, in June 1972 and the remaining three in September [D9512/5/29], leaving Buckminster yard empty of locomotives for the first time in three quarters of a century.' IRS *Bulletin* No.148 [October 1972] included an undated report stating that 'Dave Needham noted at Gretton Brook [Corby] shed 21 and 23 from Buckminster'; whilst undated, the 'surrounding' reports were all dated June/July 1972. However, a sighting of all five locomotives at Grantham on 31 August 1972 alternatively suggests that all five of the Class 14s were moved together in late-August/early-September.

The jury is still out as to whether the Class 14s were moved en-masse or as two separate movements. New sighting information for Buckminster and Corby is required for this critical time period.

D9529, S&L(M) Buckminster (Sewstern Loco Shed), 26 August, 1968. First day at Buckminster after arrival from Hull; at this point D9529 was still owned by BR. (M.J. Leah [IRS])

D9515, S&L(M) Buckminster (Sewstern Loco Shed), 25 April 1969. (Rail-Online)

D9512 with D9552 behind, S&L(M) Buckminster, 1970. (Transport Topics)

D9552 (21), S&L(M) Buckminster (Stainby sidings), 28 September 1969. 'S&L' on cab side. IRS railtour. (Robin Barnes)

Below left: D9552 (21), Mill Lane Crossing, north of Buckminster Sidings, September 1970. En route from Market Overton quarry to the BSC/BR exchange point at Stainby Sidings. 'S&L' now painted out; in fact the locomotive looks to have been re-painted in overall dark green livery. (John Ford (David Ford Collection))

Below right: D9515 (22), Ex-BR Saxby to Bourne branch (WRC 'Buckminster 95' tour), 1 January 1972. Believed to be just east of Buckminster Sidings. Overall dark green. (Transport Treasury [John Tolson])

D9515 (22), BSC Buckminster, 14 September 1971.
Believed to be Pains Sidings, north of the Market Overton quarry, on part of the 'extended' Buckminster system. D9515 is undertaking local engineering duties shunting ballast brought in on two 'work-weary' *Grampus* wagons.
(Peter Foster)

D9552 (21), BSC Buckminster, 14 September 1971.
Same location as the previous photograph and, therefore, also believed to be Pains Sidings. The loaded BR iron-ore wagons appear to be being propelled eastwards along the ex-BR line towards Buckminster Sidings, prior to haulage on the 'proper' Buckminster route to Stainby, thereby avoiding the necessity of running-round the train en route. (Peter Foster)

6.3 Harlaxton Quarries.
Class 14s at Harlaxton:
D9503/41/8 (3).

Period of Class 14 productive activity: November 1968 - February 1974 (locomotives departed by road August 1974).

The BSC quarry line ran southwards from Casthorpe Junction, on the Belvoir Junction-Denton branch, to a cliff top (over 200ft above Casthorpe), with a reversing point at Swine Hill en route and gradients as steep as 1 in 20 on the final section; allowing for the reversal, this represented a journey of approximately 3¼ miles. The cliff top 'complex' included the Workshops, Locomotive Shed, marshalling yards and access to the various quarries developed progressively on the Harlaxton system (i.e. No.1 Pearson's, No.2 Welby, No.3 Swine Hill, No.4 Hungerton, No.5 Catholic, No.6 Jenkinson's and No.7 Stroxton).

By the time of the arrival of the Class 14s in November 1968, Nos.1-3/5 quarries had ceased production and No.6 was proving to yield only poor quality ore (and was road-operated only in any case); as a consequence the efforts

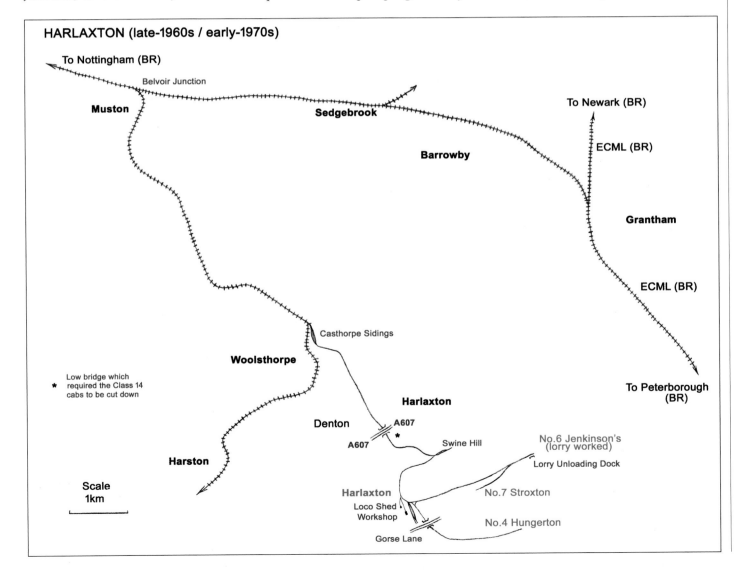

Harlaxton Quarries.

of the Class 14s were concentrated on No.4 quarry (approximately 1¼ miles from the 'complex'), plus No.7 (approximately 2 miles away, including a reversal) when it opened in 1969. The Class 14s were supported by Drewry and Sentinel shunters. Train loadings on the steeply graded 'main line' were restricted as follows:

Class 14	0-6-0DH (650hp)	20 full	30 empty	)
Drewry	0-6-0DH (375hp)	16 full	25 empty	) BR 27t tipper wagons
Sentinel	0-4-0DH (311hp)	12 full	20 empty	)

Prior to commencement of duties, the three Class 14s (D9503/41/8) had their cab roofs reduced in height from 13ft to 12ft 8in to facilitate safe passage through the short tunnel under the A607 Grantham Road.

Initially the Class 14s retained their BR two-tone livery, lion & wheel emblems and running numbers until June 1970 when the locomotives were repainted into Brunswick green livery and renumbered No.25 to No.27 (D9503/41/8 in order).

The ex-BR locomotives were found to be heavy on rail wear, and lubricators were fitted at key points; in addition a short cut off was laid between the Hungerton and Stroxton branches in Summer 1970, at the point where they divided near the yard. This was installed to enable the Class 14s to be reversed periodically to equalise wheel-flange wear. No reference has been found regarding braking difficulties on the severely graded 'main line' down to Casthorpe Sidings.

In 1971, the bulk of the ore was being transported to Stanton, Shelton and Bilston, and, with the closure of the Buckminster quarries in 1972, to Scunthorpe as well. However, with the depressed state of the steel industry generally and the decision to use foreign ore in the new 'Anchor' plant at Scunthorpe contraction and ultimate closure became inevitable. No.7 quarry closed in May 1973.

The final closure date of Harlaxton was geared primarily to that of Stanton Ironworks, the principal customer, and as a consequence quarrying ceased at No.4 quarry on 14 February 1974 coincident with the closure of Stanton. D9548 (No.27) performed the main line duties to Casthorpe Sidings on the final day.

The demolition of the quarry lines and the 'main line' from the cliff-top back to Casthorpe exchange sidings left D9503/41/8 marooned on the cliff top. Most of

D9503, S&L(M) Harlaxton, 23 December 1968. Reduced height cab to allow passage under the A607 Grantham Road bridge. (Pete Stamper [IRS])

D9541(No.26), BSC Harlaxton (WRC 'Harlaxton 95' tour), 19 June 1971. Casthorpe Junction. (Transport Treasury [John Tolson])

D9541(No.26), BSC Harlaxton (WRC 'Harlaxton 95' tour), 19 June 1971. Typical quarrying scenery. Top soil removed, exposing the ironstone layer ready for excavation. Very basic trackwork which constantly had to be slewed towards the receding rock face to assist loading of wagons by mechanical shovels. (Transport Treasury [John Tolson])

the track had been lifted by the end of April 1974. The marooning of the Class 14s at Harlaxton seems strange, precluding their transfer to Corby by rail; however, the comment 'the tyres are not in good enough condition to travel by BR' in IRS *Bulletin* No.171 explains their movement to Northamptonshire by road in July/ August 1974.

D9523, BSC Glendon East, 30 March 1978.
(Kevin Lane)

6.4 Glendon Quarries.
Class 14s at Glendon East:
D9520/3/49 (D9523 throughout, D9520 until 1970, plus D9549 for a short period in 1973/4).

Period of Class 14 productive activity: December 1968 - December 1979.

Ironstone mining in the Glendon area was first recorded in 1863, and over the next 117 years involved quarries distributed across an area of about four square miles.

The 1960s and 1970s saw the closure of all the remaining individual ironstone quarries in the area except for Glendon East and those directly connected to the Corby Works railway system. At Glendon East, the Bridge quarry was the main area of activity, supplemented by Geddington, re-opened in 1967, and Barford East from 1977 (see map on page 215). With Glendon East being less than 5 miles from Corby, the possibility of linking it to the Corby system at Little Oakley was considered in 1969 but was never implemented; Glendon East retained its railway independence until closure, requiring BR to move its iron-ore north via the Midland route to Corby.

When Stewarts & Lloyds (Minerals) purchased their fleet of twenty-three Class 14 locomotives, two were allocated to Glendon (D9520/3), and were the last to be received from BR in December 1968. These two were numbered 24 and 25 in the Corby Minerals fleet respectively. The '25' on D9523 was microscopic, stencilled in very small figures on the footplate fuel tanks at 'A' end; the BR number was retained. Presumably the same

applied to D9520 (24) although photographs of D9520 whilst at Glendon have not been found to prove this.

In reality, one of the big 650hp diesels was sufficient to handle the traffic, leaving the other idle at the shed; this was considered to be inefficient, so D9520 was sent to Corby in January 1970 and a small 0-4-0 311hp Rolls Royce 'Sentinel' ('MAUD') was provided as the spare instead even though its haulage capability was 50 per cent of the remaining Class 14. Initially, the Class 14 handled 16 empties to the quarry and eight loaded unassisted when returning, although in 1971 nine loaded wagons were noted with the use of the Sentinel as banker as far as the weigh-bridge and in 1975 train loads of ten wagons were being handled unassisted by D9523.

In 1973, plans were made to increase production at Glendon and as a consequence the 'Sentinel' was replaced by D9549 (33) from Corby. Subsequently, it was decided to allocate three six-wheel 450hp Rolls Royce 'Steelman' locomotives (Nos. 18-20) to Glendon with one (No.20) arriving in June 1974 for trials, replacing D9549. Unfortunately, the 'Steelman' with its shorter wheelbase and flangeless centre wheels made it susceptible to derailments and the transfer of the other two was delayed until modified wheels could be made. In the event, however, no more arrived.

At Glendon East, flange wear on the sharp curves was a major issue. Correspondence from Greg Evans illustrates the point: 'D9523 was re-wheeled here; presumably the new wheels came from one of the cannibalised locos at Corby'.

D9523, BSC Glendon East, 18 April 1979. The microscopic '25' number is just discernible on the footplate fuel tank. (Anthony Sayer)

D9523, BSC Glendon East, 18 April 1979. Note the slightly lower than 'standard' position for the 'Plant Registry' plaque on the cab front. (Anthony Sayer)

He recalls conversations with the Glendon Traffic Foremen, one of whom said that 'the Class 14 was a mighty fine loco, just the flange wear to cope with'.

D9523 retained the BR two-tone green livery throughout its time with BSC. D9523 *may* have been allocated new number '46' in the Corby series in October 1974, but this was never carried in practice.

Production at Glendon East ended in December 1979 with D9523 bringing out the last wagons of iron-ore on 31 December. Closing down procedures started immediately utilising D9523 exclusively. The two remaining locomotives (D9523 and the 'Steelman') at Glendon departed 'dead' for Corby on 28 May 1980, hauled by a BR locomotive.

6.5 Corby Quarries.
Class 14s at Corby:

Initially D9507/16/32/3/7/9/42/7/9/51/3/4, plus D9544 for spares.	(13)
Plus D9520 ex-Glendon East (1970)	(1)
Plus D9510/5/29/53 and spares loco D9512 ex-Buckminster (1972)	(5)
Plus D9503/41/8 ex-Harlaxton (1974)	(3)
Plus D9538 for spares ex-Ebbw Vale, South Wales (1976)	(1)
Plus D9523 ex-Glendon East (1980)	(1) (24)

Period of Class 14 productive minerals activity: October 1968-January 1980.

Subsequent site clearance and Tube Works activity: 1980/1.

6.5.1 Operations.

Quarrying for iron around Corby started in the 1880s with the Lloyds Ironstone Company becoming a major player. Output expanded considerably as a result of the logical progression of Lloyds into iron-making from 1910. In 1923 the tube-making company Stewarts & Lloyds Ltd acquired controlling interest in the Lloyds Ironstone Company, and further vertical integration into steelmaking was inevitable. Steel production in Corby commenced in 1934. Over time, quarrying activities extended several miles from Corby in a number of directions, particularly to the north and east.

As mentioned previously, the mineral operations of Stewarts and Lloyds were separated from the core iron and steel-making activities in 1949. By the early 1950s the quarries close to the Corby steelmaking were largely exhausted and as a consequence quarrying operations extended further afield and the railway network expanded with it. The added focus brought by the S&L(M) organisation resulted in the development of fewer but significantly larger and deeper mines, supported by sophisticated heavy-duty drag-line and shovel equipment, a fully-signalled railway infrastructure and a deliberately 'fit-for-purpose' locomotive fleet.

By the mid-1950s S&L(M) were operating ten major quarries in support of the Corby steelmaking operation; although quarries closed through exhaustion, others opened to compensate, such that there were still ten quarries operational in 1961. By 1964 the Corby system had reached its maximum geographical extent with system extensions to Oakley and Wakerley. By 1968, the time of the arrival of the Class 14s from BR, the number of quarries had reduced to nine. The quarries operated during the reign of the Class 14s are listed below together with mileages from the Corby Ironworks involved.

Quarry (quarries in bold were open until final closure in January 1980)	Direction from Corby Works	Approx. distance from Corby Ore Crushing Plant (miles)
Oakley	S	5¾
Cowthick (closed 1971, substituted)	SE	4½
Barn Close Extension (opened 1976)	E	2
Priors Hall	E	3¼
Brookfield Cottage	NE	4¾
Park Lodge	N	3¾

Quarry (quarries in bold were open until final closure in January 1980)	Direction from Corby Works	Approx. distance from Corby Ore Crushing Plant (miles)
Harringworth Lodge (opened July 1977)	N	4¾
Sibley's (closed 1976, exhausted)	N	5¾
Shotley	N	5¾
Wakerley (closed early 1977, substituted)	N	6½
Earltrees (closed 1973, exhausted)	NW	1

Once again we see the rationale for deploying Class 14s as trip-freight and shunting locomotives with sufficient power to haul sizeable payloads.

As the table indicates, seven quarries were still operational at the beginning of 1980 (when the Corby mineral operation finished), albeit with closures and openings during the intervening period since 1968. Through a major part of the 1970s, only four or five quarries were required to operate to meet steel production demands, and as a consequence at any one time there was never the full complement of quarries in use. In reality, some of the quarries could have been closed down with production concentrated at fewer sites, but given the expensive equipment deployed, management preferred to operate the quarries in rotation, partly to ensure that all equipment was maintained in a serviceable condition and also to produce the correct blend of ore for the blast furnaces.

The development of major fully-integrated steel works on coastal or near-coastal sites (e.g. Redcar and Scunthorpe, for example) during the 1970s, utilising imported ore with an iron content of over 60 per cent, was the death-knell for inland steel-making operations dependent on local ore with an iron content of only around 25 per cent.

Oakley and Harringworth Lodge were served by trains on 2 January 1980, and Shotley, Park Lodge and Harringworth Lodge on 4 January 1980, the final day.

Iron and steel-making activities at Corby finished in April (following a 3-month national strike) with the last iron tapped on 22 April 1980. Feedstock for the Tube operations subsequently came in the form of hot-rolled steel coils from Lackenby Works (Teesside).

Track-lifting on the quarry routes commenced almost immediately (with D9537 [52] being use in the main) and by the end of 1980 most of the rails had been taken up.

Gretton Brook Locomotive Shed was brought into use in 1954 specifically for S&L(M) locomotives and was another manifestation of the segregation of the mineral activities from the 'heavy-end' iron and steel-making activities; this shed had eight parallel roads and was capable of holding 40 steam locomotives, fully capable of housing the full fleet of Class 14s when they arrived. Gretton Brook undertook most repair and maintenance work, although the removal/replacement of major items of equipment and wheelset changes requiring the use of overhead cranes was undertaken at Pen Green

Workshops; facilities at Corby were sufficient to avoid locomotives being moved to BR depots for tyre-turning as was the case for the NCB Ashington fleet.

Most operations at Corby were between 0600 and 1400hrs (Monday to Saturday) and at other times locomotives were invariably kept inside the shed. One locomotive operated 24 hours transferring iron-ore between the North Bank sidings and the ironworks ore-crushing facilities. When not working the only locomotives kept outdoors were the 'demics' held for spares purposes, these being dumped at the east end of the shed.

Corby Minerals drivers kept their own locomotives, a tradition going back to steam days; this situation may go a long way to explaining the excellent condition of the Class 14s at Corby, certainly compared with their sisters based at NCB Ashington.

During the time of the Class 14s, all movements of trains were controlled by Gretton Brook. With up to nine working quarries it was impossible to rely on the basic operating methods practiced at the smaller systems. Colour light signalling was installed all over the system and at quarry junctions and loops train crews had to telephone Control for permission to proceed.

Corby Quarries (North).

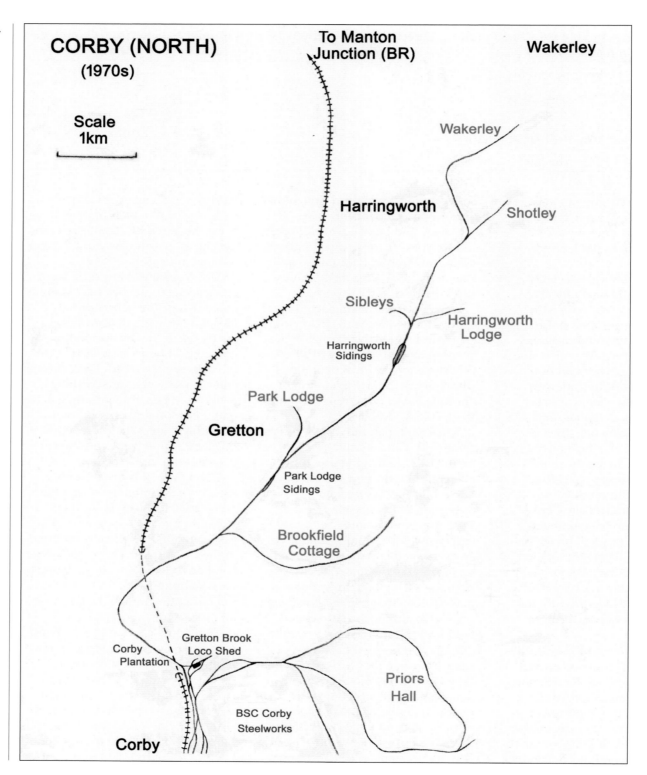

CORBY (NORTH)
(1970s)

Scale
1km

To Manton
Junction (BR)

Wakerley

Wakerley

Harringworth

Shotley

Sibleys

Harringworth
Lodge

Harringworth
Sidings

Park Lodge

Gretton

Park Lodge
Sidings

Brookfield
Cottage

Corby
Plantation

Gretton Brook
Loco Shed

Priors
Hall

BSC Corby
Steelworks

Corby

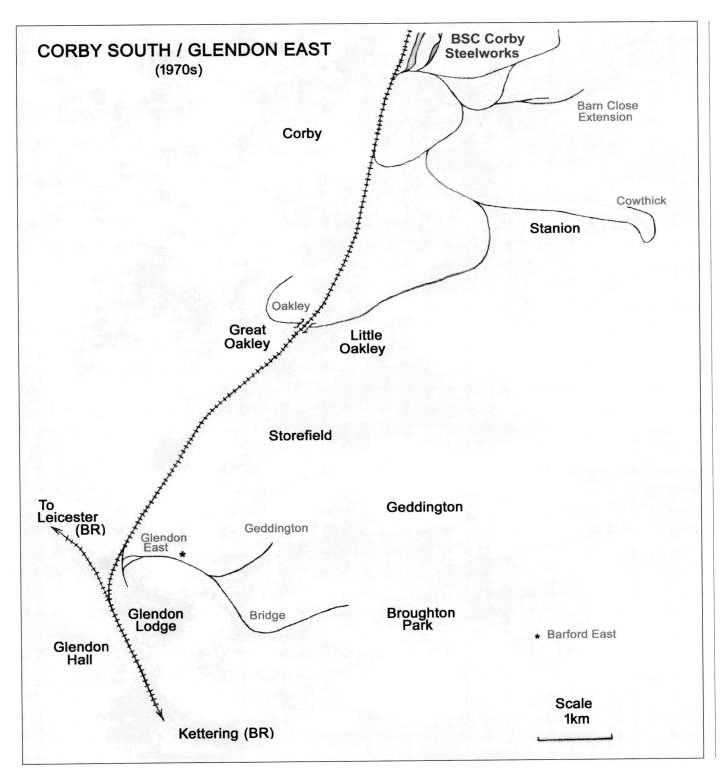

CORBY SOUTH / GLENDON EAST
(1970s)

BSC Corby
Steelworks

Corby

Barn Close
Extension

Cowthick

Stanion

Oakley

Great
Oakley

Little
Oakley

Storefield

Geddington

To
Leicester
(BR)

Glendon
East

Geddington

*

Glendon
Lodge

Bridge

Broughton
Park

* Barford East

Glendon
Hall

Scale
1km

Kettering (BR)

Corby Quarries (South)
and Glendon East
Quarries.

Corby Iron/Steelworks Map (1:10000 1974/85 combination). Detail of the Corby Steelworks (bottom), Pen Green Workshops (marked '1') and Gretton Brook shed (marked '2') areas. Strangely, the 1965 BOS Plant development (marked '3') to the right of the map is missing! (© Crown Copyright and Landmark Information Group Ltd 2020 (www.Old-Maps.co.uk Ref. 285815400))

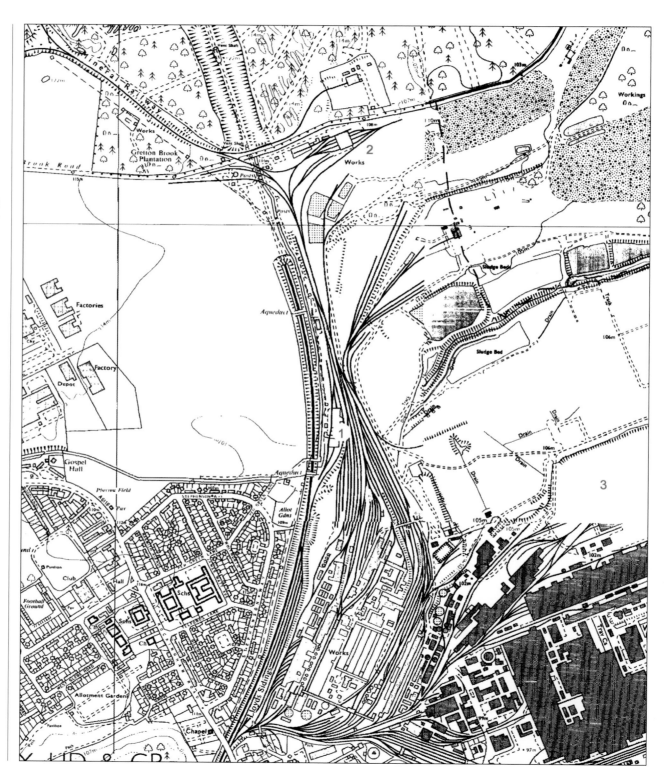

6.5.2 Enter the Class 14s.

In the 1960s, Stewarts & Lloyds (Minerals) experimented with various diesel locomotives including a Yorkshire Engine 'Indus' 0-8-0 locomotive and several variants of the Rolls-Royce 'Sentinel' (0-6-0DH and 6wDH) designs, with the preferred design for a 'squadron' order being the 445hp 6wDH locomotive. However, when S&L learnt of the availability of redundant BR 650hp Class 14 locomotives, trials with two locomotives were undertaken at Buckminster; these proved successful and ultimately twenty-three locomotives were bought from BR.

The December 1968 edition of the *Railway Observer* commented that:

'It has been reported from an unofficial source that nineteen Class 14's from Hull have been sold to an iron and steel works at Corby (presumably Stewarts & Lloyds). Four others have been sold to the same firm for spares.'

The twenty-three Class 14s were bought in two lots, eight for Buckminster/Harlaxton (see above) and fifteen for Corby/Glendon. A Corby Purchase Requisition dated 7 November 1968 specified twelve Class 14s at £3,250 each (i.e. D9510/20/3/32/3/7/42/7/9/ 51/3/4) and three at £1,000 each (D9507/12/6) to cover the Corby/ Glendon requirements. Two further documents relating to the fifteen Corby/Glendon locomotives are illustrated opposite and overleaf; of the fifteen, the twelve priced at £3,250 each were bought as 'runners' with the additional three priced at £1,000 each purchased to make one good locomotive, with

the residual two cannibalised as a source of spares.

The BSC Northern & Tubes Group Board authorised the purchase of the fifteen locomotives on 5 December 1968. The extremely low gross amount paid for the twelve 'runner' locomotives was less than 8 per cent of the as-new out-turn Swindon Works production cost four years earlier. No wonder that BSC was able to calculate the incredibly high 56 per cent return on the capital invested. According to David Hartley (*Industrial Railway Record*, 243): 'The entire Class 14 fleet was purchased for less than the cost of

one 600hp "Steelman"'; certainly, Corby acquired their 15 Class 14s at less cost than the price of one new ex-Swindon, arguably *considerably* less given that the Swindon cost excluded any profit element.

It will be noted that the Corby documentation referred to above made no reference to D9544 which was delivered to Corby with a seized engine and used by BSC as a source of spares. Two possibilities arise here:

- D9512, mentioned above as a Corby purchase, was actually delivered to Buckminster for spares. It maybe that D9544 was the nominated spares

Stewarts & Lloyds internal document.
Justification for the purchase of 15 Class 14 locomotives at Corby and Glendon East Quarries.
(Courtesy Greg Evans)

STEWARTS AND LLOYDS MINERALS LIMITED.

Diesel Locomotives .... £42,000.

An opportunity has arisen to purchase 15 secondhand 650 h.p. Paxman Diesel Locomotives from British Rail, as follows:-

$$12 @ £3,250 = £39,000$$
$$* \ 3 @ £1,000 = £ 3,000$$
$$£42,000$$

* These three will make one good locomotive with the remaining parts being held as spares.

Following trials these locomotives have been found satisfactory and well suited for ironstone haulage in the quarries and will almost complete the transfer to diesel locomotives throughout the Minerals Company. (8 have been purchased previously.) The estimated savings will be £23,700 per annum, giving a return of 56%.

The cost of the diesel locomotives new was about £45,000 each. They were built in 1964 and have had comparatively little service with British Rail.

Brigstock.
19th November, 1968.

BRITISH STEEL CORPORATION

NORTHERN AND TUBES GROUP

TUBES AND PIPES DIVISION

From:	M.J. Shirley, CORBY.	To:	See below
Our ref:	MJS/CB.	Your ref:	

| Subject: | NOTIFICATION OF CAPITAL AUTHORISATION | Date : | 9th. December, 1968 |

The Northern and Tubes Group Board at its meeting on 5th. December 1968 gave final sanction to the following capital schemes submitted on behalf of Stewarts and Lloyds Minerals Ltd.

	Amount £
Fifteen Paxman diesel locomotives	42,000

Sent to:-

J.L. McLaren Esq.	Brigstock
N.T. Kitchin Esq.	Brigstock
J. Glen Esq.	Corby
P. Smith Esq.	Corby

1 0 DEC 1968

donor for Buckminster but was subsequently transposed with D9512 and moved to Corby as a consequence, or,

- Gordon Kobish (*Railways Illustrated*, September 2014) suggests that D9544 was actually given away by BR following the agreed sale of twenty-two other locomotives by S&L.

D9507 and D9516, the other two Class 14s specifically mentioned as spares locomotives in the Corby documentation, both saw service at Corby.

With respect to the newly-arrived Corby Class 14 contingent, E.S. Tonks (*The Ironstone Quarries of the Midlands (Part VI The Corby Area)*) commented that, despite

BSC internal document. Notification for the authorisation of capital expenditure of £42,000. The first arrival at Corby was D9539 which had been booked to run light from Hull to Stewarts & Lloyds, Corby, on 7 October 1968. D9507/16/32/7/44/9/53/4 followed in November 1968, with D9533/42/7/51 arriving in December. D9520/3 moved to Glendon East in December 1968. (Courtesy Greg Evans)

servicing of the locomotives at Hull Dairycoates by BR prior to despatch: 'The BR locomotives were in poor condition when received after their long storage, but when they had been cleaned up and generally refurbished, proved ideal for the work, amply justifying their purchase and upholding the fine record of Swindon.'

As a consequence of this bulk acquisition, steam operation on the Corby mineral system ceased in January 1969. The March 1969 edition of the *Railway Observer* reported: 'Steam power finally succumbed to diesel traction in January, the last steam working being an IRS tour of the line from Gretton Brook to Wakerley Dock on Saturday, 11th January'.

6.5.3 Financial Analysis.

It is worth analysing the finances to illustrate the bargain from which BSC was able to benefit.

During the period 1968-69, the BR Supply Committee appended a document 'BRB Record of Sales over £25,000 made by Supplies Manager' to the monthly meeting minutes. There were frequent entries relating to locomotive sales to scrap merchants. These documents were of use from an financial auditing and transparency point of view but are only of limited use to railway historians due to the fact that entries were generally groupings of locomotives, of varying types, from various origins, and destined for several merchants, becoming fairly meaningless as a consequence. However, the documents were useful in four respects:

1. An entry dated 25 April 1968 was much more specific and included the sale of twenty-nine Class 21 (D61xx) locomotives by competitive tender to two scrap merchants (MacWilliam and Barnes & Bell); the combined sale value was £32,000, with the highest individual tendered price being £1,410. With the 'dry' weight of a Class 21 being 66.75tons, this implies £21.12 per ton.

2. A similar entry for 10 April 1969, included the sale of sixteen Classes 15 (D82xx) and 16 (D84xx) locomotives this time to Cohen and Cox & Danks; the combined sale was £31,000 with fifteen of the sixteen locomotives sold at £1,925. The 'dry' weight of a Class 15 was 66tons, giving a calculated scrap value of £29.17 per ton.

3. Another entry, dated 9 October 1969, registered the 'specially negotiated sale' of seven Class 77 (E2700x) locomotives to the Netherlands State Railways (NS). The total value was £37,750 made up of six locomotives at £5,000, one at £2,750 and spares at £5,000.

4. No sales of locomotives to other UK nationalised companies ever appeared in the Supply Committee appendices. For most locomotive purchases, the sales were for small numbers of locomotives to numerous destinations which would never reach the £25,000 recording threshold. However, the sale of fifteen Class 14s to BSC Corby at £42,000 might have been expected to register.

The fifteen Corby Class 14s were sold in November/December 1968. As scrap these locomotives would have attracted a sale value of approximately £1022 (i.e. 48.4 'dry' tons x £21.12 [see note 1 above]). This figure equates to the actual BSC price paid for three of the locomotives, with the twelve 'runners' at approximately three times the scrap value.

By mid-1969, the scrap value of a Class 14 would have risen to £1411 (i.e. 48.4tons x £29.17 [see note 2]); using the same multiplier used in the previous the theoretical price for a 'runner' would have been £4,200. This latter number represents an interesting aside, given the oft quoted (but officially unsupported) sale figure of £4,000 for Class 14s sold from the Western Region to the NCB North East Area.

For me, the key point here is that the sale values (£42,000 for the fifteen and £3,250 for the 'runners') both grossly understate the true value of the locomotives i.e. the true Economic Value to the Customer (EVC). These locomotives were less than four years old, with a normal expected life of over twenty years, and had considerable residual operating value. In addition, the expense incurred by BR for experiments and modifications to improve the locomotives were ignored. On top of this, the price made absolutely no recognition of how much BSC would have had to pay for new or nearly new 'Steelman' locomotives.

The EM2 electric locomotive E27002 sold to the NS for spares might have expected to yield £2,900 at scrap value (100tons 'dry' weight x £29.17), which it very nearly did, but the price agreed for the six 'runners' was less than twice the scrap value, although it should be remembered that these locomotives were over fifteen years old at the time of sale. They did, however, have an 'enhanced' EVC to the NS given the avoidance of buying new locomotives and that they provided a quick solution to their motive power shortage.

By extension, point number (4) above suggests that sales to other UK nationalised companies were never put out to competitive tender and were subject to Government intervention, with the movement of assets between two nationalised companies being covered by (pre-arranged?) transfer-pricing arrangements. Hence, why we see the lowest sale price as scrap value and the sales value of 'runners' being some multiplier of the scrap value (or 'scrap value plus') rather than a calculated EVC figure. Quite why it was accepted that BR was penalised and BSC benefitted is unclear.

6.5.4 Operations.

On arrival at Corby and Glendon, the fifteen Class 14s were renumbered 24-30/2-8 (with D9544, the spares locomotive, presumably allocated 31 but never carried). At face value the numbers seemed to be allocated in a random manner, although in reality there was some logic applied:

D9539	Delivered 10/68	Received S&L number 30
D9544	Delivered 11/68	Allocated 31 (spares loco)
D9537/49/53	Delivered 11/68	Received 32/33/34 respectively.
D9507/16/32/54	Delivered 11/68	Received 35/36/37/38 respectively.
D9533/42/47/51	Delivered 12/68	Received 26/27/28/29 respectively.
D9520/3	Delivered 12/68	Received 24/25 respectively.

The logic, therefore, was that locomotives were re-numbered in BR number order for each successive batch delivered, starting from 30-38 but then jumping back to 24-29 for the later deliveries.

One of the two original Glendon Class 14s (D9520) was transferred to Corby in May 1970 where it could be better utilised, increasing the Corby fleet to fourteen including spares locomotives. D9549 spent a short period at Glendon East from October 1973, returning to Corby in June 1974 when replaced by a Rolls Royce 'Steelman' locomotive.

In time, all of the operational Class 14s at Corby were painted all-over dark green with the fleet number in white on a square black-painted panel carried on the cab-sides.

In addition to the spares locomotives, the May 1972 edition of the *Railway Observer* stated that 'Two sets of spares had been bought from Cohen's, Kettering, and were taken from D9509/19 by BSC fitters.'

With the closure of the Lincolnshire quarries, the five Class 14s at Buckminster and the three at Harlaxton all gravitated to Corby (in 1972 and 1974 respectively) to join the fourteen already there. By the end of 1974 with a collective fleet of twenty-two locomotives (plus D9523 at Glendon) the availability of spares was largely secured.

Corby locomotives 24/6-30/2-8 were renumbered 45/47-52/64/54-58, in that order, in October 1974. This was triggered by the incidence of several locomotives with duplicated numbers on the Corby system (including D9533 and D9541 [ex-Harlaxton] both numbered 26, and D9542 and D9548 [also ex-Harlaxton] both numbered 27). D9544 was again not included in the new number series given its donor status.

The locomotives formerly at Buckminster were renumbered in a separate block 59-63, out of sequence from 21, 23, 20, 22 and D9512 respectively. Similarly, the former Harlaxton locomotives were renumbered in the 65-67 block from No. 25, No.26 and No.27 respectively.

This renumbering ensured no duplication of numbers in the Class 14 fleet, but it did generate a number of interesting questions:

- D9523 (25) never seems to have been officially allocated the number 46 (which logically it should have) and it certainly never carried it. Why? Glendon independence, perhaps? Or, just forgotten about? Or because, being just one of only two locomotives at Glendon, it was largely irrelevant!
- IRS *Bulletins* Nos.187 and 188 (both April 1975) indicate

that D9553 (ex-34) became 46, although subsequent lists recorded it as 54. Did D9553 ever actually carry the number 46?

- Why did D9549 (33) become 64, rather than the more logical 53? This locomotive had previously worked at Glendon for a short period between October 1973 and June 1974 and may have been re-numbered separate from the original Corby fleet (like the Buckminster and Harlaxton locomotives). So why wasn't the same logic applied to D9520?
- When 33 was renumbered 64 it was positioned *between* the new ex-Buckminster and ex-Harlaxton fleet number ranges. Why? Glendon alphabetically between Buckminster and Harlaxton, perhaps?
- Why was the number 53 totally ignored, given that it was not used by any other locomotive on the Corby minerals system?
- Whilst D9544 was not renumbered, D9512, another spares donor, was renumbered to 63. Why the inconsistency? Lack of wheels on D9544, perhaps?

There may have been reasons for these apparent anomalies, but any rationale has now been lost in the mists of time; my comments above are pure conjecture! Ultimately, however, the inconsistencies or 'errors' never really needed to be corrected!

In 1976, D9538 arrived from BSC Ebbw Vale as a source of spares.

This locomotive retained its Ebbw Vale 160 number and was never re-numbered in the Corby series given its donor role.

D9523 finally joined the Corby contingent in May 1980 after the closure of Glendon East, and indeed the whole Corby minerals operation.

A full list of the 24 locomotives which ultimately ended up at Corby are listed below:

Class 14s at BSC Corby.

S&L No. (to 10/74)	BSC No. (from 10/74)	S&L Plant No.	Ex-BR No.	First Allocation	Comments
24	45	8311/24	D9520	Glendon East	To Corby 05/70
25	–	8311/25	**D9523**	Glendon East	Presumably 46 allocated, although never carried
26	47	8311/26	D9533	Corby	
27	48	8311/27	D9542	Corby	
28	49	8311/28	D9547	Corby	
29	50	8311/29	D9551	Corby	
30	51	8311/30	D9539	Corby	
(31)	–	8311/31	**D9544**	Corby	Presumably 31 allocated, although never carried. Presumably BSC No. never allocated. Source of spares at Corby from outset
32	52	8311/32	D9537	Corby	
33	64	8311/33	D9549	Corby	Why not allocated 53? Classified as 'import'? To Glendon East 10/73; to Corby 06/74
34	54	8311/34	D9553	Corby	IRS Bulletins 187/188 show re-numbering to 46
35	55	8311/35	D9507	Corby	
36	56	8311/36	D9516	Corby	
37	57	8311/37	D9532	Corby	
38	58	8311/38	D9554	Corby	
20	61	8411/20	D9529	Buckminster	To Corby 09/72
21	59	8411/21	D9552	Buckminster	To Corby 06/72
22	62	8411/22	D9515	Buckminster	To Corby 09/72
23	60	8411/23	D9510	Buckminster	To Corby 06/72
–	63	8411/24	D9512	Buckminster	S&L No. never carried. Source of spares at Buckminster from outset To Corby 09/72
No.25	65	8411/25	D9503	Harlaxton	To Corby 07/74
No.26	66	8411/26	D9541	Harlaxton	To Corby 07/74
No.27	67	8411/27	D9548	Harlaxton	To Corby 07/74
	160		D9538	Ebbw Vale	Numbered 160 in Ebbw Vale series. To Corby 04/76 as source of spares.

Notes:

1. D9512(63), D9538 (160) and D9544 never worked at Corby.
2. It is also highly likely that D9503 (65), D9510 (60), D9541 (66) and D9552(59) also never worked at Corby, after their arrival from Buckminster /Harlaxton. If this is true, then only three locomotives from the Buckminster/ Harlaxton group saw further use after cessation of work there i.e. D9515/29/48.
3. D.C. Strickland, in Supplement 3 & 4 (December 1983) to his book *Locomotive Directory* (March 1983) stated:

'A 8441 prefix was added when all locos congregated at Corby …but not carried (TBC)'.

Roger Harris repeated this in his book *The Allocation History of BR Diesels and Electrics, Part Five* (April 2005), stating:

'After the fleet of BSC locos was concentrated at Corby, the location number was changed to 8441, and the plant item numbers re-allocated in the range 45-67. For example: D9520 was originally 8311/24 then became 8441/45, whilst D9512 (originally 8411/24) became 8441/63.'

The revised Plant Nos. indicated by Strickland and Harris also appeared in an article on the Class 14s in the December 2006 edition of *The Railway Magazine* but have never appeared in any IRS publication. Greg Evans and his close BSC contacts are unaware of any Plant No. changes and Adrian Booth from the IRS warns:

'My advice to you is to be very wary of this information … I have received many letters over the years about Corby, and to the best of my recollection I have never once heard anything about this 8441 numbering.' (email, October 2020)

In the Quarries.

D9537 (52), BSC Corby, 8 November 1975.
Prior's Hall quarry. (Adrian Booth)

D9548 (67), BSC Corby, Undated. (Geoffrey Starmer [IRS])

D9507 (55), BSC Corby, 16 November 1975. Oakley Quarry. (Kevin Lane)

D9507 (55), BSC Corby, 16 November 1975.
Oakley Quarry. (Kevin Lane)

D9553 (54), BSC Corby, 15 August 1979. Prior's Hall Quarry. (Geoffrey Starmer [IRS])

Between the Quarries and the Ironworks.

D9537 (52), BSC Corby, 8 November 1975.
(Adrian Booth)

D9537 (52), BSC Corby, 29 September 1977.
(Kevin Lane)

D9549 (64), BSC Corby
(en route to Oakley),
23 August 1979.
(Kevin Lane)

D9549 (64) passing
D9554 (58), BSC Corby,
23 August 1979.
(Kevin Lane)

D9553 (54), BSC Corby Gretton Brook, 10 July 1976. (Tony Skinner)

D9515 (62), BSC Corby, 14 July 1979. Near Gretton Brook. (Transport Treasury [John Tolson])

D9548 (67), BSC Corby, 14 July 1979. Near Gretton Brook. One of the ex-Harlaxton machines. (Transport Treasury [John Tolson])

D9548 (67), BSC Corby, 3 November 1979. (Lewis Bevan)

D9549 (64), BSC Corby, 18 April 1979. After my footplate ride from Harringworth Lodgel quarry to Corby Works. I just wish that I had taken a photograph of the train in the quarry itself. Too excited to get on board the 'Paxman' to worry about things like that, I guess! Full complement of Corby modifications: twin spotlights on nose-end, flashing roof lights and buffer beam lifting lugs, chains and shunting pole clips. (Anthony Sayer)

6.5.5 Locomotive Issues and Modifications.

Many of the issues suffered by BR with the Class 14s were also experienced by BSC. The replacement of aluminium-alloy cylinder heads with cast-iron continued during the 1970s. With respect to the Paxman 'Ventura' engine David Hartley commented, via a letter in the *Industrial Railway Record* (243), that:

'… in this design of engine the alloy head does not sit directly on the engine block, it only rests on the top of the liner, clamping the liner into the block. The fault with the alloy heads was the design of the aluminium-bronze valve seats (four off per head) which were screwed into the cylinder heads. It was these which caused the major cylinder head failures with catastrophic results. Eventually the British Steel Corporation replaced these with cast-iron cylinder heads in 1976. These heads cost £1,000 each at this time but they transformed to locomotive dramatically. Not all locomotives were modified and D9516, at least, is known to have retained alloy heads into preservation.'

Mike Browett, the driver of D9548 (67) at Corby, lists the following issues with respect to the Corby Class 14s:

• Valve seats on the aluminium alloy heads,
• Turbo-charger brackets (broken bolts).
• Split exhaust joints.

The familiar issues! Mike also commented that D9549 (64) carried aluminium alloy heads to the end of operations in early 1980, which begs the question … did D9549 take its alloy heads to Spain when exported in 1981?

Hartley also commented that overheating problems suffered by the Class 14s were identified as being:

'due to a design fault in the cooling system which allowed an air pocket to cause significant flow problems within the system. The problem was overcome by the fitting of a vent valve on the radiator header tank.'

6.5.6 Detail Differences.

Various external modifications were carried out on the BSC Class 14s particularly those which saw use at Corby; details are provided in the table below:

BSC-Operated Class 14s: Detail Differences.

S&L No. (to 10/74)	BSC No. (from 10/74)	S&L Plant No.	Ex-BR No.	Flat Cab Roof Profile	Bonnet-end Headlights		Flashing Cab Roof Lights	Footplate Brackets ('A' End)	Lifting Lugs (Buffer Beam)	Safety Chains (Buffer Beam)	Shunting Pole Clips (Buffer Beam)	Comments
					Large Single	Small Pair						
Buckminster (Bm)												
20		8411/20	D9529	N	Y*	N*	N*	Y*	N*	N*	N*	
21		8411/21	D9552	N	N	N	N	Y*	N	N	N	Sp(subseq)
22		8411/22	D9515	N	Y	N	N	Y	N	N	N	
23		8411/23	D9510	N	Y*	N*	N*	Y*	N*	N*	N*	
–		8411/24	D9512	N	N	N	N	N	N	N	N	Sp(outset), DNW-Bm
Harlaxton (Hx)												
No.25		8411/25	D9503	Y	Y	N	N	Y	N	N	N	
No.26		8411/26	D9541	Y	Y	N	N	Y	N	N	N	
No.27		8411/27	D9548	Y	Y*	N*	N*	Y*	N*	N*	N*	
Glendon East (GE)												
24	–	8311/24	D9520	N	N*	Y*	N*	N*	Y*	Y*	Y*	
25	(46)	8311/25	D9523	N	N	Y	N	N	Y	Y	Y	
Corby (Cb)												
24	45	8311/24	D9520	N	N	Y	Y	N	Y	Y	Y	Ex-GE
26	47	8311/26	D9533	N	N	Y	N	N	Y	Y	Y	Sp(subseq)
27	48	8311/27	D9542	N	N	Y	N	N	Y	Y*	Y	Sp(subseq)
28	49	8311/28	D9547	N	N	Y	Y	N	Y	Y	Y	
29	50	8311/29	D9551	N	N	Y	Y	N	Y	Y*	Y	
30	51	8311/30	D9539	N	N	Y	Y	N	Y	Y	Y	
–	–	8311/31	D9544	N	N	N	N	N	Y	N	N	Sp(outset), DNW-Cb
32	52	8311/32	D9537	N	N	Y	Y	N	Y	Y	Y	
33	64	8311/33	D9549	N	N	Y	Y	N	Y	Y	Y	
34	54	8311/34	D9553	N	N	Y	Y	N	Y	Y	Y	
35	55	8311/35	D9507	N	N	Y	Y	N	Y	Y	Y	
36	56	8311/36	D9516	N	N	Y	N	N	Y	Y	Y	
37	57	8311/37	D9532	N	N	Y	N	N	Y	Y	Y	Sp(subseq)

S&L No. (to 10/74)	BSC No. (from 10/74)	S&L Plant No.	Ex-BR No.	Flat Cab Roof Profile	Bonnet-end Headlights		Flashing Cab Roof Lights	Footplate Brackets ('A' End)	Lifting Lugs (Buffer Beam)	Safety Chains (Buffer Beam)	Shunting Pole Clips (Buffer Beam)	Comments
					Large Single	Small Pair						
38	58	8311/38	D9554	N	N	Y	Y	N	Y	Y	Y	
20	61	8411/20	D9529	N	Y	N	N	Y	Y	Y	Y	Ex-Bm
21	59	8411/21	D9552	N	N	N	N	Y	N	N	N	Ex-Bm, DNW-Cb
22	62	8411/22	D9515	N	Y	N	Y	Y	Y	Y	Y	Ex-Bm
23	60	8411/23	D9510	N	Y	N	N	Y	N	N	N	Ex-Bm, DNW-Cb
–	63	8411/24	D9512	N	N	N	N	N	N	N	N	Ex-Bm, DNW-Cb
No.25	65	8411/25	D9503	Y	Y	N	N	Y	N	N	N	Ex-Hx, DNW-Cb
No.26	66	8411/26	D9541	Y	Y	N	N	Y	N	N	N	Ex-Hx, DNW-Cb
No.27	67	8411/27	D9548	Y	Y	N	Y	Y	Y	Y	Y	Ex-Hx
	160		D9538	N	N	N	N	N	N	N	N	Ex-Ebbw, DNW-Cb

Abbreviations:

Y / N	Yes / No. Green highlighting reinforces "Y" entries, and blue highlighting indicates 'surprising' "N" entries (see Notes below).
Sp(outset)	Used for spares from outset.
Sp(subseq)	Subsequently used for spares in later years.
DNW-Xx	Did not work at specified location.
*	Assumed

Notes:

1. Flat cab roof profile.
   Harlaxton modification to allow passage under the A607 Grantham road.
2. Single (large-diameter) bonnet-end headlights.
   Standard Buckminster/Harlaxton fitment from 1970/71, although they were not fitted to D9512 (spares loco from outset) and D9552 (subsequent spares locomotive at Buckminster).
   No photographic evidence has been found of D9510/29/48 with large single headlights whilst at Buckminster/ Harlaxton, although they were all noted with this modification at Corby. Given Corby favoured the small diameter twin headlights, it is assumed that D9510/29/48 received the single headlights whilst at Buckminster/Harlaxton.
   All locomotives noted with the large headlights at Buckminster and Harlaxton retained this feature throughout their time at Corby.
3. Pair of (small-diameter) bonnet-end headlights.
   Standard Corby fitment, although not fitted to D9544 (spares loco).
4. Flashing cab roof lights.
   Later fitment on remaining operational locomotives at Corby.
   D9515 and D9548 (ex-Buckminster and Harlaxton respectively) were fitted during their time at Corby, although strangely D9529 was not despite being operational at Corby until the end.
   Original Corby locomotives D9516/32/3/42, plus spares loco D9544, were not fitted with roof lights. D9516 is a surprising omission given its rebuilding from a spares locomotive at purchase to a fully operational locomotive, surviving until the end of operations at Corby. D9532/3/42 were early traffic casualties and missed out on receiving this modification as a consequence.
5. Footplate Brackets ('A' end).
   Standard Buckminster/Harlaxton fitment although the purpose of these brackets is unknown. Only D9512, the spares donor at Buckminster, was not fitted with this modification.

6. Buffer-Beam Lifting Lugs.
   Standard fitment for all of the original Corby Class 14s. Also fitted to D9515/29/48 on arrival from Lincolnshire. The other Buckminster/Harlaxton locomotives were never fitted with lugs supporting my theory that D9503/10/41/52 (plus spares loco D9512) never worked at Corby. Somewhat strangely, the Corby spares locomotive, D9544, received lugs, the only modification received by this machine.

7. Buffer-Beam Chains.
   Another standard Corby feature to enable these locos to operate plate-laying trains. The mess van was always positioned next to the loco, and, as a safety measure, extra chain couplings were deployed to prevent runaways. Although photographic evidence has not been found for D9542/51 carrying chains, it is assumed that they were fitted.
   Photographic evidence indicates that D9523 at Glendon was fitted with brackets for the chains to be attached, but not the actual chains.
   As with the lifting lugs, ex-Lincolnshire D9515/29/48 were fitted with chains on arrival at Corby, but D9503/10/2/41/52 were not.

8. Shunting-pole clips.
   Standard Corby fitment. Two clips were attached to the upper part of the buffer beam to carry shunter's coupling poles. Once again, of the ex-Buckminster/Harlaxton contingent, D9515/29/48 were the only recipients. Whilst at Buckminster/ Harlaxton, shunting poles were rested across the buffers shanks and drawhook.

9. Lamp-Irons.
   Given their Hull origins, all of the BSC Class 14s (with the obvious exception of D9538) would have been expected to carry the BR-style forward-facing lamp irons. In fact, D9529, at least, retained its WR-style sideways-facing lamp-irons both at Hull and in industry. As far as is known the lamp-irons were never used at the various BSC sites.

D9547 (49), D9516 (56) and D9554 (58, with accident damage to cab), BSC Corby, 20 September 1977. Gretton Brook shed. (Lewis Bevan)

D9520(45), BSC Corby, 3 November 1979. Gretton Brook shed. Note the removal of the exhaust cowling, exposing the slightly off-centre exhaust pipe beneath. (Lewis Bevan)

D9515 (62), BSC Corby, 12 June 1978. Outside Pen Green Workshops. Main route from the northern quarries to Corby Steelworks on embankment. (Martin Shill [IRS])

6.5.7 Locomotive Crew Opinions.
The following is an extract from a letter received from Greg Evans who has spent many years researching Northamptonshire ironstone quarrying:

'I can recall the loco crews at Gretton Brook telling me the Class 14s were much preferred in the quarries over the 'Steelman' locos. The RR locos were prone to derailment with their shorter wheelbase. I was told that the 'Steelman' cabs were better though. The Class 14s were much better all-round 'pullers', when compared with the 'Steelman'; the Class 14 crews got more tonnage bonus because of this. I have heard it said that the Class 14s could be rough-riding - that said, some of the minerals tracks left a lot to be desired!

'As time went on spares from Paxman became ever more difficult to obtain - hence the engine swapping, etc, at Gretton Brook.'

David Hartley comments(*Industrial Railway Record*, 243):

'The 'Steelman' locomotives were not as successful as was hoped and the four Corby examples did not perform as required; in particular having disc brakes as opposed to wheel tread brakes and suffering with adhesion issues on poor rail conditions. For a locomotive that was not designed for the work at Corby, the Class 14s turned out to be exceptional locomotives, if only for the fact that they used half the quantity of fuel compared to a 'Steelman'.'

6.5.8 Class 14 Fleet Status 1977-80.
As already mentioned, the large size of Gretton Brook shed enabled all locomotives to be kept inside, including those between duties as well as those sidelined for spares recovery.

Corby spares locomotive, D9544, was dumped outside following wheelset 'recovery' by August 1970.

The next tranche of 'hopeless-case' Class 14s to be moved outside were all locomotives transferred to Corby from other sites over the previous five years; a Corby visit report dated 29 December 1977 in IRS *Bulletin* No.230 (March 1978) recorded that 'Outside Gretton Brook shed, OOU, were 160, 63 ... 59, 65 and D9544'. The editor commented that 'this is a change as only the last [D9544] has been outside up to now'. D9512 (63, Buckminster spares loco) and D9552 (59) had previously been at Buckminster, D9503 at Harlaxton, and D9538 (160) at Ebbw Vale.

These were the last locomotives moved out of Gretton Brook shed before the mass exodus of December 1980. However, over the years locomotives in the shed were progressively cannibalised to keep the remaining fleet in operation. Three IRS *Bulletin* reports illustrate the situation during the final two years of Corby Minerals operations:

Gretton Brook, 15/07/78:

BR Nos.	BSC Nos. (respectively)	Status
D9507/15/29/37/48/9	55/62/61/52/67/64	Useable.
D9520/51	45/50	Useable (Repair Bay).
D9539/42/7/53	51/48/49/54	Stopped awaiting repairs.
D9510/6/32/3/41/54	60/56/57/47/66/58	Supplying parts for useable locos.
D9503/12/38/44/52	65/63/160/D9544/59	Dumped outside shed, OOU.
D9532	57	Not listed.

Gretton Brook, 03/08/79:

BR Nos.	BSC Nos. (respectively)	Status
D9515/6/37/9/48/9/53/4	62/56/52/51/67/64/54/58	Working.
D9507/20/9/51	55/45/61/50	Other workable locos.
D9510/32/3/41/2/7	60/57/47/66/48/49	Stored in shed (dismantled).
D9503/12/38/44/52	65/63/160/D9544/59	Dumped outside shed, OOU.

Gretton Brook, 29/12/79:

BR Nos.	BSC Nos. (respectively)	Status
D9515/6/29/37/48/9/51/3/4	62/56/61/52/67/64/50/54/58	Workable in shed.
D9507/39	55/51.	Repair Bay.
D9510/32/3/41/2/7	60/57/47/66/48/49	OOU in shed.
D9503/12/38/44/52	65/63/160/D9544/59	Dumped outside shed, OOU.
D9520	45	Not listed.

Notes:

1. The locomotive *status* information provided above was in all probability defined by the IRS correspondents concerned rather than anything officially provided by BSC. Hence the differing definitions and how locomotives were assigned. However, the reports certainly give a valuable insight into general condition of the fleet.
2. As already mentioned, it is believed that D9503 (65), D9510 (60), D9541 (66) and D9552 (59) never worked at Corby following arrival from Buckminster and Harlaxton. D9512 (63) and D9538 (160), acquired as spares locomotives from BR and BSC Ebbw Vales, certainly did not.
3. D9532/3/42/7 were relatively early casualties from the operational fleet.
4. D9507 and D9516, bought as spares locomotives, were ultimately rebuilt and entered traffic.

6.5.9 Re-engining Proposal.

During the late 1970s BSC were in negotiation with Hunslet Engine Co. regarding the fitment of Rolls Royce DV8T engines similar to the engines deployed in the 'Steelman' locomotives and, indeed, in two of the Clayton Class 17s (D8586/7). Following a visit to Corby on 15 July 1978, John Scholes reported that:

'Two of the D95xx are to be re-engined next year and four more the year after'. (IRS *Bulletin* No.250)

Howard Johnston (*Rail Enthusiast*, April 1982) went a stage further:

'Plans were formulated to re-engine them with Rolls-Royce power units. Three engines were ordered, and one was in fact delivered to Corby.'

Rail Enthusiast (August 1982) clarified the point:

'New Rolls Royce DV8TCE power units might have been fitted, and wheelsets and transmissions overhauled, on the basis of three per year from 1978.

'The work might have gone to loco builders Thomas Hill of Rotherham, who took a gamble and ordered three engines for the 1978 batch. Refusal of BSC management to approve the work, or of Rolls-Royce to cancel the engines, brought headaches. Two units eventually went to 'Steelman' locos built for ICI Billingham … while the third is still on the shop floor, possibly for 'Steelman' 10277 recovered for rebuilding from BSC Scunthorpe.'

Johnston, this time in his book *Preserved BR Diesel and Electric Locomotives*, 1992, suggested that conversion of the locomotives would additionally involve 'most controversial of all, altering the body outline more to the Hunslet shape'.

The impending closure of Corby Iron and Steelmaking in 1980 resulted in the abandonment of the project.

6.5.10 Iron/Steelmaking Closure and Post-Minerals Locomotive Usage.

Following the closure of the Corby Minerals operation in early-1980, the disposal of locomotives was a fairly long drawn out affair, due to a number of factors:

(a) short-term locomotive demands, i.e. for:
  • site clearance and demolition work (quarry track-lifting),
  • short-term Tube Works requirements.
(b) the general market for the sale of complete locomotives at this time being in the doldrums.

Site-Clearance and Demolition Work.

Track lifting of the Minerals lines commenced in April 1980. The IRS *Bulletin* No.291 (August 1980) reported on the 'Farewell to Corby' rail-tour which ran on 17 May 1980:

'Track lifting commenced immediately the strike was over, but Mr. M.J.C. Jones (Minerals Operations Manager) had arranged for a through route to be available to Wakerley terminus … With 52 at the front and 61 at the rear, we went off [from Gretton Brook], noting en route that nearly all sidings and branches to quarries (Brookfield Cottage, Park Lodge, Harringworth Lodge … and Shotley) had been taken up … At present four crews are being kept on for track-lifting, after which a programme of restoration will begin. By August rail traffic will probably cease.'

Based on a visit on 9 September 1980, IRS *Bulletin* No.297 (December 1980) reported: 'Track-lifting in the quarries is almost complete …'; *Bulletin* 321 (December 1981) (based on a visit 15 August) further reported 'Most of the former quarries have been landscaped … Track from Gretton Brook extends as far as Brookfield Plantation.'

Class 14s were heavily involved in demolition work with D9537 (52) being the major participant, supported by at least D9523 and D9549 at various times.

Tube Works Operations.

Following the cessation of iron and steel making at Corby, feedstock for the Tube Works arrived in the form of hot-rolled coil from Lackenby Coil Plate Mill (Teesside). Trains arrived in 20-wagon rakes of 102-tonne BAA wagons with a train payload of up to 1,400 tonnes. Initially these trains were delivered to the BR/BSC Corby South Exchange Sidings and then hauled by BSC motive power to the Tube Works for discharge.

From February 1981 and following a major track upgrade between the Exchange Sidings and the Tube Works, BR motive power (invariably pairs of Class 37s) hauled the trains from Lackenby directly into the Tube Works, obviating any need for BSC locomotives.

In the intervening period between about May 1980 and February 1981, however, Tube Works locomotives were used for the transfer work. Greg Evans comments:

'Once stocks of Corby-produced ingots had been used up, Corby Tube Works commenced running on hot-rolled coil from elsewhere – trains from Lackenby became the mainstay. The normal works locos (EEV/GECT six-wheelers) had a job stopping the BAA wagons on the journey from Corby South Exchange Sidings into the Tube Works Slitting Plant, so three Class 14s were picked to do this job. Some wag thought even these locos would have trouble braking the BAAs loaded with Lackenby coils so D9510 (60) was converted to a 'brake-tender'. It had an ingot dropped-in in place of the engine and was to be used coupled to loco 50. I am told it was used as such for two days only.'

D9520/49/51 were the three selected 'runner' locomotives, supported by D9510 as the brake-tender. Trains were to be operated on the basis of two locomotives on the front (runner plus brake-tender) and one on the rear. At face value this looks like an excessive provision of power; however, horse power wasn't the issue, braking power most certainly was! It should be noted that the Class 14s were (at best) vacuum-braked fitted or (more likely) not fitted with any operational train braking capability at all. The BAA wagons were (by definition) air-braked only and, therefore, totally incompatible with the Class 14s from a braking point of view. The trains were effectively unfitted and completely reliant on locomotive braking.

D9551 (50, operational) and D9510 (60, prospective brake-tender) were transferred to the Tube Works fleet in July 1980. The IRS *Bulletin* No.292 (October 1980) recorded: 'If the experiment is a success another pair may be similarly treated'. The selection of D9510 was on the basis of good wheelsets (i.e. thick tyres). D9520/49 followed in September 1980.

According to Greg Evans 'The Class 14s did not last long on this job, however, as just before BR commenced running directly into the works, the EEV/GECT fleet had taken over again.'

Dates for Class 14 locomotives allocated to the Tube Works fleet are as follows:

Loco. No.	Joined Tube Works fleet	Comments
D9510 (60)	10/07/80	Brake-tender project (subsequently abandoned). Noted at Steelworks Disposal Site on 21/01/81.
D9520 (45)	xx/09/80	Runner. Noted on Tube Works Loco Shed on 21/01/81.
D9549 (64)	xx/09/80	Runner. Noted on Tube Works Loco Shed on 21/01/81. Noted at Steelworks Disposal Site on 09/05/81.
D9551 (50)	xx/07/80	Runner. Noted working at Tube Works on 21/01/81. Noted at Steelworks Disposal Site on 09/05/81.

Other Class 14s were noted carrying out duties on Corby Works from time to time, as follows:

Loco. No.	Dates	Work undertaken
D9515 (62)	08/05/80	'Shunting steel bar stock'. (BRD3)
	27/05/80	Shunting work. (EBay photo)
D9529 (61)	07/80	Working in steelworks (solo), based at Gretton Brook. (IRS292)
	10/80-12/80	
D9537 (52)	09/80-10/80 (at least)	Site-clearance work (North Bank); shunting redundant wagons for disposal. Working ballast trains, based at Gretton Brook (after completion of demolition work).
D9549 (64)	13/05/80	Ballast train duties (see photograph page 239).
	07/80	Working in steelworks (solo), based at Gretton Brook (IRS292); then to Tube Works (see above).

Railtour Finale.

D9529 (61), Wakerley (IRS Ironstone Special), 17 May 1980. (Transport Treasury [John Tolson])

D9537(52) and D9529 (61), Wakerley (IRS Ironstone special), 17 May 1980. (Transport Treasury [John Tolson])

After the Ore.

D9549 (64), BSC Corby, 13 May 1980. D9549 moving towards the South Exchange sidings with three Tarmac wagons of ballast, presumably as part of track strengthening to accommodate the heavy steel coil trains from Teesside. (Jim Wade [IRS])

D9551 (50), BSC Corby, 24 October 1980. The new (albeit temporary) order. Redundant blast furnaces on the sky-line. Hot-rolled coil feedstock for tube-making now being brought in from Lackenby Coil Plate Mill (Teesside) using 102t gross air-braked BAA coil-carriers. D9551 provides rear-end brake power for the transit between the South Exchange Sidings and the Tube Works Slitting Bay. (Jim Wade [IRS])

6.5.11 Disposal.

Disposal details of the twenty-four BSC Class 14s which had ultimately all congregated at Corby are given below:

Scrapped at Gretton Brook (shed yard)	D9503 / 44 / 52	(3)
Scrapped at Corby Steelworks Disposal Site	D9507 / 10 / 2 / 32 / 3 / 8 / 41 / 2 / 7 / 54	(10)
Exported to Spain (via Hunslet, Leeds)	D9515 / 48 / 9	(3)
Preserved	D9516 / 20 / 3 / 9 / 37 / 9 / 51 / 3	(8) (24)

Gretton Brook Shed Yard.
Immediately following closure of the Minerals operation in January 1980 locomotives were kept inside Gretton Brook shed, except, of course, for the group of five long-term 'demic' Class 14s, and the four which migrated to the Tube Works in the Summer 1980.

Three of the derelict Class 14s outside Gretton Brook shed were cut-up on site in September 1980 (i.e. D9503 (65), D9544 and D9552 (59)).

On 29 December 1980 there was a mass exodus of sixteen Class 14s from Gretton Brook shed to the Steelworks Disposal Point (see later).

D9537 (52), apparently the favourite of the Minerals fleet, was kept back at Gretton Brook for a short while to perform any remaining shunting duties such as positioning wagons for scrap, etc.; it was moved to Pen Green shops in August 1981 and was last used on 27 October 1982 prior to being sold into preservation.

Gretton Brook shed itself was sold in September 1982 to Corby Freight & Storage Ltd (a subsidiary of Knights of Old Ltd).

D9512(63), D9552(59) and D9503(65), BSC Corby, 22 October 1974. Yard to the east of Gretton Brook shed. (Alistair Ness)

D9512 (63), BSC Corby, 18 April 1979. Gretton Brook shed yard. (Anthony Sayer)

**D9538 (160), BSC
Corby, 18 April 1979.**
Gretton Brook shed yard.
(Anthony Sayer)

**Partially dismantled
D9538(160) and D9512
(63), BSC Corby,
17 May 1980.** (Transport
Treasury [John Tolson])

BSC Steelworks Disposal Site, Corby
On 29 December 1980, sixteen Class 14s from Gretton Brook shed were transferred to the Ingot Handing Plant (Soaking Pits and Stripping Bay lines) of the No.1 Strip Mill; this was used as a 'concentration point' for surplus Minerals and Steel Plant locomotives ahead of final disposal. Between 19 September and 17 November 1981 the locomotives were moved from inside storage at the No.1 Strip Mill to the outside yard immediately to the south-west

Two more 'demics', D9544 and D9503 (65), BSC Corby, 17 May 1980. (Transport Treasury [John Tolson])

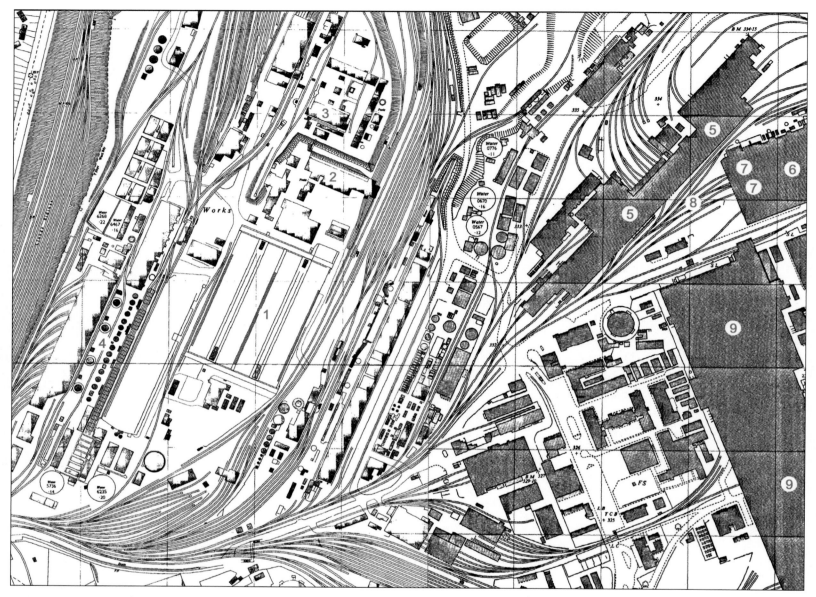

Corby Steelworks Map (1:2500 1963/64).

1. Ore Beds.
2. Ore Crusher.
3. Sinter Plant.
4. Blast Furnaces (x4).
5. Bessemer Plant (closed 1965 and superseded by the BOS Plant (just off map to the north-east)).
6. No.1 Strip Mill.
7. Ingot Handing Plant (Soaking Pits and Stripping Bay lines) (where the Class 14s were stored between end-December 1980 and circa October 1981).
8. Outside Area (where Class 14s were stored from circa October 1981 until finally scrapped or sold for export/ preservation (progressively up to February 1983).
9. Tube Works.

of the Strip Mill, adjacent to the Old Bessemer Plant, to allow the demolition of the Strip Mill to commence. This may have occurred on 9 October 1981 when 'Steelman' 20 (RR10273) was noted 'shunting locos around'. (IRS *Bulletin* 325)

It is important to note that many publications record the storage area for the Class 14s during the 1981/82 period as the Old Bessemer Plant but this was not the case, although the Bessemer Plant did form the backdrop to many of the photographs taken of the locomotives dumped in the outside storage area. A more accurate generic description was the 'Steelworks Disposal Site', or, more specifically, the No.1 Strip Mill area.

Disposals in detail:

BSC No.	S&L Plant No.	Ex-BR No.	Disposal Details
45	8311/24	D9520	Preserved: to NYMR 16/03/81 (believed direct ex-Tube Works; by rail)
–	8311/25	D9523	Preserved: to GCR 17/10/81 (ex-Steelworks Disposal Site)
47	8311/26	D9533	Scrapped: Corby Steelworks Disposal Site 09/82
48	8311/27	D9542	Scrapped: Corby Steelworks Disposal Site 08/82
49	8311/28	D9547	Scrapped: Corby Steelworks Disposal Site 08/82
50	8311/29	D9551	Preserved: to WSR 05/06/81 (ex-Steelworks Disposal Site)
51	8311/30	D9539	Preserved: to GWR 23/02/83 (ex-Steelworks Disposal Site)
–	8311/31	D9544	Scrapped: Corby (Gretton Brook) 09/80 (by 24/09/80)
52	8311/32	D9537	Preserved: to GWR 23/11/82 (ex-Pen Green Workshops)
54	8311/34	D9553	Preserved: to GWR 23/02/83 (ex-Steelworks Disposal Site)
55	8311/35	D9507	Scrapped: Corby Steelworks Disposal Site 09/82
56	8311/36	D9516	Preserved: to GCR 17/10/81 (ex-Steelworks Disposal Site)
57	8311/37	D9532	Scrapped: Corby Steelworks Disposal Site 02/82
58	8311/38	D9554	Scrapped: Corby Steelworks Disposal Site 08/82
59	8411/21	D9552	Scrapped: Corby (Gretton Brook) 09/80 (by 24/09/80)
60	8411/23	D9510	Scrapped: Corby Steelworks Disposal Site 08/82
61	8411/20	D9529	Preserved: to NYMR 16/03/81 (ex-Steelworks Disposal Site; by rail)
62	8411/22	D9515	To Hunslet, Leeds xx/12/81 (ex-Steelworks Disposal Site)
63	8411/24	D9512	Scrapped: Corby Steelworks Disposal Site circa 02/82
64	8311/33	D9549	To Hunslet, Leeds 14/11/81 (ex-Steelworks Disposal Site)
65	8411/25	D9503	Scrapped: Corby (Gretton Brook) 09/80 (by 24/09/80)
66	8411/26	D9541	Scrapped: Corby Steelworks Disposal Site 08/82
67	8411/27	D9548	To Hunslet, Leeds 19/11/81 (ex-Steelworks Disposal Site)
160	–	D9538	Scrapped: Corby Steelworks Disposal Site 09/82

D9541 (66), BSC Corby (No.1 Strip Mill), 19 September 1981. A case of what might have been! The locomotive on the left is Rolls-Royce 'Steelman' 445hp 6wDH '20' (Works No.10273) which arrived new at Corby in December 1968. It was trialled successfully on the ore trains from the local quarries and looked to be the successor to Corby's steam fleet; however, the sudden availability of the (very cheap) BR Class 14s soon put paid to any further 445hp locomotives from Rolls-Royce. '20' spent its BSC 11-year career working on the Corby and Glendon East systems before being retired to the Corby Works Disposal Site for store in December 1980. '20 'survived to see another day, however, being sent to work at Bardon Hill Quarries, Coalville, in September 1982, after a short period of re-fettling at Thomas Hill (Rotherham) Ltd at Kilnhurst. D9541, on the other hand, was scrapped in August 1982, so, ultimately, '20' had the last laugh! One other fact of interest is that the Rolls Royce engine in '20', the DV8N model, was very similar to the power units used in Clayton Class 17 Nos. D8586 and D8587 i.e. engines which might have been the substitute for the Paxman 6ZHXL engines in the next 100 Type 1s after D8616, had it been developed and tested early enough. Instead D8617-D8716 morphed into English Electric-built D8128-99 and D8300-27 (please see my Clayton offering of 2021). (Douglas Johnson)

D9523, BSC Corby (No.1 Strip Mill), 19 September 1981. With what looks like D9538 (160) behind. D9523 escaped to the Great Central Railway at Loughborough on 17 October 1981. (M. Liston)

General view of the Corby Steelworks Disposal Site (in front of No.1 Strip Mill and adjacent to the old Bessemer Plant [left]), 17 November 1981. (Martin Shill [IRS])

D9515 (62) and D9548 (67), BSC Corby Steelworks Disposal Site, 17 November 1981. D9542 (48) and D9533 (47) lurk on the left. (Martin Shill [IRS])

D9515 (62) and D9548 (67), BSC Corby Steelworks Disposal Site, 17 November 1981. D9548 being prepared for movement away from Corby to Hunslet, Leeds. (Martin Shill [IRS])

D9515 (62) and D9548 (67), BSC Corby Steelworks Disposal Site, 17 November 1981. D9515 pushing D9548 onto a low-loader for despatch to Hunslet, Leeds. (Martin Shill [IRS])

D9539 (51), D9553 (54), D9547 (49) and YE2894 (30) on the left track, and D9541 (66), D9542 (48), BSC Corby Steelworks Disposal Site, 17 November 1981. The old Bessemer Plant provides the backdrop. (Martin Shill [IRS])

D9541 (66), D9542 (48) and D9533 (47), plus D9512 (63) out of view behind 'Steelman' 20, BSC Corby Steelworks Disposal Site, 17 November 1981.
(Martin Shill [IRS])

D9507 (55), D9538 (160) and D9532 (57), BSC Corby Steelworks Disposal Site, 17 November 1981. D9554 (58) on the extreme right.
(Martin Shill [IRS])

D9533 (47), D9542(48) and D9541(66), BSC Corby Steelworks Disposal Site, 23 February 1982. (MasonPhenix19 Collection)

D9541 (66), D9542 (48) and D9533 (47), BSC Corby Steelworks Disposal Site, 21 May 1982. Note the extent of demolition of the No.1 Strip Mill building (gable-end and pipework) since the November 1981 photographs; this explains the early scrapping of D9512 (63) and D9532 (57), in February 1982, these two being located closest to the Strip Mill building. (Tom Dovey [IRS])

D9507(55) and D9538(160), with D9533(47), BSC Corby Steelworks Disposal Site, 25 August 1982. Total carnage! Apart from locomotive destruction, the north-eastern end of the Bessemer Plant building has now been completely destroyed. Compare with photograph on page 250. (Eric Tonks [IRS])

'Demics' in Detail (Sources: Eric Tonks, IRS *Bulletins* and Archives).
Gretton Brook Loco Shed:

25/09/73	D9512/44 (dismantled; outside shed)
07/10/76	D9544 (dismantled; outside shed)
	D9510/6/52 (56/9/60) (dismantled, inside shed)
30/04/77	D9512/38/44 (63, 160, D9544)
29/12/77	D9503/12/38/44/52 (59/63/5, 160, D9544) (outside shed)
04/02/78	D9503/12/38/44/52 (59/63/5, 160, D9544) (outside shed)
06/04/78	D9503/12/38/44/52 (59/63/5, 160, D9544)
15/07/78	D9503/12/38/44/52 (59/63/5, 160, D9544) (outside shed)
	D9510/6/33/41/54 (47/56/8/60/6) (supplying parts for useable locomotives), plus possibly D9532 (57)
03/08/79	Working: D9515/6/37/9/48/8/53/4 (51/2/4/6/8/62/4/7)
	Workable: D9507/29/51 (50/5/61)
	Stored in shed, dsm: D9510/32/3/41/2/7 (47/8/9/57/60/6)
	Dumped behind shed: D9503/12/38/44/52 (59, 63/5, 160, D9544)

29/12/79	Repair Bay: D9507/39 (51/5)
	Workable in shed: D9515/6/29/37/48/9/51/3/5 (50/2/4/6/8/61/2/4/7)
	OOU in shed: D9510/32/3/41/2/7 ((47/8/9/57/60/6)
	Dumped behind shed: D9503/12/38/44/52 (59/63/5, 160, D9544)

Gretton Brook (after cessation of ironstone working):

16/04/80	In shed: D9507/10/5/6/32/3/7/9/41/2/7/9/51/3/4 (47-52/4-8/60/2/6/7), plus D9520/9/49 (45/61/4) out working.
16/08/80	Dumped behind shed: D9503/12/38/44/52 (59, 63/5, 160, D9544)
09/09/80	'A scrap gang was due to arrive that day to begin cutting up the derelicts at the back of the shed.' (IRS297)
24/09/80	'Eric Tonks.....found that 59 (*D9552*), 65 (*D9503*) and D9544 had been scrapped.' (IRS297)
26/11/80	In shed: D9507/15/6/23/9/32/3/7/9/41/2/7/8/53/4 (47-9/51/2/4-8/61/2/6/7, D9523)
	Outside shed: D9512/38 (63, 160)
	Not listed (at Tube Works): D9510/20/49/51 (45/50/60/4)

Corby Steelworks Disposal Site (No.1 Strip Mill):

29/12/80	Inside Ingot De-scaling Plant: D9507/12/5/6/23/9/32/3/8/9/41/2/7/8/53/4 (47-9/51/4-8/61-3/6/7, 160, D9523)
	Tube Works: D9510/20/49/51 (45/50/60/4)
	Gretton Brook (in shed): D9537 (52)
21/01/81	Near Bessemer Plant (inside): D9507/12/5/6/23/9/32/3/8/9/41/2/7/8/53/4 (47-9/51/4-8/61-3/6/7, 160, D9523)
	Near Bessemer Plant (outside): D9510 (60)
	Outside Tube Works shed: D9520/49 (45/64)
	Tube Works (working): D9551 (50)
	Gretton Brook (in shed): D9537 (52)
09/05/81	Bessemer Plant (outside): D9510/6 ((56/60)
	Bessemer Plant (inside): D9507/12/5/23/32/3/8/9/41/2/7-9/51/3/4 (47-51/4/5/7/8/62-4/6/7, 160, D9523)
	Not listed: D9537 (52) at GB, D9520/9 (45/61) to preservation.
01/08/81	Near Bessemer Plant: D9507/10/2/5/6/23/32/3/7/8/9/41/2/7-9/53/4 (47-9/51/4-8/60/2-4/6/7, 160, D9523)
	Not listed: D9551 (50) to preservation.
27/08/81	Ingot De-scaling Plant: D9507/10/2/5/6/23/32/3/8/9/41/2/7-9/53/4 (47-9/51/4-8/60/2-4/6/7, 160, D9523)
	Gretton Brook: D9537 (52)

19/09/81	Bessemer Plant (inside): D9507/12/5/23/32/3/8/9/41/2/7-9/53/4 (47-9/51/4/5/7/8/62-4/6/7, 160, D9523)
	Bessemer Plant (outside): D9510/6 (56/60)
	Pen Green Workshops: D9537 (52)
09/10/81	'At the former Ingot Descaling Plant.....20 (RR10273) was shunting locos around.' (IRS325)
17/11/81	Disposal Point (outside): D9507/12/5/32/3/8/9/41/2/7/8/53/4 (47-9/51/4/5/7/8/60/2/3/6/7, 160), plus
	D9548 (67) being loaded-up for movement to Hunslet, Leeds.
	Not listed: D9549 (64) to Hunslet, D9516 (56) and D9523 to preservation
23/01/82	Bessemer Plant (all in the open awaiting disposal): D9507/10/2/32/3/8/9/41/2/7/53/4
	Not listed: D9515/48 to Hunslet,

Locos in order recorded by Eric Tonks:

49 (D9547)	Minus parts of engine & some bodywork	(nearest Strip Mill)
54 (D9553)	Complete	
51 (D9539)	Complete	
…..		
66 (D9541)	Minus parts of engine	
48 (D9542)	Minus parts of engine	
47 (D9533)	Minus parts of engine	
63 (D9512)	Minus parts of engine	(nearest Strip Mill)
…..		
57 (D9532)	Minus engine	(nearest Strip Mill)
160 (D9538)	Minus parts of engine & some bodywork	
55 (D9507)	Minus parts of engine & some bodywork	
…..		
60 (D9510)	Minus engine	
…..		
58 (D9554)	Minus engine	

12/04/82	Bessemer Plant: D9507/10/33/8/9/41/ 2/7/53/4 (47-9/51/4/5/8/60/6, 160)
	Not listed: D9537 (52) (Pen Green Workshops?), D9512/32 (57/63) (cut-up).
21/04/82	Steelworks Disposal Site (outside): D9507/10/33/8/9/41/ 2/7/53/4 (47-9/51/4/5/8/60/6, 160
	Pen Green Crane Depot: D9537 (52)
	Disposal Site locomotives in order recorded by Tom Dovey:
	Line 1 (immediately adjacent to the Bessemer Plant): 51, 54, 49, plus other industrials.
	Line 2: 66, 48, 47.
	Line 3: one industrial ('Steelman' 20).
	Lines 4 & 5: mix of industrials, plus 55, 60, 160, 58.

19/05/82	Old Bessemer Plant (all in the open awaiting disposal): D9507/10/33/8/9/41/2/7/53/4 (47-9/51/4/5/8/60/6, 160)
	Not listed: D9537 (52) (Pen Green Workshops?)
08/06/82	Outside Ingot Plant: D9507/10/33/8/9/41/2/7/53/4 (47-9/51/4/5/8/60/6, 160)
25/08/82	Bessemer Plant: D9507/33/8/9/53 (47/51/4/5, 160)

'The rest of the stock at the Bessemer Plant was being cut up by Shanks & McEwan as soon as the engines have been removed for resale by a local man. Locos 51 and 54 have been set aside for possible resale, and 52 and 32 remain at Pen Green shops. Scrapping started at the beginning of August and few, if any, will remain at the end of the month.' (Eric Tonks/IRS337)

Eric Tonks' notebook states: 'David Hartley [BSC fitter] is stripping the engines out, then Shanks & McEwan cut them up'.

Not listed: D9510/41/2/7/54 (48/9/58/60/6) (cut-up)

20/11/82	'51/4 alongside the remains of the former Bessemer Plant, looking a bit out of place amongst all the scrap.' (IRS346)

Not listed: D9507/33/8 (47/55, 160) (cut-up)

10/03/83	'With the departure of these two locomotives (D9539 [51] and D9553 [54]).....there are now no locos left at the old Bessemer Plant store.' (IRS Archive)

Notes:
1. BSC Nos. are listed in numerical order and **DO NOT** equate with the *order* of the BR numbers.
2. References to Bessemer Plant are incorrect as already explained but are quoted here as they were recorded as such in notebooks or documents.
3. D9512 (63) and D9532 (57) were cut-up around February 1982. Eric Tonks reported that '63 (D9512) … has been cut up as it was in the way of the demolition of a nearby building.' The same reason probably applied of D9532.
4. At least three of the four locomotives which had worked at the Tube Works were transferred to the Steelworks Disposal Site (D9510/49/51); the fourth, D9520, is believed to have been despatched for preservation direct from the Tube Works shed.

6.6 BSC Ebbw Vale.

	Arrived	Departed
D9538	22/02/71 (from BR Swindon Works)	xx/04/76 (to BSC Corby (for spares)

The fully-integrated steel works at Ebbw Vale in Monmouthshire (now Gwent) was nationalised in 1967 to become part of the British Steel Corporation; after various early re-organisations Ebbw Vale became part of the BSC Strip Mills Division (Tinplate). BSC's subsequent rationalisation strategy centred around concentration on large-scale iron and steelmaking facilities using high-grade imported iron-ore. In South Wales, Port Talbot and Llanwern (Newport) became the two key steelmaking sites and the small less-efficient facilities were closed. For Ebbw Vale this meant the closure of the blast furnaces and converter shop in July 1975, and concentration on the production of specialist tinplate products.

It will be recalled that Class 14s were used to bank Newport-Ebbw Vale iron-ore trains from Aberbeeg up the valley to the steelworks during the late-1960s. The BR Class 14s disappeared in 1968, only for one to re-appear on 22 February 1971, now owned by the British

D9538 (160), BSC Ebbw Vale, 25 April 1975. Vacuum brake pipe missing. Out of use.
(Pete Wilcox)

Steel Corporation (after a short period in Essex at Shell Haven Refineries, at Thames Haven, Stanford-le-Hope, and via repairs at Swindon Works).

D9538 handled the iron-ore traffic at the works, but was described in the IRS *Bulletin* No.190 as being 'not heavy enough for the heaviest duties'; in edition No.193 it was stated that 'the larger wheels tend to make her slip with heavy loads, and the Sentinels are preferred.' *Bulletin* No.179 had already described D9538 as 'finished and not to be repaired'. With the closure of the 'Heavy-End'

at Ebbw Vale only nine locomotive duties remained and D9538's fate was sealed.

D9538 was purchased internally by BSC Tubes Division, Corby, as a source of spares for its own fleet of Class 14s, arriving there in April 1976.

Chapter 7

OTHER INDUSTRIAL USERS

7.1 Cement Works.

7.1.1 APCM Hope Cement Works, Hope, Derbyshire.

	Arrived	Departed
D9505	26/09/68 (ex-50B Hull Dairycoates)	05/05/75 (for export)
D9534	xx/10/68 (ex-50B Hull Dairycoates)	05/05/75 (for export)

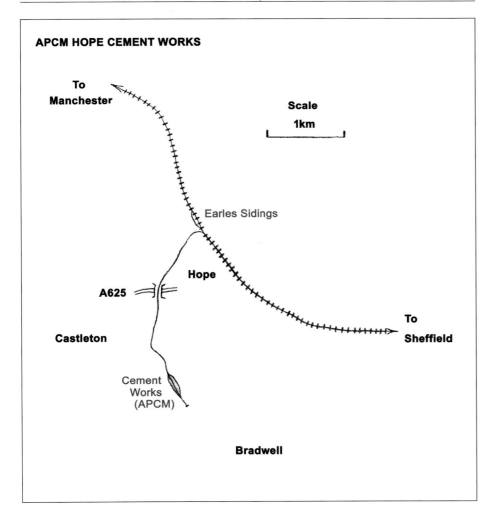

APCM HOPE CEMENT WORKS

Cement production at Hope is based around locally extracted limestone, and imported coal for the kilns. A railway between the Cement Works and Earles Sidings, on the Manchester-Sheffield line (via Edale), facilitates the import of coal and the export of cement products.

Class 14s were located at Hope during the period September 1968 and May 1975.

By January 1969, whilst still in its as-delivered BR livery, D9534 had received the name *Eccles* as a transfer and D9505 may have been similarly treated with the name *Michlow*. At a later date the two locomotives were repainted in an overall green livery with reduced-size black/yellow chevron warning panels and yellow buffer beams (see page 85); D9505 and D9534 became numerically anonymous but the names *Michlow* and *Eccles'* were retained and proper nameplates were carried. Michlow is an area in the town of Bradwell and Eccles similarly a part of Hope, both near to the Cement Works.

By March 1973 *Eccles* (D9534) was yielding spares to keep *Michlow* operational. The situation regarding spare parts had reached a somewhat critical point by this time and ultimately both locomotives were laid-up awaiting parts.

Hope's association with ex-BR Type 1 locomotives continues to this day with the long-term deployment of Class 20s.

APCM Hope.

D9520 (in the guise of D9534 'ECCLES'), Hope Cement Works, 6 September 2014. A slightly 'fraudulent' photo due to the fact that only two photographs have been found illustrating Class 14s at Hope (see page 85). An Open Day was held at the Cement Works in 2014, with D9520 invited to attend; it masqueraded as both D9534 (the side shown here) and D9505 'MICHLOW' (the other side). (SlightlyReliable70 2010-2015)

7.1.2 APCM, Westbury, Wiltshire.

	Arrived	Departed
D9526	xx/01/70 (ex-86A Cardiff Canton)	03/04/80 (to West Somerset Railway)

APCM bought D9526 with a view to general shunting duties at their Westbury terminal including the building-up of heavy block train consists for subsequent movement by BR.

D9526, APCM Westbury Cement Works, 26 March 1976.
(Peter Wilcox)

7.2 Petroleum Complexes.
7.2.1 Gulf Depot, Roath Docks, Cardiff.
Refinery officially opened 10 August 1968.

	Arrived	Departed
D9530	Circa 09/69 (ex-86A Cardiff Canton)	26/09/69 (to Gulf Oil Refining Ltd, Waterston, via 86A)

The following observations and non-observations need to be noted:

86A Cardiff Canton: 21/07/69, 19/10/69, 26/10/69.

Not listed 02/08/69, 10/08/69, 18/09/69.

87E Landore: 29/11/69

These sightings suggest that D9530 made a brief visit to Cardiff Roath Docks, for local trials, in August/September 1969, with the subsequent movement to Waterston taking place in November, via short stop-overs at Cardiff Canton and Landore.

7.2.2 Gulf Oil Refining Ltd, Waterston, Milford Haven, Pembrokeshire.

	Arrived	Departed
D9530	26/09/69 (ex-Gulf Depot, Roath Docks, Cardiff), or, xx/11/69 or xx/12/69 (ex-86A Cardiff Canton (see above)	xx/10/75 (to NCB Mardy Colliery, via BR Cardiff Canton)

See comments in Section 7.2.1 above. A perhaps less likely scenario is that D9538 arrived at Waterston on 26 September 1969 but had to return to Landore for attention.

D9530, Gulf Oil, Waterston, 1970.
(Transport Topics)

7.2.3 Shell Haven Refineries, Thames Haven, Stanford-le-Hope, Essex.

	Arrived	Departed
D9538	xx/04/70 (ex-86A Cardiff Canton)	To BSC Ebbw Vale (via Swindon Works) xx/01/71

D9538 was purchased by Shell UK Ltd to handle 100-ton tank wagons at its Shell Haven installation. Very little information has been found regarding D9538 whilst under Shell ownership, but given the short time spent at Thames Haven, it would appear to have been considered as unsuccessful or unsuitable. It was resold to the British Steel Corporation which the *Railway Observer* (July 1971) attributed to prohibitive flame-proofing costs.

D9538 retained its BR livery and identity throughout its time with Shell.

7.2.4 BP Refinery Ltd, Grangemouth, Scotland.

	Arrived	Departed
D9524	xx/07/70 (from 86A Cardiff Canton)	09/09/81 (to Scottish RPS, Falkirk)

D9524 was bought in July 1970 for the movement of oil tank wagons around the BP Refinery complex and assembling trains of up to 800tons for BR to transport onwards to destinations in Central Scotland. D9524 suffered a number of significant failures and was generally reported as being heavy on maintenance.

In 1974, the locomotive was substantially modified by Andrew Barclay (Kilmarnock) with the aim of improving availability, providing air-braking capability consistent with the modern wagons being shunted and enhancing its safety credentials within the refinery environment. The following modifications have been largely derived from Kevin A. McCallum's section on D9524 in P.J. Hembrey's booklet *Class 14: The Cinderellas of the Diesel-Hydraulic Era*:

- Replacement Dorman 8QT engine (500hp at 1800rpm), with flame-proofing protection.
- Reduced voltage electrical system (with both 12V and 24V quoted), replacing the 110V system.
- Ingersoll-Rand compressed air system installed for engine starting.
- Air-brake equipment fitted (vacuum brakes and exhausters removed), with two Broomwade belt-driven compressors used to supply both the locomotive and train brakes.
- Replacement of the auxiliary generator with a Broomwade B6 single-cylinder air compressor driven by a Lister diesel engine.
- Revised cooling water temperature and oil pressure control arrangements to prevent engine damage.
- Serck/Behr hydrostatic fan locked-out with the fan operated at constant speed.
- Cab control desk rebuilt in simpler form with a single instrument display replacing the duplicated display.
- Fuel capacity reduced to 250gals, and locomotive weight reduced to approximately 48tons.

The existing transmission and final drive were retained and seem to have worked satisfactorily despite the engine speed range being widened to 500-1800rpm.

It is believed that D9524 received its distinctive light blue livery at this time.

It is unclear whether D9524 received the modifications at Barclay's works in Kilmarnock or by their staff at Grangemouth; given the scale of work undertaken, the former would appear most likely but no sighting evidence has been found to prove this.

Despite the major up-grade, D9524 seems to have spent a considerable amount of time out of traffic. A catastrophic engine failure and problems with bringing the locomotive fully up to the latest industry safety standards ultimately led to its withdrawal and sale into preservation.

Chapter 8

SUCCESS IN INDUSTRY

Use of the Class 14s by the NCB at Philadelphia, Ashington, Burradon/Weetslade and Backworth, and by the BSC at Corby, Harlaxton, Buckminster and Glendon East proved to be very successful and it was only the rationalisation of the coal and steel industries which ultimately led to the demise of the locomotive fleets. The Class 14s found their designed niches at all of these locations, to the point that they became very highly regarded by the drivers. The sometimes Machiavellian efforts of the Ashington drivers to retain their 'Paxmans' despite the continued efforts of senior management to deploy the cheaper and more basic Barclay industrial locomotives was testament to the regard they had for the 'Paxmans' on the Leading turns.

Success was arguably directly proportional to the size of the operation, with the large systems at Northumberland and Corby enabling the locomotives to fully demonstrate their trip-freighting capabilities as well as yard shunting. At these locations, where the Class 14s virtually monopolised operations, the fitters became total experts and were able to keep the locomotives in good operational condition despite their exacting duties and challenging operating environments. Maintenance

facilities generally were fairly good, particularly so at Gretton Brook (Corby), a facility which could easily compete with anything BR could offer. The large fleet sizes justified the stocking of parts to support locomotive availability, often topped-up by a bank of spares from redundant sisters specifically acquired for that purpose.

Smaller concerns, however, with alternative motive power and less extensive maintenance facilities, seemed to adapt less readily and most sold them on.

J.K. Lewis in his book *The Western's Hydraulics*, highlights the fact that the Class 14s were still by no means perfect:

'As on BR, the D9500s led mixed careers in private-ownership. Mechanical reliability continued to be poor though much improved over that endured by BR, principally due to the use of improved cylinder heads, and more reliable ancillaries, in conjunction with the regular inspection of known problem areas such as radiators and heat exchangers.

'Whilst less arduous duties [debatable in my view!] coupled with more rigorous maintenance routines succeeded in reducing the incidence of major failures, the mechanical

fragility of the design was never truly exorcised.'

This latter point ultimately led BP at Grangemouth to change the Paxman engine for a Dorman, and the British Steel Corporation at Corby would in all probability have moved over to Rolls-Royce engines had rationalisation of the industry not intervened.

P.J. Hembrey is more complimentary about their industrial service:

'As if to confound those who dismissed them on BR as unsuccessful, all the mechanical faults which had dogged them began to disappear. The cylinder head problem was cured by the replacement of aluminium alloy with cast-iron. The turbo-blower problem was cured [certainly improved] by re-designing the mounting brackets ... It must not be forgotten that BR ironed out most of the teething troubles and bore the financial penalties...

'With their new owners they earned a reputation for reliability and economical fuel consumption, their rugged construction has been praised, and they seem to possess that elusive quality which affords a high degree of availability.'

Chapter 9
EXPORT

9.1 Belgium and (possibly) Italy.
9.1.1 Preamble.
D9505/35 were sold to Sobemai NV, Maldegem, Belgium in May 1975; IRS *Bulletin* No.523 (January 1992) described Sobemai as being 'Dealers, with a large workshop …' One of the aims of the buyer was to refurbish locomotives and hire or sell them for further use. This certainly happened with D9505, finding use in Belgium, but the ensuing history of D9534 became somewhat 'opaque' with onward export to Italy a possibility.

The following sources of information have been accessed in the compilation of this Section:

- *Ex-BR Diesels in Industry*, Handbooks 3BRD-8BRD, Adrian Booth, IRS, 2019.
- *Diesel Dilemmas* web page, Topic: *Class 14 Exports*, Peter Hall, RCTS.
- *The Railway Magazine*, p57, *Exiles 'Fit and Well'*, Guido Baetons.

9.1.2 En route to Belgium.
On 5 May 1975 D9505/34 departed Hope by rail en route to Harwich for export; they were subsequently sighted at 31B March depot on 10 May. The June 1975 edition of the BLS *British Locomotives* magazine states:

'On 10/5 (1975), two ex-BR diesels D9505 + D9534 were seen on a low loader in a siding south of March …'

This suggests that onward movement from March to Harwich was by road; however, the ITS *Ipswich Transport Journal* (June 1975) contradicts this with the following entry:

'… the most unusual train to pass through Ipswich during May was that of 9X35 00.35 March (Up Yard) to Parkeston on Saturday 10th. This out-of-gauge load, restricted to 25mph and hauled by 37044, was composed of two privately-owned diesel locomotives from Hope (Earles Sidings), these locos being ex-BR Class 14s D9505 and D9534 .'

It could be construed from this that D9515/34 arrived at Harwich on 10 May, given the short distance between Ipswich and Harwich. However, both 8BRD and *Diesel Dilemmas* indicate arrival at Harwich on 10 July 1975. An exact date of shipment from Harwich to Zeebrugge has never been published but the two Class 14s are known to have arrived at Zeebrugge by 9 August 1975, with

movement to Maldegem at some point thereafter.

9.1.3 D9505.
Whilst at Sobemai NV, D9505 was overhauled and subsequently sold on to Suikergroep NV, Moerbeke-Waas for use at their sugar factory. Sightings were sparse, with two at Maldegem (both 1976) and then an eight-year gap until seven sightings at Moerbeke between 1984 and 1997! Guido Baetons explains:

'The Class 14 is used to shunt wagon-loads of sugar beet from the station to the sugar beet factory at Moerbeke-Waas, 15 miles north-east of Gent … the reason for the locomotive's reclusiveness - it works only during the beet-lifting season, from October until December.'

The last known sighting of D9505 at Moerbeke was on 22 June 1997 with an associated comment 'not used for while'. 8BRD records it as scrapped on site in 1999.

9.1.4 D9534.
If D9505 was a 'reclusive', then D9534 was an 'enigma'!

A report submitted by Mike Kennard to the IRS regarding a visit to Sobemai NV on 1 May 1976 stated that D9534 was 'being overhauled' and had been 'sold to Italy' based on information supplied by the Sobemai guide. This was never subsequently reported in the IRS *Bulletin* although the *Railway Observer* (September 1976) reports 'D9534 undergoing repairs, resold to a company in Italy' on the same date.

From the third edition of the IRS *Ex-BR Diesels in Industry* books (3BRD), D9534 is recorded as 'sold to an industrial user near Milan, Italy, 1976', and, from 5BRD as 'working at a steelworks near Brescia, by May 1997'.

Peter Hall has undertaken a considerable amount of research on D9534 and has posted the following information on his excellent *Diesel Dilemmas* site:

'Interestingly, as a result of enquiries made in 2018, we have been told by Sobemai NV, that D9534 went to a terminal to shunt Ambrogio Transporti SPA wagons, although it's not clear that was who it was sold to. Reggio Emilia was mentioned as the location but no reference to Ambrogio having an involvement there has so far emerged. Ambrogio do have a site at Gallarate, Lombardy which is roughly 25 miles north-west of Milan, but this appears not to have opened until 1984. They also have a site at Candiolo, on the outskirts of Turin. Subsequent enquiries were made with Ambrogio Transporti SPA who stated they had never owned the locomotive.

'Italian Board of Trade documents seen by those researching this topic indicate that during 1976 and 1977 no locomotives were imported from any Benelux companies. However, these documents indicate that during 1976 a 50ton locomotive was imported from and also exported back to Switzerland. Could it be this was D9534 with a Swiss company acting as intermediary? That being the case, the locomotives stay in Italy was short-lived and perhaps it subsequently saw use in Switzerland or was exported elsewhere from there or returned to Italy later.

'By 2000 the IRS in '5BRD' were recording it as 'working at a steelworks in the Brescia area by May 1997'. This suggests that if it was originally at Gallarate or Candiolo it had been sold on and left there by 1997. Intriguingly the IRS in '6BRD'[2007] add 'extant June 2003' and in '7BRD' [2007] 'scrapped October 2005'. These references suggest someone knew where it was located between 1997 and 2005 and was keeping tabs on it … It should be noted though that the locomotive is not listed in *Deutsche Lokomotiven in Italien* by Frank Glaubitz and Micheal Ulbricht, published in 2003, and the authors, despite having extensive knowledge of industrial railway sites in Italy have no knowledge of the locomotive whatsoever. Similarly, no British enthusiast that has made contact and has visited Italy searching for ex-BR diesel-shunting locomotives exported to Italy has ever reported seeing or knowing anything about the whereabouts of this locomotive.'

Correspondence between Mark Jones and myself during September 2020 concluded with the following comment from Mark:

'There is a strong case for the loco never arriving in Italy. I have two friends who live in Milan; one gentleman has been involved with industrial railways since the 1950s and did have a few connections within FS (loco examiners). He does not know of a Class 14 arriving in Italy.'

It is very strange that there are absolutely no 'definitive' sightings of D9534 after 27 June 1976 at Maldegem, either in Belgium or Italy; by 'definitive' I mean the crucial three components of a quality sighting (i.e. locomotive identity, exact location and full date). And, similarly, no photographic records either over a period spanning approximately thirty years! As regards the 'less-definitive' sightings, I do seriously wonder whether these are instances of confusion with other centre-cab locomotives of European origin.

D9534 is clearly a case of 'Disposal not Proven', or more accurately, 'History Not Proven' after May 1976!

My *theory*, for what it is worth, is that D9534 was 'lifted' in the Sobemai Workshops for recovery of the thicker wheelsets for use under D9505 (which was subsequently repaired for use by Suikergroep) and later scrapped at Sobemai. Thus, if Italy was ever a possibility, as indicated by Sobemai in May 1976, then this deal presumably fell through.

If readers can provide any further help on this subject, please contact Peter Hall with any post-1976 information or photographs.

9.1.5 Locomotive Histories.

D9505

D9505, Sobemai NV, Maldegem (Belgium), 27 June 1976. APCM all-over dark green livery, with the position of the 'MICHLOW' nameplate discernible on the cabside. This photograph was sold as depicting D9534 but the locomotive pictured is actually D9505; it was recorded as such by Mike Kennard on 1 May 1976 in exactly this position, with exactly the same 'detritus' surrounding it! D9534 suffered damaged grab rails in the shunter's recess at 'B' end (see pages 27 and 85); such damage is not evident here. Thin wheel sets compared with photograph of D9505 in May 1996 (see below). (Transport Treasury [John Tolson])

Below left: **D9505, Suikergroep Sugar Factory, Moerbeke-Waas, near Gent, Belgium, 7 June 1987.** Air-braked, fitted by Sobemai NV. The black window frames give the impression of larger windows. It looks operational but the connecting rods are removed and tracks are rusty! Out of season for sugar beet traffic. (Robert von Hirschhorn)

Below right: **D9505, Suikergroep Sugar Factory, Moerbeke-Waas, near Gent, Belgium, 25 May 1996.** Note the 'Spoonful of Sugar' logo on the cab side and the wing mirror by the shunter's recess. Probably stored out of use; also possible is that the flanges of the centre wheels have been removed to assist traversing sharp corners! (Mark Jones)

Movements:
Exported from Harwich: xx/05/75. To Sobemai NV, Maldegem, near Bruges, Belgium.
Overhauled by Sobemai NV.

Sold to Suikergroep NV, Opperstraat, Moerbeke-Waas sugar factory, near Gent.
At Suikergroep NV, Moerbeke-Waas: scrapped on site xx/xx/99.

Sightings:
Zeebrugge port, Belgium: Arrived by 090875
Sobemai NV, Maldegem, near Brugges, Belgium:
010576 (yard, wtg reps)/270676 (yard, wtg reps). Not
listed 280681.
Suikergroep NV, Moerbeke-Waas, nr Gent, Belgium:
071284/070687/ 220687 (wkg)/ 231090 (wkg)/ 111091

(wkg)/ 281192/ 071294/ 250596/ 220697 (spare, not
used for a while). Not listed: 130801.

Disposal: Disposal not proven.

Liveries and Numbers:
Three liveries:
1. Orange livery with broad yellow band above footplate level. Additional broad yellow band on buffer beam below
   buffers. No alpha/numeric identity. See photograph on page 265 (07/06/87); similarly noted on 23/10/90 and
   11/10/91 (M. McDonald photographs).
2. Same orange/yellow livery but with revised front-end style. Large yellow panels inside black 'frame'. No alpha/
   numeric identity. See photographs dated 28/11/92 (RM0695) and undated (RI1114).
3. All-over yellow livery, with inverted-'V' black/yellow chevrons on buffer-beam, black handrails on bonnet
   top, red grab-rails for shunter's recesses, and red wheels and coupling-rods. Suikergroep logo on cab sides. See
   photograph dated 07/12/94 (RM0695): no alpha/numeric identity. See also photograph dated 25/05/96 (page
   265) with UIC No. 98 8820 22202-4 applied.

Detail Differences:
Headcode box still fitted 28/11/92, removed by 25/05/96.
Headlight fitted (by 25/05/96).
Air-brake fitted; vacuum-brake removed.
Shade over side cab windows.
Wing mirrors fitted below just sole-bar level immediately behind the shunter's recess at 'A' end (by 28/11/92).

Notes:
1. Visit to Belgium (*Sobemai NV, Maldegem*), 09/08/75. 'The two D95xx from APCM Hope were expected shortly,
   having already arrived at Zeebrugge.' (IRS *Bulletin* No.201, April 1976)
2. Overhauled 1994 (RM0695). Second overhaul resulted in a number of changes i.e. livery change to all-over yellow,
   application of UIC Nos., removal of headcode boxes and fitment of headlights.
3. 'The [sugar beet] season usually ended mid-December and in 1993 a SNCB switcher was rented. Unfortunately
   this factory closed after the 2007 season and it is now completely demolished.' (Wim de Ridder, Letter, RI1114).

D9534

Movements:
Exported from Harwich: xx/xx/75. To Sobemai NV, Maldegem, near Bruges, Belgium.
Overhauled by Sobermai NV.

Sold to an industrial user near Milan, Italy, 1976 (3BRD).
Additional comment (8BRD): 'This may be Ambrogio Transporti SPA, Gallarate, Lombardy, near Milan.'
Working at a steelworks near Brescia, by May 1997 (5BRD).
Extant June 2003 (6BRD).
Scrapped 10/2005 (7BRD), or, believed scrapped (8BRD).

Sightings (Belgium):
Zeebrugge port, Belgium: Arrived by 090875
Sobemai NV, Maldegem, nr Brugges, Belgium: 010576 (Workshop, lifted; resold to firm in Italy)/270676.
Not listed 280681.

Sightings (Italy):

Approx. 5 miles east of Milan Central station (south side of Verona/Venice line): Summer 1983 (Rail 0185)

Disposal: Disposal not proven.

Liveries and Numbers:
Noted in APCM colours on 27/06/76. Subsequent liveries, if any, not known.

Detail Differences:
Not known.

Notes:
1. As Note 1 for D9505 (see page 266).
2. See Section 9.1.4.

9.2 Spain.
9.2.1 Preamble.
Three Class 14s were exported to Spain during June 1982; the locomotives concerned, D9515/48/9, had all previously seen industrial use with the British Steel Corporation. It is useful to remind readers of the previous history of these three, because their earlier industrial locations of activity resulted in external detail differences which allowed their later identification when in Spain (when all *previous* alpha-numerical identification had been obliterated under a coat of yellow paint). Relevant details are as follows:

D9515	BSC Buckminster	Single bonnet-end spotlights, solebar brackets (x3) at 'A' end.
D9548	BSC Harlaxton	Single bonnet-end spotlights, solebar brackets (x3) at 'A' end, plus, reduced-height cab and exhaust stack.
D9549	BSC Corby	Twin bonnet-end spotlights.

Changes once in Spain, particularly regarding spotlights, blurred matters over time, but at least the solebar brackets remained a constant.

The following sources of information have been accessed in the compilation of this Section:

- *Ex-BR Diesels in Industry, 8BRD*, Adrian Booth, IRS, 2019
- *Industrial Railways and Locomotives of Spain*, Paul Spencer, IRS, 2018 (plus amendments).
- *No Way to Treat a Teddy Bear*, Don Townsley, *Railway Bylines*, December 2013.
- *When Shall We Three Meet Again*, Industrial Railway Record, No.240, March 2020 (Cliff Shepherd, IRS) and follow-up letter from David Hartley in No.243, December 2020
- *Diesel Dilemmas* web page, Topic: *Class 14 Exports*, (Peter Hall, RCTS)
- *Continental/Overseas* forum, Topic: 'Spanish Class 14s' (Peter Hall, RM Web).

9.2.2 Preparation for Spain.
D9515/48/9 were sold to infrastructure company Cubiertas y MZOV SA (CMZ) (formed in the 1980s by the merger of Cubiertas SA and MZOV SA) through agents Aikin Española SA, with a view to deployment on RENFE construction work on the new Northern line between Madrid Atocha to Madrid Chamartín.

According to David Hartley (a BSC fitter at the time) the initial selection of D9515/48/9 was on the basis of their 'having recently rebuilt engines and new tyres fitted'. Hunslet Engine Co., Leeds received the contract to re-gauge

the locomotives from 1435mm (4ft. 8½ in) to the Iberian 1672mm (5ft. 6in.) gauge on 4 November 1981 (Don Townsley) and the three locomotives were moved to Leeds during November/December 1981. The work involved removing the wheelsets, jackshaft, gearbox and brake-gear and manufacturing new axles, jackshaft and brake rigging. Cab roof-mounted flashing lights were removed. The locomotives were re-painted with an all-over yellow body (including nose-ends), inverted 'V' chevron buffer beams, black underframes and red coupling rods and jackshaft.

Whilst at Hunslet, D9549 suffered the ignominy of falling onto its roof during a lifting operation (see accompanying photographs). Adrian Freeman comments:

D9515/48/9 'arrived at Hunslet in November 1981 whilst I was doing my apprenticeship in the Erecting Shop and the work involved removing the wheelsets, jack drive gearbox and brake gear for modification to suit Spain's 5' 6' gauge. There were lifting points on the buffer-beams but, with these parts removed, the locos were very top heavy and whilst moving D9549 down the Erecting Shop with the overhead cranes, a mishap occurred on Wednesday 25 November 1981; fortunately nobody was injured.'

As it turned out the damage to the cab was superficial and the locomotive was repaired prior to export. Further details of the mishap are provided in Townsley's 'Railway Bylines' article.

Townsley states that 'Despatch of the three re-gauged locomotives …

took place on 2 April, 16 April and 11 June 1982 but without reference as to which was which as no identifying numbers were provided. D9515/48/9 were exported from Goole Docks during June 1982, although whether individually or as a group is unknown.

David Hartley again:

'I then travelled to Spain in July 1982 and commissioned the locomotives on behalf of the agent, Aiken Española SA of Madrid, but had no contact with the locomotives after that.'

9.2.3 Usage?
Although purchased for use on infrastructure trains in the Madrid area, it is not known whether they actually saw service as intended. Such has been the paucity of sightings of the Class 14s in Spain that it has been impossible to ascertain their usage with any accuracy at all; between 1982 and 1989 only an average of five photographs and/or sightings per locomotive have been found, all at Madrid Chamartín (either stabled or stored). D9515/49 were photographed at Madrid Chamartín in January and April 1988; the IRS publication 8BRD lists D9548 as being at Chamartín in January 1988 and may well have still been there in April (although not photographed). D9515 has never been seen again!

In the IRS *Bulletin* No.462 (November 1988) Michael Poulter supplied the following commentary:-

'The locomotives were supplied to Cubiertos y MZOV for a ballasting contract on RENFE. It is believed that they were not used on this project and have been stored for about two years in the centre road of the new Madrid station. Aikin Española SA, Caidos Division, Azul, 16 Madrid were trying to find a buyer for these locos. (This company were agents acting on behalf of the original purchaser - Ed.).'

If this report was correct, then it would indicate that Aikin Española were unsuccessful in finding a buyer because D9548/9 were subsequently rejuvenated (and repainted) for further use with CMZ. D9548 was noted repainted in December 1989 and D9549 similarly in June 1990. When noted on these dates D9548 was operating at Curtis (Galicia), with D9549 at Santiago de Compostela (both near Coruña, north-west Spain). D9549 was later photographed at L'Aldea-Amposta-Tortosa in north-east Spain on 27 May 1996.

When repainted, D9548 and D9549 finally received some form of identification, as follows:

D9548	P-602-03911002-CMZ (also reported as carrying UIC No. 93 71 1310 602-8 by 1998)
D9549	P-601-0-3911-003-CMZ.

It has been suggested that D9515 became P-603-03911-001-CMZ but no photographic evidence exists to support this.

On 28 April 1997 CMZ merged with Entrecanales y Távora SA to form NECSO (NECSO Entrecanales Cubiertas SA).

From 1997 sightings of D9548 and D9549 continued to be few and far between. D9548 was last noted and photographed at Sagrera, Barcelona in June1998, apparently still in use.

D9549 was later sold and moved to Industrias Lopez Soriano, Calle de Miguel Servet, Zaragoza (north-east Spain), a scrap metal merchant and trader. 8BRD states that this move was 'by circa 2000' which amply shows how vague the information is on this subject. Earliest photographic evidence positions D9549 at Lopez Soriano, Zaragoza in August 2002 and the latest on an unspecified date in 2007.

9.2.4 Disposal.
The demise of D9515 and D9548 is distinctly unclear. Spencer lists both locomotives as scrapped in October 2002, with no location or scrap merchant mentioned. 8BRD understandably uses the phrase 'by October 2002' which although more vague is probably a more accurate description.

Peter Hall asks the 'key' question:

'How was it established that D9515 was scrapped fourteen years after it was last seen in Madrid? The answer might be that when asked in 2003, Industrias Lopez Soriano, who then had D9549 in their Zaragoza yard, said they had scrapped two others, presumably this and D9548.'

With D9549 dumped for approximately seven years at a scrap merchant's premises in Zaragoza, one would have thought that this was where it was finally dismantled. 8BRD implies that this was indeed the case with scrapping taking place in March 2007, but Spencer indicates disposal at Constantí, Tarragona, during the same month.

My personal view is that all three Spanish Class 14s should be categorised as 'Disposal Not Proven'.

Peter Hall will be updating his RCTS Class 14 web page as new information surfaces. If you can assist, please make contact, and, for those others interested in the subject, I encourage you to visit Peter's excellent site from time to time for any developments.

9.2.5 Locomotive Histories.

D9515

Above left: **D9515 Hunslet Engine Co., Leeds, 28 May 1982.** Buckminster headlight retained. Angle brackets in place of buffers. (Adrian Freeman)

Above right: **D9515, Goole Docks, 16 June 1982.** Securing to vessel deck appears to be via the angle brackets. Note the 'resting' position of the spotlight on the 'A' end bonnet roof. (Chris Davis)

D9515, Madrid Chamartín, 29 January 1988. (Phil Wormald)

Sale:
Sold, 11/1981 by BSC Corby, to Cubiertas y MZOV SA, with Aitken Española SA, Madrid acting as intermediaries.

Movements:
To Hunslet Engine Co Ltd, Leeds: xx/12/81 (for overhaul, conversion to 5ft 6in gauge and repainting).
To Goole Docks: xx/xx/82.
Exported to Bilbao, Spain: circa 16/06/82.

Arrived Madrid Chamartín: xx/xx/xx.
Passed to infrastructure company Curbiertas and MZOV (CMZ).
Following a merger in 1997, the owner became NECSO Entrecanales Cubiertas SA.
Scrapped: unknown location, believed by 10/02.

Sightings:
Hunslet, Leeds: 270382 (ex-Corby condition, numbered 62; on wheels, rods removed)/ 280582 (repainted; on wheels, rods fitted)
Goole Docks: 160682 (on-board ship)

Madrid Chamartín: 170683/231084 (OOU)/ 070286 (stored)/ 290188/ 020488

Liveries and Numbers:
All-over yellow inc. bonnet-ends and headcode box glass, black/yellow chevrons on buffer-beam, red coupling-rods.
N.B. Very small yellow areas at top corners of the buffer-beam chevrons.
No known numbers.

Detail Differences:
Vestigial brackets (x3) on the solebar at 'A' end (both sides), a left over from Buckminster.
Large Buckminster single spotlight retained on each nose-end (ex-Hunslet); last photograph/sighting of D9515 on 02/04/88 shows retention of this spotlight. N.B. No triple colour light-clusters fitted (when sighted 07/02/86, 29/01/88 and 02/04/88).

Notes:
1. Last sighting of this locomotive was at Madrid Charmartín on 02/04/88 by which time no spotlight/light-cluster modifications had been made; renumbering to the (presumably) allocated number P603-0 3911-001-CMZ had also not taken place.
2. **Disposal not Proven.**

D9548

**D9548(67) and
D9549 (64), Hunslet
Engine Co., Leeds,
27 November 1981.**
Harlaxton headlight
and reduced-height cab
retained. (Adrian Freeman)

**D9548, D9515 and
D9549, Madrid
Chamartín, 7 February
1986.** (Phil Wormald)

D9548 (P-602-03911002-CMZ), Curtis, 6 December 1989. New lights on nose ends and also new light clusters on buffer beams. Repainted (and numbered) since 1986. (Luis Rentero Corral)

D9548 (P-602-03911002-CMZ), Sagrera Goods Yard, Barcelona, 19 June 1998. A similar photograph, previously published in the IRS 5BRD publication and on the RCTS *Diesel Dilemmas* web page, has generated a considerable amount of debate over the years. The CMZ number on the original print is clearly visible confirming it to be D9548, but why did the owner go to the effort of changing the Harlaxton reduced-height roof back to the original curved profile (albeit without the top-access hatch cover)? (Kevin Prince)

Sale:
Sold, 11/1981 by BSC Corby, to Cubiertas y MZOV SA, with Aitken Española SA, Madrid acting as intermediaries.

Movements:
To Hunslet Engine Co Ltd, Leeds: 19/11/81 (for overhaul, conversion to 5ft 6in gauge and repainting).
To Goole Docks: xx/xx/82.
Exported to Bilbao, Spain: circa 06/82.

Arrived Madrid Chamartín: xx/xx/xx.
Passed to infrastructure company Curbiertas and MZOV (CMZ).
Numbered P602-03911-002-CMZ.
Following a merger in 1997, the owner became NECSO Entrecanales Cubiertas SA.
To Curtis, Galicia (~30km SE of Coruña, NW Spain): xx/xx/xx.
To Sagrera, Barcelona (NE Spain): xx/xx/xx.
Scrapped: unknown location, by 10/02.

Sightings:
Hunslet, Leeds: 271181 (ex-Corby condition, numbered 67; on wheels, rods fitted)/ 270382 (repainted)

Madrid Chamartín: 170683/231084 (OOU)/ 070286 (stored)/ xx0188. Not photographed by Phil Wormold 290188 or by EddieB xx0488.
Curtis, Galicia: 061289
Sagrera, Barcelona: 190698

Liveries and Numbers:
All-over yellow inc. bonnet-ends and headcode box glass, black/yellow chevrons on buffer-beam, red coupling rods.
N.B. Large yellow areas at top corners of the buffer-beam chevrons.
No identification (07/02/86).

Repainted: by 12/89 (ex-Works condition per Luis Rentero Corral's photograph).
No. on fuel tank box ('A' end): **P602-03911-002 CMZ** (06/12/89 and 19/06/98).
Also quoted as carrying UIC No. **93 71 131 0602-8** (19/06/98).

Detail Differences:
Vestigial brackets (x3) on the solebar at 'A' end (both sides), a leftover from Harlaxton.
Harlaxton flat top cab roof retained until at least 1989 (sighted 06/12/89) but replaced by a round-top profile roof (without hatch cover) by 1998 (sighted 19/06/98).
Large spotlight on nose ends (ex-Hunslet) (sighted 07/02/86); replaced by:
Twin spotlights in single oblong frame on nose-ends and triple colour light-clusters on buffer beam (sighted 06/12/89 and 19/06/98).

Note:
1. **Disposal not Proven.**

D9549

D9549 (64) Hunslet Engine Co., Leeds, 20 November 1981. Rods and wheels removed; resting on timber bearers. Jackshaft still to be removed to facilitate re-gauging. (Adrian Freeman)

D9549 (64), Hunslet Engine Co., Leeds, 27 November 1981. D9549 following a crane incident whilst moving the locomotive down the Erecting Shop. Miraculously the damage sustained was only superficial. (Adrian Freeman)

D9549, Hunslet Engine Co., Leeds, 11 March 1982. None the worse for wear! Corby twin-headlights retained. (Adrian Freeman)

D9549 and D9515, Madrid Chamartín, 29 January 1988. Additional light clusters fitted above D9549's buffer beam, presumably in anticipation of further work. Shabby condition with draw-hook missing. (Phil Wormald)

D9549, Santiago de Compostela, Spain, June 1990. This superb photograph is another one which has generated a huge amount of debate over the years, specifically regarding the identity of the locomotive. The large single Buckminster/ Harlaxton-style spotlight suggested D9515 and it was believed that it couldn't be D9549 given that this locomotive was exported from the UK with the Corby-style twin spotlights. However, spotlights were easily changed as indeed was the case here (possibly from D9548 which had lost its big headlights by this time and which had a similarly clamping arrangement to that seen here). The defining factor is the lack of the three brackets on the solebar at the 'A' end (furthest from the camera), another feature unique to locomotives which operated from Buckminster and Harlaxton; in Spanish terms D9515 and flat-roofed D9548 operated at Buckminster and Harlaxton (respectively), whereas D9549 only ever operated at Corby and hence never received the solebar brackets. The pictured locomotive has clearly received a recent re-paint and the painter obviously went to extreme lengths to do a decent job, including painting the redundant Corby safety chains, now neatly slung from the shunting pole clips. Complete rejuvenation since the January 1988 photograph at Chamartín. (David Henderson)

D9549 (P601-0-3911-003-CMZ), L'Aldea-Amposta-Tortosa, 27 May 1996. New bonnet roof headlights; fitted by 16 July 1991. Cubertias sticker on cab side. Number (60, or possibly 80) on cab door. (Luis Rentero Corral)

Sale:
Sold, 11/1981 by BSC, Corby, to Cubiertas y MZOV SA, with Aitken Española SA, Madrid acting as intermediaries.

Movements:
To Hunslet Engine Co Ltd, Leeds: 14/11/81 (for overhaul, conversion to 5ft 6in gauge and repainting).
To Goole Docks: xx/xx/82.
Exported to Bilbao, Spain: circa 06/82.

To Madrid Chamartín: xx/xx/xx.

Passed to infrastructure company Curbiertas and MZOV (CMZ).
Numbered P-601-03911-003-CMZ.
Following a merger in 1997, the owner became NECSO Entrecanales Cubiertas SA.

To Santiago de Compostela (~50km SW of Coruña, NW Spain): by 06/90.
To L'Aldea-Amposta-Tortosa (~150km/50km SW of Barcelona/Tarragona, NE Spain): by 05/96.

To Industrias Lopez Soriano, Calle de Miguel Servet, Zaragoza (~200km W of Tarragona, NE Spain): by circa 2000 (8BRD).
At Industrias Lopez Soriano, Zaragoza (assumed): Scrapped: xx/03/07 (8BRD).
or,
To Constantí, N of Tarragona (~200km E of Zaragoza, NE Spain), where scrapped 03/07 (IRLSpain).

Sightings:
Hunslet: 201181 (ex-Corby condition, numbered 64; off wheels, rods removed)/ 271181 (overturned, hanging from crane)/ 110382 (repainted; off wheels)/ 270382 (repainted; on wheels, rods to re-fit)

Madrid Chamartín: 170683/ 231084 (OOU))/ 070286 (stored)/ 290188/ 020488

Santiago de Compostela: xx0690 (wkg)/ 160791 (wkg)
L'Aldea-Amposta-Tortosa: 270596
Industrias Lopez Soriano SA, Zaragoza: xx0802/ 180103/ 070503/ 110605/ xxxx07

D9549 (P601-0-3911-003-CMZ), Industrias Lopez Soriano SA, Zarragoza, Spain, 18 January, 2003. Shabby condition once again! Note the buffers dumped in the battery box. Number (70) on the cab door, on the opposite side of the locomotive (see previous photograph); it has been suggested that '70' was another locomotive identity but given the differing numbers on each side this seems unlikely. (Mark Jones)

Liveries and Numbers:
All-over yellow inc. bonnet-ends and headcode box glass, black/yellow chevrons on buffer-beam, red coupling rods. N.B. Large yellow areas at top corners of the buffer-beam chevrons.
No identification (07/02/86).

Repainted: circa 06/90 (ex-Works condition per David Henderson's photograph).
No. on fuel tank box ('A' end): **P-601-03911-003-CMZ** (possibly xx/06/90, and all subsequent sightings).

Detail Differences:
Twin spotlights on bonnet-ends (ex-Hunslet) (sighted 07/02/86 and 29/01/88); replaced by:
Large spotlight on bonnet-ends (sighted xx/06/90) (possibly transferred from D9548 which had replacement twin spotlights in a single oblong frame fitted by 06/12/89); replaced by:
Twin spotlights in oblong frame on bonnet-ends (sighted 16/07/91 and all subsequent sightings).
Triple colour light-clusters on buffer-beam (sighted with these clusters on 29/01/88 (at Chamartín), xx/06/90 and all subsequent sightings). N.B. Not fitted on 07/02/86.

N.B. No vestigial brackets (x3) on the solebar at 'A' end (both sides), unlike the other two Class 14s exported to Spain.

Notes:
1. Incident at Hunslet Engine Co. Ltd., Leeds: 25/11/81.
2. **Disposal not Proven.**

9.3 Turkey.

Howard Johnston in his book *Preserved BR Diesel and Electric Locomotives* (1992) makes reference to the fact that D9539 (BSC 51) and D9553 [54] were the last locomotives in the Corby complex 'awaiting export to Turkey'. The deal subsequently fell through but this potential sale may explain why these two locomotives were shunted together and positioned a short distance away from the other members of the fleet in the Corby Steelworks Disposal site about October 1981. It was at this time that all condemned locomotives were removed from inside the No.1 Strip Mill to the outside yard immediately south-west of the Strip Mill, adjacent to the Bessemer Plant.

9.4 Middle-East.

When five Class 14s were put up for tender by the National Coal Board towards the end of 1983, interest was apparently expressed in purchasing them for use in the Middle-East. Paul Green in a letter to the IRS dated 15 December 1983 commented:

'The five engines awaiting disposal at Ashington Colliery (Nos.37/36/9/8/6) are according to the Traffic Manager to be inspected with a view to purchasing all five engines. Out of these will be made two good engines which would then be re-gauged and sent to the Middle East.'

Quite how much credence can be given to this is unknown because the timing of the letter seems to be significantly out of synchronisation with the following:

* The Ashington Loco Shed Daily Report (8 November 1983) (see page 144) show all five locomotives as 'Mechs taking parts off'; the report for 9 November reads 'Scrap for spares only.'
* A letter by John Wade to the IRS (8 November 1983) reported: 'These five locomotives were all officially withdrawn the week before I visited [on 25 October] by Head Office, the shed staff having a month to take useable spares off before the scrap merchants tender and dispose of the remains of these locos.'

All locomotives were physically scrapped in January 1984.

Chapter 10

PRESERVATION

Locomotives Preserved: D9500/2/4/13/6/8/20/1/3-6/9/31/7/9/51/3/5 (19).
Vacuum-brakes only: D9500/2/13/8/21/5/6/37/9/51/3/5
Fitted with air-brakes: D9504/16/20/3/4/9/31.

D9524 (numbered 14901), Bury Bolton Street, East Lancashire Railway, 26 July 2014. Modified both internally and externally. BFY livery (including yellow cab), plus double-arrow emblems and TOPS numbers. 'Domino'-style head-code boxes. Re-engined (again), hence the 14/9 reclassification. Dual-braked. (Anthony Sayer)

**D9555 (9101/57),
D9518 (No.7) and
D9521 (No.3), Rutland
Railway Museum,
Cottesmore,
29 November 1987.**
(Anthony Sayer)

**D9521 (14021),
Swanage Railway,
Swanage, September
1994.** Railfreight grey,
TOPS numbering
(including the bonnet end
repeaters). (John Law)

IN CASE OF FIRE
SHUT DOWN DIESEL ENGINE
THEN PULL HANDLE
TO FULLEST EXTENT

D9551, Severn Valley Railway, 18 June 2021. Cab controls (see Chapter 4 of my earlier Class 14 book "Their Life on British Railways" for further details) including the 'twin' deadman's pedals; the pedals are duplicated on the other side of the control desk. The two steps within the cab which have to be traversed to climb over the transmission/gearbox cardan shaft are visible in the 'portrait' photo. (Anthony Sayer)

Chapter 11

FURTHER EXCURSIONS INTO INDUSTRY (2001–10)

11.1 Channel Tunnel Rail Link (CTRL).

11.1.1 CTRL1 (2001/2).

Two Class 14s, D9504 and D9529 (numbered 14029) based on the Kent & East Sussex Railway, were hired out by the Forsythe-Stratton partnership (the owners of the two locomotives), subsequently Stratrail Ltd, during the period July 2001 and December 2002, for use on work associated with the Channel Tunnel Rail Link (CTRL1) being constructed between Cheriton (Folkestone) and Fawkham Junction. Work was essentially restricted to shunting at the temporary yard at Beechbrook Farm, near Ashford, including the marshalling of incoming ballast and rail trains ready for movement onto the high-speed 'trace', and, the re-assembly of discharged wagons ready for removal by BR.

The Class 14s were chosen in preference to other shunting power due to their enhanced ability to cope with the on-site gradients and heavy consists; the 40mph maximum speed provided the additional insurance of being capable of going out onto the CTRL proper to rescue a failed works train, a duty undertaken on at least one occasion. The two locomotives concerned had already been fitted with air brakes making them fully compatible with all stock requiring movement; larger compressors were fitted to upgrade their braking capability.

11.1.2 CTRL2 (2004-7).

D9504 and D9529 (14029) were also involved with yard shunting work associated with the construction of CTRL2 between Ebbsfleet and London St. Pancras during the period June 2004 to April 2007. Two yards were involved, one at Dagenham (Essex) and the other at Swanscombe (Kent). Unlike Beechbrook Farm, the Class 14s spent a sizeable amount of time working engineering trains on the 'trace'.

11.1.3 Other Work.

Other 'industrial' work undertaken by D9504 and D9529 included:

- Chatham Docks (2003). Shunting the storage and distribution centre set up here for handling steel reinforcing bar required for the Heathrow Airport Terminal 5 project.
- Tilbury Docks (2003, 14029 only). Short term handling of trainloads of scrap destined for export.
- March Whitemoor Yard (2004, D9504 only). Re-construction of part of the Whitemoor site as Network Rail's new material distribution centre for the Anglian area.
- Aggregate Industries Ltd, Bardon Hill (2008-10). Movements between the quarry and the BR exchange sidings.

11.1.4 Locomotive Histories.

D9504

D9504, Dagenham (CTRL2), 27 May 2005. (Rail-Online)

D9504, March Whitemoor Yard, 2 March 2004. (Peter Foster)

Movements and hire periods:

To CTRL Beechbrook Farm: 01/08/01 (ex-KESR, hire)
To Medway Ports, Chatham Dockyard: xx/02/03 (hire)
To NVR: 04/04/03
To EWS Toton: 07/01/04 (tyre-turning)
To NVR: 09/01/04
To Victa Rail, March: 15/01/04 (hire)
To NVR: 08/04/04
To CTRL Swanscombe: 15/06/04 (hire)
To CTRL Dagenham: 02/11/04 (hire)
To NVR: 24/02/05
To CTRL Dagenham: by 03/05/05 (hire)
To NVR: xx/xx/05
To CTRL Swanscombe: 07/11/05 (hire)
To NVR: 13/01/06
To CTRL Dagenham: 02/03/06 (hire)
To NVR: 25/01/07
To Aggregate Industries Ltd, Bardon Hill: 16/01/08 (hire)
To NVR: 10/02/09

Sightings:
Beechbrook Farm (CTRL1): 091101 (shunting)/140602/ 300902/ 190103 (Detling, wiring train, deputising for failed Class 20)
Medway Ports, Chatham Dockyard: Nil.
BR Toton: Nil.
Whitemoor Yard, March: 280104/120204/ 200284/ 020304/ 250304
Swanscombe (CTRL2): 090904 (Ebbsfleet)
Dagenham (CTRL2): 201104/270505/ 200406 (Stratford International)/ 101006 (Stratford International)
Aggregate Industries Ltd, Bardon Hill: Nil.

Detail Differences:
Bonnet-end mounted single square spotlight.

D9529 (14029)

D9529 (numbered 14029), Dagenham (CTRL2), 27 February 2005. (Rail-Online)

Movements and hire periods:

To CTRL Beechbrook Farm: 10/07/01 (ex-KESR, hire)
To NVR: xx/04/02
To CTRL Beechbrook Farm: 28/06/02 (hire)
To Tilbury Docks: 02/01/03 (hire)
To Medway Ports, Chatham Dockyard: 01/03/03 (hire)
To NVR: 14/07/03
To CTRL Dagenham: 19/07/04 (hire)
To NVR: 19/09/04
To EWS Toton: 17/11/04 (tyre-turning)
To NVR: 29/11/04
To CTRL Dagenham: 23/02/05 (hire)
To CTRL Swanscombe: xx/09/05 (hire)
To NVR: 14/02/06
To CTRL Dagenham: 07/09/06 (hire)
To NVR: 29/09/06
To CTRL Swanscombe: 24/01/07 (hire)
To NVR: 24/04/07, then KESR: 30/05/07, then NVR: 29/12/08
To Aggregate Industries Ltd, Bardon Hill: 07/01/09 (hire)
To NVR: 09/10/10

Sightings:
Beechbrook Farm (CTRL1): 160801/230801/ 130901/ 031001/ 301001/ 140102/ 300902. OOU 201201-010802 for engine repairs.
Tilbury Docks: Nil.
Medway Ports, Chatham Dockyard: Nil.
Dagenham (CTRL2): Nil.
BR Toton: 171104 (on low-loader)
Dagenham (CTRL2): 110305/270205/ 240405/ 290505
Swanscombe (CTRL2): 200487 (Ebbsfleet)
Aggregate Industries Ltd, Bardon Hill: Nil

Detail Differences:
Bonnet-end mounted single square spotlight.

Chapter 12

CONCLUDING REMARKS

British Railways' ability to sell the majority of the redundant Class 14s to the National Coal Board and the British Steel Corporation was somewhat fortuitous, enabling these organisations to bring forward the displacement of steam power at some of their key facilities by at least five years. It will be remembered from my first book that the construction of up to 400 Class 14s was originally envisaged in the very early days before design work commenced. Circumstances determined that only fifty-six were actually built during 1964/65, with all subsequently withdrawn by the Spring of 1969. Whilst forty-eight were sold into industry, the sale of significantly more than this number, had they been built, would have been a serious challenge. In just the same way that on BR the Class 14s covered a niche at the bottom-end of the traffic spectrum, so on the NCB and BSC they were very much top-end niche (i.e. railway *systems*, rather than stand-alone local collieries or steelworks). Maybe a few more railway *systems* in the NCB North

East Area could have been found to suit the Class 14s, but not many.

The ridiculously low sale prices paid by the NCB and BSC is the subject which continues to amaze me. To secure less than 8 per cent of their original construction cost after only four years of use is the most scandalous part of the Class 14 story as far as BR was concerned, particularly considering (i) the money spent on rectifying faults for the eventual benefit of the subsequent users, and, (ii) the comparative cost of new industrial shunters from the 'trade'. One can only assume that 'agreed' transfer-pricing arrangements between Nationalised companies were responsible for this very curious situation.

NCB and BSC made good use of their acquisitions and, with good maintenance, the removal of unnecessary equipment and, at Corby, the use of dedicated drivers, they managed to achieve reasonably good levels of availability and operational economy, although it should be recognised that the cheap purchase price enabled the

acquisition of spare locomotives as insurance against failures or instances of low availability. Less success was achieved with companies which purchased only small numbers, but for the big operators the situation was quite different as Adrian Booth (*Railway Bylines*, August/September 1997) summarised very well:

'With a diet of regular work and planned maintenance they were an outstanding success. They were reliable, popular with their crews, economical at the pumps, and were strong and rugged for the hard work in the coal mines and ironstone quarries.'

Ultimately, the rationalisation of the steel and coal industries led to their demise in their last two strongholds, but at least some Class 14s managed to reach twenty-two years of service.

As with previous books I have a 'Wish List' of information requirements to fill in gaps in the Class 14 story; any help with my list will as always be very much appreciated:

Sightings/photographs:

D9505	Belgium, particularly after 22/06/97.
D9515	Spain, particularly after 02/04/88.
D9534	Belgium, particularly after 27/06/76, and, Italy (if indeed this loco did actually move there).
D9535	BR livery, whilst operating at NCB Burradon.
D9548	Spain, particularly after 19/06/98.
D9549	Spain, particularly after 11/06/05.

'14s at 50' celebrations, Ramsbottom, East Lancashire Railway, 26 July 2014. Nine Class 14 locomotives on the 19.00 Bury Bolton Street to Ramsbottom service. 5850hp of Type 1 power; absolutely awesome! In order the locomotives are: D9531, D9520, D9513 (38), D9555, D9521, D9526, D9539, D9524 (14901) and D9537. (Anthony Sayer)

SOURCES AND REFERENCES

Books:

a) Industry (Industrial Railway Society publications).

Ashworth, P.J., Bendall, I. & Plant. K., *Industrial Railways & Locomotives of Lincolnshire & Rutland*, IRS, 2010.

Booth, A.J., *Ex-BR Diesels in Industry*, IRS. Seven editions: 2nd edition, 1981; 3rd edition, 1987; 4th edition, 1991; 5th edition, 2000; 6th edition, 2007; 7th edition, 2011; 8th edition, 2019. (2BRD-8BRD)

Bridges, A., *Industrial Locomotives of Scotland*, IRS, 1976.

De Havilland, J., *Industrial Locomotives of Dyfed & Powys*, IRS, 1994.

Hill, G. & Green, G., *Industrial Locomotives of Gwent*, IRS, 1999.

Hill, G., *Industrial Locomotives of Mid & South Wales*, IRS, 2007. (ILMSW)

Mountford, C.E. & Charlton, L.G., *Industrial Locomotives of Durham*, IRS, 1977.

Mountford, C.E. & Charlton, L.G., *Industrial Locomotives of Northumberland*, IRS, 1983.

Mountford, C.E. & Holroyde, D., *Industrial Railways and Locomotives of County Durham; Part 2 The National Coal Board and British Coal*, IRS, 2009. (IRLCD)

Spencer, P., *Industrial Railways and Locomotives of Spain*, IRS, 2018. (IRLS)

Tonks, E.S., *Former BR Diesel Locomotives in Industrial Service* (1st edition), IRS, 1972.

Waywell, R., *Industrial Locomotives of Buckinghamshire, Bedfordshire and Northamptonshire*, IRS, 2001. (ILBBN)

Waywell, R. & Jux, F., *Industrial Railways & Locomotives of Essex*, IRS, 2011.

Waywell, R. & Holroyde, D., *Industrial Railways and Locomotives of the Northumberland Coalfield*, IRS, 2020. (IRLNC)

Yardley, V.J., *Industrial Locomotives of Yorkshire', Part A: 'The National Coal Board including Opencast Disposal Points & British Coal in West and North Yorkshire* (Interim Pocket Book 8A), IRS, 2002.

b) Industry (other publishers)

Tonks, E.S., *The Ironstone Quarries of the Midlands*, Runpast Publishing:
   Part VI *Corby Area*, 1992 (IQM6); Part VII *Rutland*, 1989 (IQM7); Part VIII *South Lincolnshire*, 1991 (IQM8).

Railway Bylines Collection 2006-2007, Irwell Press, 2006, specifically:
   pp4-27, 'Worth Going Back For' (Backworth recollections), P. Johnson.

c) Other.

Hembry, P.J., *Class 14: The Cinderellas of the Diesel-Hydraulic Era*, D&EG, 1980.

Johnston, H., *Preserved BR Diesel and Electric Locomotives*, Silver Link, 1992.

Magazines:

Industrial Railway Record (published by the Industrial Railway Society) (IRRxxx), specifically:

No.112, March 1988, pp205-215, *The Ashington Railway System*, C.E. Mountford.

No.134, September 1993, pp182-192, *Decline of Steam at Ashington*, T.Scott.

No.142, September 1995, pp21-33, *Northumberland Paxmans*, T. Scott.

No.187, December 2006, pp441-449, *British Oak, Crigglestone*, C. Shepherd.

No.188, March 2007, pp492-496, *Hope Cement Works Visit*, C. Shepherd.

No.232, March 2018, pp319-324, *Corby Iron and Steel Works*, R. Horne.

No.240, March 2020, pp131-137, *When Shall We Three Meet Again*, C. Shepherd.

No.243, December 2020, pp284-7, Correspondence, G. Evans, D. Hartley and P. Spencer.

Bulletin, Industrial Railway Society (IRSxxx).

Railway Bylines, specifically:
August /September 1997, pp214-221, *The Fall and Rise of the Paxmans*, A.J. Booth.

September 2006, pp478-481, *Backworth: Steaming into the 1970s.*

December 2013, pp32-35, *No Way to Treat a Teddy Bear*, D. Townsley.

The Railway Magazine (RMxxxx), specifically:
June 1995, p57, *Exiles 'Fit and Well'*, G. Baetens.

December 2006, pp41-45, *Teddy Bears: the locos BR put to bed early*, A. Flowers.

Railways Illustrated (RIxxxx), specifically:
October 2008, 74-77, *Partners in Industry*, N. Pallant.

November 2008, pp68-71, *Industry's Bear Necessities*, P. Dunn.

August 2014, pp56-59, *The Bear Facts*, P. Dunn and G. Kobish.

September 2014, pp56-59, *Life left in the old Bears!*, G. Kobish and P. Dunn.

November 2014, p84, In Box: *Class 14s at work in Belgium*, W. de Ridder.

Rail Enthusiast / Rail (RExxxx), specifically:
April 1982, pp46-49, *Swindon's Black Sheep*, H. Johnston.

August 1982, p54, *Corby Torch.*

September 1982, pp29-31, *Teddy Bears' Picnic*, P. Kelly.

January 1987, pp39-42, *Ashington: Land of the Class 14s*, J. Furness.

08/01/14-21/01/14, pp46-51, *Class 14s: the unlikely survivors*, D.N. Clough.

Traction, specifically:

August 2005, pp51-53, *14 Finale*, M. Leah.

Today's Railways UK, specifically:
May 2013, pp28-32, *The Class 14 Diesel-Hydraulics: The Most Successful Failures Ever*, P. Abell.

Heritage Railway, specifically:
No.191, 3-30 July 2014, pp76-81, *Teddy Bear Jubilee*, F. Kerr.

Model Rail, specifically:
No.105, June 2007, *Class 14 Teddy Bears*, B. Jones.

Classic Diesels & Electrics (CD&Ex), specifically:
No.5, pp52-55, *Iron Mighty!*, P. Winter.

No.18, pp23-28, *Ready, Teddy, Go!*, C. Neill.

No.33, pp4-11, *Fabulous Fourteens*, G. Kobish.

The Railway Observer, RCTS (1963-87). (ROxxxx)

Bulletin, LCGB.

Journal, SLS.

Railway Locomotives, BLS.

The Big Four, Worcester Locomotive Society (WLS), specifically:

No.48, Winter 1972, pp15-16, *History of the Paxmans Part 2*, A.J. Booth.

Link, Engine Shed Society (ESS).

Archive Sources:
NCB Northumberland Area, Internal Railways Committee, October 1967-December 1973 (courtesy Trevor Scott).

NCB Ashington Loco Shed Daily Reports (courtesy Trevor Scott). (AshDR)

Websites:

RCTS *Diesel Dilemmas*, specifically: *Class 14 Exports*.

RM Web, specifically: *Spanish Class 14's*.

Sightings/Observations:
A.J. Booth, D. Burrell, J. Carter, T. Dovey, H. Earl, B. Embleton, C. Fisher, C. Foster, A. Freeman, B. Galloway, P. Gradidge, P. Green, A. Griffith, D. Johnson, H. Johnston, M. McDonald, K. McGowan, R.N. Pritchard, T. Scott, T. Skinner, J. Wade, B. Webb, P. Wilcox, MasonPhenix19, and Shed Master Archives.

D9555(9107/57)_D9518(No.7), NCB Ashington, 28 February 1987. (Bruce Galloway)

D9500, NCB Ashington, 28 February 1987. (Bruce Galloway)

PAXMAN ENDPIECE

D9525 (507), NCB Ashington, 7 February 1986. 507 had just been re-instated to traffic after 20 months or so inactivity, which included the installation of a new/refurbished engine. The locomotive suffered a period of low engine oil pressure but once this problem had been rectified, it carried on in traffic until October/November 1986 before suffering from the perennial problem of a fractured turbo-charger bracket. (Steve Carter)

Initial Class 14 Re-numbering at NCB Ashington.

The table on pages 131 and 132 illustrates how the Ashington Class 14s were re-numbered from 9312/100 *down to* 9312/90 (or the abbreviated 100 to 90 as recorded on many NCB reports) as 'new' locomotives progressively arrived from BR. It has always intrigued me why they were numbered *downwards*. During another meet-up with Trevor Scott (the day before submission of the final book proof!) he explained the reasoning. In 1969 the Ashington standard-gauge diesel fleet comprised 9312/101 (Yorkshire Engine Co.) and 9312/102 and 103 (both NBL), so logically the Class 14 arrivals should have been numbered upwards starting from 9312/104. However, it was realised that a number of 3ft.-gauge diesel locomotives, numbered 9306/103 to 108 were operated at the nearby Ellington and Bates collieries. So to avoid any potential (pure locomotive number) confusion the 'Paxmans' were allotted numbers in the range 100 downwards to 90, thereby keeping the standard-gauge stock together numerically. This was done despite the Plant Registry 9306 prefix actually being sufficient to have kept the fleet numbers unique.